THE · BIG
FOOD & DRINK
BOOK

THE · BIG
FOOD & DRINK
BOOK

MICHAEL BARRY, JILLY GOOLDEN

& PETER BAZALGETTE

BBC Books

Acknowledgements

The authors are grateful to Deborah Collinson, Grahame Dudley, Heather Holden-Brown, Susie Magasiner, Anna Ottewill, Frank Phillips and Chris Weller for their assistance in the preparation of this book.

The authors would also like to thank the following for their help:

Diana Bazalgette, Fisher Dilke, David Edwards, Hattie Ellis, Angela Gillmore, Helen Hawken, Gloria Morris, Moyra Rose and Dr Tom Sanders.

Published by BBC Books,
a division of BBC Enterprises Limited,
Woodlands, 80 Wood Lane
London W12 0TT

First published 1993
© Bazal Productions Ltd, Crafty Cooking Ltd and Jilly Goolden 1993
The moral rights of the authors have been asserted

ISBN 0 563 36787 3

Design and Art Direction
by Grahame Dudley Associates
Illustrations by Barbara Hampton
Food photography by Nick Carman
Styling by Jane McLish
Home Ecomonist Maxine Clark

Set in Helvetica and Aster by
Ace Filmsetting Ltd, Frome

Printed and bound in Great Britain by
Butler and Tanner Ltd, Frome

Colour separation
by Dot Gradation Ltd, Chelmsford

Jacket printed by
Lawrence Allen Ltd, Weston-super-Mare

contents

NOTES ON THE RECIPES

1 Follow one set of measurements only, do not mix metric and Imperial.

2 Eggs are size 2.

3 Wash fresh produce before preparation.

4 Spoon measurements are level.

5 A tablespoon is 15 ml; a teaspoon is 5 ml.

6 Adjust seasoning and strongly-flavoured ingredients, such as onions and garlic, to suit your own taste.

7 If you substitute dried for fresh herbs, use only half the amount specified.

8 Where soy sauce is listed for a recipe we recommend Japanese soy sauce (*shoyu*). It is high quality and half-way between light and heavy Chinese soy.

A NOTE ON SAFETY

Some of the food preparation in this book, particularly in the chapters on fish, meat and vegetables, involves the use of sharp kitchen utensils. Take extra care when using these implements and always follow the instructions carefully.

FAN OVENS AND AGAS

All the recipes in this book can be cooked in an Aga or fan oven. Of course each requires a rather different approach to cooking. As a guide, for fan ovens reduce the temperature by 20°C (68°F). For an Aga, use the roasting oven for temperatures above 180°C (350°F), using the bottom of the oven for gas mark 4, 180°C (350°F) and the top of the oven for gas mark 7, 210°C (425°F). Use the slow oven for lower temperatures.

CONVERSION TABLES

Weights	Volume	Measurement	Oven Temperatures
15 g (½ oz)	5 ml (1 teaspoon)	1 cm (½ inch)	gas mark ¼, 110°C (225°F)
25 g (1 oz)	15 ml (1 tablespoon)	2.5 cm (1 inch)	gas mark ½, 120°C (250°F)
50 g (2 oz)	120 ml (4 fl oz)	5 cm (2 inches)	gas mark 1, 140°C (275°F)
75 g (3 oz)	150 ml (5 fl oz)	7.5 cm (3 inches)	gas mark 2, 150°C (300°F)
100 g (4 oz)	300 ml (10 fl oz)	10 cm (4 inches)	gas mark 3, 160°C (325°F)
150 g (5 oz)	450 ml (15 fl oz)	13 cm (5 inches)	gas mark 4, 180°C (350°F)
175 g (6 oz)	600 ml (1 pint)	15 cm (6 inches)	gas mark 5, 190°C (375°F)
200 g (7 oz)	750 ml (1¼ pints)	18 cm (7 inches)	gas mark 6, 200°C (400°F)
225 g (8 oz)	900 ml (1½ pints)	20 cm (8 inches)	gas mark 7, 220°C (425°F)
250 g (9 oz)	1.2 litres (2 pints)	23 cm (9 inches)	gas mark 8, 230°C (450°F)
275 g (10 oz)	1.5 litres (2½ pints)	25 cm (10 inches)	gas mark 9, 240°C (475°F)
300 g (11 oz)	1.75 litres (3 pints)	28 cm (11 inches)	
350 g (12 oz)		30 cm (12 inches)	
375 g (13 oz)			
400 g (14 oz)			
425 g (15 oz)			
450 g (1 lb)			
550 g (1¼ lb)			
675 g (1½ lb)			
900 g (2 lb)			

The Food and Drink team have set out to create the essential guide to eating and drinking at home.

how to use this book

The guiding principle of this book is that food is all about pleasure, as well as sustenance and good health, so the easier it is to prepare the better. All the recipes and ideas therefore embody the short cuts and crafty tips for which Michael Barry is famous.

All the major ingredients used in Britain are included, with the best advice on what to buy and some great recipes for you. All are carefully designed to be easy to make and most are eminently affordable. But there are also the odd luxuries and grand recipes for special occasions.

As you will see from the contents, the chapters are organized around ingredients – from fish and shellfish, through eggs, poultry and game, on through vegetables, pasta and rice, to meat and then flour-based breads and pastries and finally, fruit and dairy products. The specific recipes are listed by course in a special recipe index at the back for your convenience. So whether you are looking for a main course idea, a starter or a pudding, you'll be able to find what you want within seconds.

 Throughout the book there are wines suggested that will go well with particular dishes. And the Enjoying Wine section (see page 257) is a simple buyer's guide giving you all the practical information you need.

7

....

Easy Entertaining (see page 299) suggests about twenty menus based on recipes in this book. The dishes have been chosen to match each other and to avoid as much of the last minute rush as possible. The Crucial Kitchen (see page 303) lists all the equipment which is essential for convenient and high quality cooking.

 Finally, throughout the book there are helpful 'fact files' on nutrition and food safety, combining the most up-to-date informaton with the most down-to-earth advice.

CHAPTER ONE

We very much
undervalue soup. It's
easy to make and it's
very economical.
Here are ten soups and
a variety of ideas about
stocks and garnishing.
But don't be afraid to
adapt them to what you
happen to have on
hand.

soups

Three key approaches to stock

1. Home-made

Five essential home-made stocks:

- **Chicken stock** Use a chicken carcass, a
bay leaf, a couple of peppercorns and a
pinch of salt. Cover with 1.2 litres (2 pints)
of water and simmer for 40 minutes then
strain.

- **Richer chicken stock** Brown the carcass in
an oven at gas mark 4, 180°C (350°F) for 10
to 15 minutes, add the washed outer skins
of a couple of onions, a stalk of celery, and
repeat as above.

- **Meat stock** Use 2 lbs beef or veal bones
(butchers will usually give you these),
brown them for 30 minutes or so in an oven
at gas mark 4, 180°C (350°F) and then make
the stock simply or with added vegetables,
as above.

- **Vegetarian stock** Use left-over cooking
water from asparagus or spinach as a base
with other chopped root vegetables
(parsnips give a strong flavour), onions and
celery, and green herbs. Cook for 25
minutes then strain.

- **Fish stock** Simmer fish off-cuts
(fishmongers will give you these for
nothing), the pared rind of a lemon, a
couple of bay leaves and a stalk or two of

Tuscan bean soup (page 11)

celery for 45 minutes. You can add the juice
of a lemon, or a tablespoon of wine or cider
vinegar.

Don't overcook stocks – after about an hour of
simmering the flavour of any stock will spoil.
These stocks form the base of several of this
book's recipes and indeed, many great recipes
of the world.

2. Cubes

Good stock cubes of all sorts are widely
available. Don't just depend on the well-
known names – some of the smaller, more
specialist companies are producing a variety
of flavours including onion, herbs, spicy
pepper, as well as fish stocks, court bouillon
and other exotica. As well as cubes, it's also
possible to buy ready-made jellied stock in the
chill or freezer cabinets of some large
supermarkets and specialist stores. They're
very good but not cheap. Many stock cubes
contain flavour enhancers such as
monosodium glutamate. Soy sauce and
anchovies contain glutamates naturally and
are effective flavour enhancers
(Worcestershire sauce relies on anchovies for
this reason).

 MONOSODIUM GLUTAMATE
It's been claimed that an excessive
intake of monosodium glutamate can
lead to 'Chinese restaurant
syndrome': dizziness and headaches. There is no
firm medical evidence for this. But those who
have high blood pressure or have had a stroke
should control their intake of sodium.

9

3. Consommé

Stock can be clarified by beating in a lightly beaten egg white, bringing it to the boil and then straining it carefully. Suitably reduced it is known in France as Consommé and drunk in its own right. A few mushrooms or herbs can be added to this for a very quick and easy soup, and it's wonderful with tomato juice as a cocktail.

Three key decisions for vegetable soup

Whole . . . chunky . . . or processed?

- Whole vegetable soups tend to be substantial and are often eaten as a main course, whether as a chowder in New England or a bean-based minestrone in Tuscany.

- Chunky soups, while substantial, are often just parts of a meal although they make a good light lunch.

- Processed soups are much more delicate although their flavours can be quite intense. You can also choose between finely processed or coarse (as the French like them).

Two whole soups

Corn chowder

This is a vegetarian alternative to the famous Cod Chowder eaten in New England. It's just as venerable and quite as delicious.

Serves 4

225 g (8 oz) potatoes, peeled and cut into ½-inch dice
225 g (8 oz) onions, peeled and diced
300 ml (10 fl oz) water
300 ml (10 fl oz) milk
1 red pepper, de-seeded and diced
1 green pepper, de-seeded and diced
350 g (12 oz) sweetcorn kernels, frozen (preferably) or tinned
Salt and freshly ground black pepper
2 teaspoons cornflour
6 cream crackers or similar biscuits
1 tablespoon chopped fresh parsley (optional)

Place the potatoes, onions and water in a saucepan with a pinch of salt and bring them to the boil. Simmer for 5 minutes. Add the milk and peppers and bring to the boil. Add the sweetcorn and simmer for 2 minutes. Season to taste with salt and pepper. Blend the cornflour with a little more water and whisk into the soup until it's thick. To serve, sprinkle each serving with a crushed cracker and, if desired, a teaspoon of chopped parsley.

WINE tip A filling, chunky soup needs rich, nutty wines to partner it. Two suggestions from Italy are Bianco di Custoza – like a richer, nuttier Soave – and Tocai di Friuli.

Tuscan bean soup

A classic version of the Minestra, this soup is eaten all over Italy but particularly in the north. Although the British tradition is to regard it as a tomato-based soup, beans are the heart of a proper Minestrone and the other vegetables are added according to season. This is a spring-time version but you can vary the vegetables to suit your taste.

Serves 4 to 6

225 g (8 oz) cannellini, borlotti or haricot beans, soaked for 6 hours
2 bay leaves
4 tablespoons olive oil
1 bunch spring onions, chopped
225 g (8 oz) carrots, diced
4 stalks celery, sliced
175 g (6 oz) peas
350 g (12 oz) spring greens, cut into ribbons
50 g (2 oz) small pasta, elbow macaroni etc.
Salt and freshly ground black pepper
1 tablespoon chopped fresh parsley
Grated Parmesan cheese to garnish

Place the beans in a saucepan and cover generously with water. Add the bay leaves and olive oil, bring to the boil and boil vigorously for 10 minutes. Simmer for 1 to 1½ hours until the beans are tender (the time depends on their age and quality). Add all the vegetables and the pasta to the beans, with enough water to make the soup liquid but not thin. Season generously, bring to the boil and simmer for 15 to 20 minutes. Stir well before serving with a sprinkling of chopped parsley and plenty of Parmesan cheese.

WINE *tip* Very Italian, so deserves a vibrant Italian red such as Chianti, Barbera or red Lambrusco; or a white with a good jab of acidity such as Frascati.

Two chunky soups

Pumpkin and tomato soup

A recipe invented in Southern Africa when there was nothing for supper but a chicken carcass, some tomatoes and a piece of ancient pumpkin. The result is quite delicious!

Serves 4

450 g (1 lb) pumpkin in shell
900 ml (1½ pints) chicken stock
2 sprigs fresh parsley, stalks separated and leaves chopped
225 g (8 oz) tomatoes quartered
Salt and freshly ground black pepper

Peel the pumpkin from its shell and cut the flesh into 1 cm (½ inch) dice. Simmer in the chicken stock with the parsley stalks for about 15 to 18 minutes until tender. If the tomatoes are large, cut them into eighths. Add these to the soup, season generously, then simmer for 5 minutes. Stir the chopped parsley into the soup to serve.

11
....

Borscht

Some Russians will tell you Borscht requires raw beetroot, others that it requires no beetroot at all. This version is easy to make and has the traditional rich ruby colour. It's nicest eaten with a substantial rye or wholemeal bread.

Serves 4

1 tablespoon cooking oil
225 g (8 oz) onions, peeled and finely chopped
225 g (8 oz) potatoes, peeled and cubed
2 carrots, grated
900 ml (1½ pints) beef stock (good quality cube is okay)
225 g (8 oz) cooked beetroot (not pickled), peeled and grated
Salt and freshly ground black pepper
1 teaspoon lemon juice (optional)
4 tablespoons soured cream
1 large dill gherkin, finely chopped

Heat the oil and sauté the onions and potatoes for 5 minutes. Add the carrots and stock, bring to the boil then simmer for 10 minutes. Stir in the grated beetroot and simmer for a further 10 minutes until the vegetables are completely cooked and beginning to fall apart. Season generously, adding a little lemon juice to sharpen it if necessary. Fill 4 bowls with soup, add a tablespoon of soured cream to the centre of each bowl, and top with a spoonful of finely chopped gherkin.

12

Three processed soups

Carrot and coriander soup

This soup offers the vivid contrast of the orange carrots and green coriander. It can be made at any time of year – if you can't find fresh coriander, freeze-dried is a very good substitute both for colour and flavour. Add that at the very end but allow enough time for the dried herb to rehydrate. A food processor or liquidizer is really essential. You can use a sieve if you've got half an hour!

Serves 4

2 tablespoons oil
25 g (1 oz) butter
450 g (1 lb) carrots, peeled and diced
1 large potato, peeled and diced
1 Spanish onion, peeled and diced
Salt and freshly ground black pepper
900 ml (1½ pints) chicken stock or water
2 tablespoons chopped fresh coriander leaves

Melt the oil and butter and sauté the carrots, potato and onion for 4 to 5 minutes. Season generously and add the stock or water. Simmer for 15 minutes until the vegetables are thoroughly cooked then purée until smoothly blended. Add the chopped coriander, check for seasoning and serve.

WINE
tip
Carrot is quite sweet, coriander is perfumed. Muscat d'Alsace is dry to offset the sweetness but highly scented to complement the coriander.

FACT FILE
BETA-CAROTENE
Carrots are particularly high in beta-carotene which our bodies convert into vitamin A (retinol). Vitamin A is important for good sight and healthy skin. It may also help to protect against heart disease and some cancers. Beta-carotene is most easily absorbed in conjunction with fat – hence the butter!

Broccoli and cheese soup

Broccoli and cheese soup

This is an unusual, smooth but robust soup using ingredients available all the year round (though broccoli is naturally in season in the summer). Adding the uncooked broccoli florets just before processing provides a slightly grainy texture, but you can, if you prefer, cook all the broccoli together. Serve the soup with wholemeal bread or crusty brown rolls.

Serves 4

1 tablespoon sunflower oil
1 medium onion, peeled and coarsely chopped
175 g (6 oz) potatoes, peeled and coarsely chopped
450 g (1 lb) broccoli
Salt and freshly ground black pepper
900 ml (1½ pints) water or chicken stock
½ teaspoon sugar
175 g (6 oz) mature Cheddar cheese

Heat the oil and fry the onion and potatoes gently until just soft. Trim the broccoli, divide into florets and cut the stems into 1 cm (½ inch) slices. Add the stems to the potato and onion mixture and fry for 5 minutes. Season generously and add half the broccoli florets and the water (or stock if you prefer a richer soup). Bring to the boil then simmer for 20 minutes until the vegetables are soft. Add the remaining broccoli florets and the sugar, cook for 1 minute then purée in a food processor or liquidizer. The bulk of the soup will be smooth but the newly-added broccoli will retain a slight grainy texture. Pour into a soup tureen and sprinkle on the cheese, stirring and turning with a ladle for a moment until the cheese is thoroughly melted into the soup.

WINE tip Sherry is the classic partner. Amontillado (that's medium) or a not-too-sweet Oloroso provides a foil for the creaminess of the cheese.

Borscht

Carrot and coriander soup

Vichyssoise

Vichyssoise is the classic French vegetable soup based on potatoes and leeks, eaten hot or cold. It can be puréed coarsely and you can leave out the cream, if you prefer. Other vegetables like carrots, onions or turnips, beans or courgettes can be added, but don't add more than two vegetables to the basic leek and potato mixture, and do try them on their own as well.

Serves 4

450 g (1 lb) leeks
2 tablespoons oil (if eating hot, 1 tablespoon oil and 1 tablespoon butter)
450 g (1 lb) potatoes, peeled and cubed
Salt and freshly ground black pepper
900 ml (1½ pints) chicken stock or water
4 tablespoons double cream

Clean the leeks by trimming and splitting them lengthways and putting them in a bowl of water or under a tap for a minute to wash away all the sand. Cut them into 2.5 cm (1 inch) lengths. Heat the oil or oil and butter and sauté the vegetables for 5 minutes. Season generously, add the stock or water, bring to the boil and simmer for 15 minutes until the vegetables are thoroughly cooked. Purée thoroughly in a food processor or liquidizer or rub it through a sieve. Stir in the cream. Before serving, stir the soup and sprinkle it with an appropriate garnish, traditionally very finely slivered bits of the green part of the leek were used. If you're eating it hot, parsley and croûtons (see right) take a lot of beating. If cold, chill for at least 2 hours.

WINE tip A dry white with plenty of oomph would provide a contrast to the cream and potatoes. Try New Zealand Sauvignon Blanc.

Five great garnishes

Garnishes can make a soup come alive. Here are five:

1. Parsley

Always finely chopped (in more rustic soups, it should not be too fine), parsley sprinkled on looks great but doesn't add much flavour. Parsley on the bottom of the bowl (as the Welsh do) with the soup poured over it produces a surprising amount of flavour. Try flat-leaved parsley when you want it chopped more coarsely.

2. Other fresh herbs

Dill and fennel are good with fish soups, basil with tomato ones, thyme and marjoram with summer vegetable soups and mint with peas. Chives go well with most things. Don't be tempted to put more than two herbs into any soup – the flavours just cancel each other out.

3. Croûtons

Croûtons are cubes of bread that have been either fried or baked till they're crisp. If you're baking, do it on a tray in an oven pre-heated to gas mark 4, 180°C (350°F) and turn them a couple of times.

If you're frying, do it in good oil and watch them like a hawk – when they've turned golden they're ready. Beware – they go on cooking even after you've taken them off the heat. Don't try to keep them as they always go soggy or stale. Try a light sprinkling of garlic or celery salt on to croûtons. Wholemeal bread makes good croûtons for substantial soups, white bread for more delicate ones. They can be cut from 3mm (⅛ inch) to 2.5 cm (1 inch) in size.

4. Yoghurt

Plain yoghurt and/or soured cream are often used as a garnish in soups. Fromage frais works well, too, providing a creamier texture. They can be blended into the soup as long as you don't bring it to the boil again before serving. By stirring them in you can produce a pretty marbled effect, particularly in soups of a vivid colour.

5. Cheese

Traditionally eaten with French onion and Mediterranean fish soups, grated cheese can give a soup substance and nutritional value.

Choose the cheese to match the soup by nationality and style – Parmesan for Italian, Gruyère for French (especially for French onion) and Lancashire or Cheshire on British chunky farmhouse soups. Never use soft cheeses in soup, only ones that can be grated.

Above: *Vichyssoise.* **Below:** *Pumpkin and tomato soup* (page 11)

Three Classic fish soups

Tom yam kung

Perhaps the most famous of all Thai soups, this is often cooked in a 'steamboat' in Thailand, a kind of moat around a charcoal chimney. However, an ordinary saucepan or a fondue set works pretty well. Although it's given here as a recipe for prawns, the soup can also be made with firm-fleshed, white fish like monkfish or haddock. The prawns have to be uncooked – you can often buy frozen, headless and trimmed ones which do very well. Many supermarkets now sell laos or galingale powder, and fish sauce.

Serves 6

2 stalks lemon grass, crushed
1 teaspoon laos or galingale powder or crushed fresh ginger root
1 fresh red chilli pepper
1.5 litres (2½ pints) water
2 tablespoons of Thai fish sauce
675 g (1½ lb) raw prawns or firm white fish
Grated rind of 1 lime
1 tablespoon lime juice
100 g (4 oz) button mushrooms
1 teaspoon oil
2 cloves garlic, peeled and chopped
2 tablespoons chopped fresh or freeze-dried coriander

Mix the lemon grass, laos powder, chilli and water in a saucepan. Bring to the boil then simmer for 15 minutes. Add the fish sauce and the prawns or fish and simmer for 5 minutes until the prawns are pink or the fish is cooked. Add the lime rind and juice and the mushrooms. Remove from the heat for 1 minute. Heat the oil and fry the garlic until soft. Pour the soup into a warm tureen, stir in the fried garlic and the coriander leaves and serve. Don't eat the chilli pepper unless you are a devotee.

The spicy oriental flavourings here cry out for the clean refreshing qualities of lager. Tiger is a good imported Malaysian brand with a smoothness and gentleness. Or try Spanish San Miguel (a favourite in the Far East).

Mediterranean fish soup

This is a simplified form of Bouillabaisse, the mixed fish soup of the Mediterranean. As most of the fish usually used are simply not available in Britain, it's been adapted significantly but it still tastes gorgeous and sunny. It is often served with *rouille*, a garlic-flavoured mayonnaise, coloured and sharpened with a teaspoon of chilli sauce.

Serves 4

4 tablespoons olive oil
225 g (8 oz) onions, peeled and finely chopped
2 cloves garlic, peeled and finely chopped
1 stalk celery, finely chopped
2 bay leaves
Small bunch fresh parsley, stalks separated and leaves chopped
17 fl oz (500 ml) passata (liquid tomato purée)
400 ml (14 fl oz) fish stock made with the fish trimmings (see page 9) or water
450 g (1 lb) of 3 kinds of fish from a choice of: red mullet, gurnard, haddock, coley, rock salmon and hake
Pinch of saffron (optional)
2 tablespoons chopped fresh parsley
Croûtons
Grated Gruyère cheese
Rouille

Heat the oil and sauté the onions, garlic, celery, bay leaves and parsley stalks for 5 minutes. Add the passata and fish stock or water, bring to the boil then simmer for 10 minutes. Cut the fish pieces (preferably skinned) into neat pieces not more than 5 × 2.5 cm (2 × 1 inch). Add them to the soup and simmer gently for 5 to 7 minutes until the fish is thoroughly cooked.

If you're using saffron strands, steep them in a tablespoon of hot water for 1 minute then add with the fish. Stir the soup gently and serve sprinkled with parsley. Offer bowls of croûtons, grated Gruyère cheese and rouille to add to taste.

Good southern French plonk such as red or rosé Coteaux d'Aix-en-Provence, Palette (Château Simone) or Tavel rosé. At a lower price – Vin de Pays des Bouches-du-Rhône.

Normandy fish soup

A smooth and creamy soup made of North Atlantic fish very similar to those available in British waters, this makes a lovely winter dish that in generous quantities only needs cheese and fruit to follow it.

Serves 4

1 tablespoon oil
1 tablespoon butter
225 g (8 oz) onions, peeled and diced
225 g (8 oz) potatoes, peeled and diced
300 ml (10 fl oz) milk
450 g (1 lb) firm white fish, haddock, cod, coley or
*   whiting*
450 ml (15 fl oz) water
1 tablespoon lemon juice
Salt and freshly ground black pepper
4 tablespoons double cream
1 tablespoon snipped fresh chives

Heat the oil and butter and sauté the onion and potato for 5 minutes. Add the milk, bring to the boil and simmer until soft. Trim and skin the fish fillets and reserve a quarter cut into neat 1 cm (½ inch) dice. Add the rest of the fish to the soup with the water, lemon juice and seasoning. Simmer for a further 5 to 6 minutes until the fish is cooked. Purée in a food processor or liquidizer. Return the soup to the pan, add the cream and the fish cubes and simmer for a further 5 minutes until the fish cubes are just cooked through. Serve with a sprinkling of chives over each bowl.

WINE tip Sancerre (on the pricey side) or a cheaper Sauvignon Blanc such as Sauvignon de Touraine. Or with a little more spice – the classy Pinot Grigio from north-east Italy.

From top: *Normandy fish soup; Tom yam kung; Mediterranean fish soup*

sauces

Here are five basic sauce recipes which you can flavour in all kinds of ways, and a fair number of suggestions as to how to make use of them. Don't be afraid to try these sauces, all in crafty versions. You will never need to buy 'cook-in sauce' again.

Three key hot sauces and oodles of their relations

1. Béchamel sauce

Béchamel is the French name for white sauce. The crafty version is very easy to make. You can use ordinary flour or cornflour. Cornflour provides a lighter sauce with a slightly more open texture but not one that will work as well on long-cooked dishes, so if you're planning to pour it over cauliflower and then bake it, a proper flour sauce is best. If it's a light sauce for coating a dish before serving, cornflour works fine.

Crafty béchamel sauce

This method is totally different from the classic way of making a white sauce but it works perfectly every time. The only key ingredient is a proper whisk (with a coil spring). It has the virtue of breaking down all the lumps in the sauce almost without effort. If you need a thick sauce, use slightly less milk.

Makes 300 ml (½ pint)

300 ml (½ pint) milk (or milk and stock for a velouté sauce)
25g (1 oz) plain flour or cornflour, sieved
25g (1 oz) butter
Pinch of freshly grated nutmeg
Salt
2 tablespoons double cream or fromage frais (optional)

Clockwise from top right-hand: *Crafty béchamel sauce; Maltaise sauce (page 20); Parsley sauce; Basic hollandaise sauce (page 20)*

Put the milk into a non-stick saucepan and whisk in the flour or cornflour until it is thoroughly blended with the milk. Add the butter and bring gently to the boil, whisking every minute or so. It doesn't require constant whisking but you must pay attention as soon as the sauce starts to thicken. When it's fully thickened and just bubbling, turn the heat right down and whisk thoroughly to ensure a smooth, silky texture. Add the nutmeg and season to taste with salt. For extra texture, add the double cream or fromage frais. If you're adding the fromage frais you mustn't boil it again after it has been added or the texture will deteriorate.

VARIATIONS

- **Mustard sauce** Two 5 ml spoons (2 teaspoons) of French Dijon-style mustard added to 300 ml (10 fl oz) of sauce makes a great spicy accompaniment to oily fish such as herring or mackerel or a gratin of root vegetables like celeriac.

- **Egg sauce** A Victorian addition, particularly used with baked or grilled fish, was a finely chopped hard-boiled egg and a teaspoon of chopped fresh parsley to 300 ml (10 fl oz) of Béchamel Sauce. This is rich and well textured.

- **Parsley sauce** The traditional English sauce for eating with fish, this is also delicious with broad beans, carrots and new potatoes. Add at least 2 tablespoons of chopped fresh parsley and a squeeze of lemon to 300 ml (10 fl oz) of sauce.

- **Mornay (cheese) sauce** When the sauce has thickened, stir in 1 heaped teaspoon of Dijon mustard and then add 50 g (2 oz) of grated Gruyère or Cheddar cheese. Stir until thoroughly melted then add 25 g (1 oz) of grated Parmesan cheese at the last moment.

- **Velouté** This is Béchamel sauce made with half milk and half stock – usually chicken or fish depending on the dish.

- **Hard or sweet white sauce** Whisk in 2 tablespoons of soft, light, Barbados brown sugar and a pinch of allspice for a superb sauce to eat with Christmas or other puddings.

20

2. Egg emulsion sauces: Hollandaise and friends

The hardest of all sauces to make? Not with a food processor or liquidizer.

Basic hollandaise sauce

This basic processor method produces a slightly lighter sauce than the more traditional egg yolk only versions. It is ideal with poached salmon or asparagus.

Makes 300 ml (10 fl oz)

2 eggs and 1 yolk
2 teaspoons lemon juice
Salt
225 g (8 oz) lightly salted butter

Put the eggs and egg yolk, lemon juice and a pinch of salt into the bowl of a liquidizer or food processor. Cut the butter into chunks and place it in a saucepan and heat steadily until the butter melts completely and foams. You will hear a hissing noise as it gives off steam. At this point switch on the liquidizer or processor and beat the eggs thoroughly. With the motor running, pour the butter in a continuous stream on to the egg mixture, discarding the white residue at the bottom of the saucepan. Tip out the residue but do not rinse the pan. Switch off the motor and pour the sauce back into the saucepan, stirring gently but continuously off the heat. Within 30 seconds the sauce will have thickened even more and is ready to serve. It can be kept warm in a bowl over a pan of water for up to 10 minutes but no more.

VARIATIONS

- **Béarnaise sauce** Substitute a tablespoon of wine vinegar for the lemon juice in the ingredients. Bring the wine vinegar to the boil with a teaspoonful each of chopped shallot and fresh tarragon. Strain out the herbs and shallot before adding the vinegar to the eggs, otherwise proceed as before. Use with steaks, grills and strong-flavoured fish.

- **Maltaise sauce** Substitute the juice of a blood orange for the lemon juice in the Hollandaise recipe. This produces a blush pink sauce used with fish and some lightly poached egg recipes.

3. Tomato sauces

The third of the hot sauce bases is a tomato one. Its wide use in various forms of Italian fast food (pizza and pasta) make it an almost universal style of cooking. But there are variations on this theme, too. The basic sauce is slightly more French than Italian in style but can be modified in a variety of ways.

Tomato coulis

This goes very well as a sauce with fish mousses or with grilled meats, and for a variety of other basic uses. For pasta, however, you need something more substantial such as Napolitana Sauce.

Serves 4

1 tablespoon butter
1 tablespoon olive oil
450 g (1 lb) very ripe tomatoes, skinned or unskinned and finely chopped
or 400 g (14 oz) tin chopped Italian tomatoes
Salt and freshly ground black pepper
Pinch of sugar
½ teaspoon freeze-dried or 1 teaspoon chopped fresh basil

Melt the butter in the oil until it stops sizzling. Add the tomatoes, stir thoroughly then turn down the heat and simmer for 10 minutes. Season generously with salt and pepper. Add the pinch of sugar (not for the sake of sweetness but to enhance the flavour), stir in the basil and serve.

THESE ARE VARIATIONS ON TOMATO COULIS

Napolitana sauce

This is the basic Italian tomato sauce and ideally should be made with fresh, sun-ripened plum tomatoes. As these are virtually unobtainable in Britain I always use tinned Italian chopped tomatoes which began life ripened in the sun. If added to browned minced meat and finely chopped onion, this is the basis for the bolognese sauce that made spaghetti famous, although it's also improved by the addition of a little chopped carrot at the beginning of the cooking period and a tablespoon or two of cream at the end of it.

Serves 4

2 tablespoons olive oil
1 clove garlic, peeled and crushed
1 × 400 g (14 oz) tin Italian chopped tomatoes
1 tablespoon concentrated tomato purée
½ teaspoon chopped fresh oregano
½ teaspoon chopped fresh thyme
½ teaspoon chopped fresh basil

Heat the oil and fry the garlic gently for 2 minutes without allowing it to go brown. Add the tomatoes and simmer, stirring for 1 minute. Stir in the tomato purée, making sure it is thoroughly blended, and simmer the mixture for 10 minutes. Stir in the herbs and allow to blend over a very low heat for another minute before using.

21

- **Mustard mayonnaise** Add 2 teaspoons of French mustard to the egg, olive oil, salt, pepper, sugar and lemon juice in the bowl before you begin to process. English mustard is much too strong for this purpose. It can be the golden mustard of Dijon, the dark, herby mustard of Bordeaux or the grainy mustard of Meaux. Whichever you use, continue with the basic recipe. The mayonnaise will have a golden colour and a pungent flavour.

- **Tomato mayonnaise** This is a mayonnaise affected more by colour than by flavour but extremely pretty as a variation, nice with light foods and pasta salads. To the egg and oil mixture, add a tablespoon of tomato purée and a teaspoon – no more – of white wine or cider vinegar and proceed as before. The mayonnaise will have a rose pink colour, and is particularly good served with shellfish and as a dressing for vegetable salads.

2. Vinaigrettes

24 The second great salad sauce is Vinaigrette. This is the name given to the mixture of oil, vinegar, and sometimes lemon juice that's the basic dressing for salads in France.
There are three ways to make it:

- In a jar where you put all the ingredients (in the correct order!), shake it and store it in the fridge.

- In a liquidizer or blender where a full emulsification of all the ingredients takes place. You can make this in bulk and store it for up to 3 weeks in the fridge.

- In the salad bowl before adding the salad ingredients.

When making it in the bowl, you can cross the salad servers over the dressing and pile the greens on top, only tossing them at the last moment. You can also put the ingredients on to the greens just before you toss and serve the salad. This works even better. Whichever way you make them, vinaigrettes can also be used to dress raw and cooked vegetables in individual servings to make up an hors d'oeuvres.

Crafty lemonette dressing

This is my favourite vinaigrette salad dressing. It uses equal proportions of fresh lemon juice and cider vinegar to produce a much lighter dressing than normal, and one that's less destructive of other flavours in the meal. The dressing will keep in a screw-topped jar in the fridge for 3 weeks, so it can be used as you need it. You can double or treble the quantities if you wish.

Makes 300 ml (10 fl oz)

2 tablespoons fresh lemon juice
2 tablespoons cider vinegar
1 teaspoon caster sugar
½ teaspoon salt
2 tablespoons olive oil
250 ml (8 fl oz) sunflower or salad oil

Mix together the lemon juice, cider vinegar, sugar and salt until the salt and sugar are thoroughly dissolved. Do not add the oil until this has taken place, whether you're using a jar, a whisk or a processor. Add the olive oil and mix thoroughly, then add the remaining salad oil and blend until thoroughly mixed.

Variations

- **Mustard vinaigrette** To the basic lemon juice and cider vinegar, sugar and salt, add a generous teaspoon of Dijon mustard – Bordeaux is probably too heavy for this, but a light grain mustard is acceptable. Mix together thoroughly before adding the oil, as before. This dressing will keep in the fridge for up to 2 weeks.

Herb vinaigrette

This is a very attractive alternative dressing. However, it won't keep for very long in the fridge if you use fresh herbs. Dried herbs seem to have much greater staying power.

Makes 300 ml (10 fl oz)

1 teaspoon very finely chopped parsley
1 teaspoon very finely chopped celery leaf
1 teaspoon very finely chopped marjoram
Pinch of finely chopped or crushed thyme
Pinch of finely chopped or crushed rosemary
½ clove garlic, crushed with salt
1 quantity crafty Lemonette Dressing (see page 24)

Mix the herbs and garlic into the vinaigrette, shake thoroughly and leave for at least 6 hours before using so that the flavours combine.

From top: *Raspberry vinegar* **(page 23);** *Mayonnaise vert* **(page 23);** *Salsa sauce* **(page 22)**

fish

Broadly speaking, we live on three or four kinds of meat, three kinds of poultry, and perhaps ten or eleven vegetables. But fish – which we eat all too rarely – offers up to twenty varieties. There is an enormous choice in flavour, texture and style of cooking. What's more, it's very good for us.

Key rules for buying and cooking fish

1. Get someone else to do the work

Most supermarkets, as well as fishmongers, now have either fish counters or are selling fish that has been pre-prepared. If you don't like heads, ask them to cut the heads off the fish for you, to trim it, to fillet it, even to skin it. You're paying – get them to do the work.

2. Buy fresh fish

This doesn't mean you need to go out on a trawler. It does mean the fish should not have been frozen solid. Whatever people tell you, frozen fish suffers a change in texture and a loss of quality. Besides, fresh fish is widely available, not least because of high speed air transport and chilling technology.

3. Cook the fish simply

Fish cooks very quickly. The delicate protein structure of its flesh should not be subjected to enormously complicated or lengthy recipes.

Simple cooking by a variety of methods listed below gets the best out of fish and leaves the texture and the flavour intact. Fish is so delicate that in many places it's eaten raw or almost raw – from Scottish smoked salmon to Whitstable oysters to Japanese sushi.

4. Don't deep-fry

Although fish and chips may be a great tradition, deep-frying at home is a smelly and cumbersome business. There are more attractive ways to cook fish.

27

BUYING FRESH FISH
To tell if a fish is fresh:
● Look at the skin – it should be moist and shiny.
● Look at the eyes – they should be full and not sunken and dried.
● Look at the gills – they should be pinky-red.
● Feel the texture and smell the odour if you are still in doubt.
Fresh fish has a firm texture and a clean bright odour – don't buy anything that doesn't.

Poached salmon (page 28)

Five of the best ways to cook fish with some recipe ideas

1. Poaching fish

Poaching is cooking fish in lightly flavoured and gently simmering water. Don't be tempted to try to cook it at a rolling boil. The French use the word '*mijouter*' which translates as 'shivering'. A good trick with poaching fish is to cut it into pieces the size and shape you want then wrap each piece in cling film and poach it in the film. This doesn't stop the fish cooking but does help it keep its shape. The liquid for poaching fish should be freshly drawn water with the juice of a lemon, a couple of bay leaves, a few peppercorns and a good teaspoon of sea or coarse salt. A sprig of parsley and a piece of celery are good additions. The liquid, which is called court bouillon, should be simmered for 10 to 15 minutes before adding the fish.

Poached turbot

28

Turbot is a very expensive fish but a delicious one for special occasions, being moist and meaty. It needs simple saucing; try Mornay Sauce (see page 20). Serve it with new potatoes and spinach or French beans.

Serves 4

4 × 175 g (6 oz) turbot fillets
1 saucepan of poaching court bouillon (see page 9)

Wrap the fillets in cling film. Bring the court bouillon to a very gentle boil. Put the fish in, allow the liquid to return to the simmer and poach for just 8 minutes before transferring the fish on to a warm plate. Unwrap the cling film, coat the turbot with Mornay Sauce and flash under the grill for 2 or 3 minutes until the sauce is just bubbling.

Poached salmon

You can poach salmon either whole, in joints (known as darnes), or as cutlets. If you're poaching a whole salmon, or a substantial piece of one, make sure you have a pan or fish kettle big enough to take it. There's no harm in cutting a salmon in half crossways in order to poach it in a medium-sized saucepan; you can reassemble it remarkably effectively afterwards.

Cooking

To poach a whole fish or a large piece of fish:

- Place it in cold poaching liquid.

- Bring it to the boil.

- Allow to simmer for just 4 minutes.

- Switch the heat off and cover it.

- If you're going to eat it hot, leave it for 15 minutes for each 450 g (1 lb).

- If you're going to eat it cold, leave it until the fish has cooled down completely before removing it from the water.

- If you're cooking cutlets, wrap those in cling film before putting into simmering water, then cook for just 10 minutes, allow to stand for 5 minutes, remove the cling film and serve.

WINE tip Hot salmon with Hollandaise needs something with a mild acidity such as an Alsace Riesling, a German Riesling or a dry Muscat from Central Europe, the south of France, or Portugal.

Serving

● Once you've put it on a serving tray, remove the skin carefully.

● If it's hot, serve it with Hollandaise Sauce (see page 20) or when blood oranges are in season a Maltaise Sauce (see page 20).

● If you're serving it cold, it's a pretty trick (after you have taken the skin off) to re-cover it with 'scales' of very thinly sliced cucumber and serve it with Mayonnaise or Mayonnaise Vert (see page 23).

● Cold salmon marries perfectly with a dill and yoghurt sauce.

● New potatoes and a cucumber salad are perfect accompaniments, hot or cold.

WINE tip A wine which has zingy acidity and enough character to match dill and yoghurt flavours: Pouilly Fumé from the Loire, or one of the excellent Sauvignon Blancs from the New World.

Above: *Bass in saffron sauce* (page 32). **Below:** *Haddock dieppoise* (page 32)

2. Baking fish

Baking is a very efficient and effective way to cook fish. You can flavour it in a variety of ways, it cooks without trouble and contains much of the smell in the oven. Although it's best for whole fish, whatever their size, it's also the technique for very good fish gratins.

Mix 450 g (1 lb) of cooked fish with 300 ml (10 fl oz) of herbed white sauce and 100 g (4 oz) of mushrooms. Sprinkle with cheese or breadcrumbs and bake in a shallow dish for 20 minutes until it bubbles.

Sprats

Sprats are incredibly cheap and very nutritious. In season, they make a very simple and popular treat for high tea or a light supper. Serve them with plenty of brown bread and butter.

Serves 4

1 tablespoon coarse salt
675 g (1½ lb) sprats
Freshly ground black pepper
1 lemon

Pre-heat the oven to gas mark 6, 200°C (400°F), and line a baking tray with a piece of foil – don't bother to oil it as the sprats are quite oily enough in their own right. Sprinkle the salt on to the foil and spread the sprats out on it in a single layer. Grind plenty of black pepper over the top and squeeze the lemon juice over the sprats. Bake at the top of the oven for 20 minutes then serve at once.

NUTRITIOUS FISH
Fish is a great source of valuable nutrients such as vitamin D, vitamin B$_{12}$ and trace elements. Oily fish such as salmon, sprats, mackerel, herring and trout are also an important source of Omega 3 polyunsaturated fats. In countries where the people eat a diet rich in oily fish, they have a relatively low rate of heart disease. Tinned fish such as sardines are good for calcium because the bones are eaten as well as the flesh.

30

Herbed grey mullet

Grey mullet is a very cheap and underrated fish that is often caught in British waters. It can taste a little muddy, but cooked in this way the herbs and the baking improve the flavour dramatically.

Serves 4

Good bunch of fresh parsley
Sprig celery leaves
2 sprigs fresh thyme
2 bay leaves
2 lemons, sliced
1 × 900 g (2 lb) grey mullet, cleaned, head removed if you choose
Salt and freshly ground black pepper
1 tablespoon butter

Pre-heat the oven to gas mark 5, 190°C (375°F). Wash the herbs and remove the leaves from the parsley. Chop the parsley leaves coarsely and set them aside. Chop the parsley stalks, celery and thyme, mix with the bay leaves and use the mixture to stuff the cavity of the fish. Oil a large sheet of kitchen foil and put a line of lemon slices diagonally across the foil. Place the fish on top, put a couple of lemon slices into the cavity, and arrange the rest of the lemon along the top of the fish. Season with salt and pepper. Sprinkle generously with the reserved parsley leaves and close the foil loosely around the fish; do not pack it down tightly but leave a little air space. Bake in the oven for 45 minutes.

To serve, remove the slices of lemon and serve the fish on a long plate. Make a sauce from the juices which have run out during the cooking, enriched with a knob of butter.

WINE *tip* Quite a flavoursome fish, so it needs a wine with a good, strong character – try South African Chenin Blanc or French dry Vouvray.

Above: *Trout with almonds and cucumber batons* (page 36). Below: *Neapolitan terrine* (page 39)

Bass in saffron sauce

An elegant dinner party dish which uses one of the grander fish that are caught in British waters. If you can't find bass or it's a bit pricey, you can substitute small, whole salmon.

Serves 6

Coarse or sea salt
1.1 kg (2½ lb) sea bass (or a whole salmon)
2 sprigs fresh parsley
2 bay leaves
2 limes
175 ml (6 fl oz) double cream
¼ teaspoon ground saffron

Pre-heat the oven to gas mark 4, 180°C (350°F) and line a baking dish with a lightly oiled sheet of kitchen foil.

Sprinkle the foil with a little salt. Sprinkle some more of the salt into the cavity of the fish and stuff with the parsley sprigs and bay leaves. Grate the rind from one of the limes and squeeze both of them over the fish. Bake in the oven for 45 to 50 minutes until the fish is just done. You can, if you wish, turn it over during this period. Transfer the fish to a serving dish and ease off the skin from the top. Pour the cooking juices into a non-stick saucepan, add the cream, the saffron, and the rind and bring to the boil. Simmer for about 5 minutes until the sauce is thick. If the sauce does not thicken sufficiently, mix a heaped teaspoon of cornflour with a little water, remove the sauce from the heat and stir in the slaked cornflour. Return to the heat and stir until thick and glossy.

To serve, carefully separate the fish into fillets at the table and coat with the sauce for each serving. This can be done in the kitchen in advance if you prefer but it's not so spectacular.

WINE tip **Bass needs a light and delicate white wine. Try a good German Riesling (if you're feeling flush), Austrian Rhine Riesling, or a Viognier from southern France (if you can find one).**

Haddock dieppoise

The trick with this and most gratins is not to cook the fish for too long and to make sure the sauce is thick enough to begin with. Otherwise the juices from the fish thin it down until it becomes a runny gravy. This recipe can also be made with plaice fillets in which case it needs to cook perhaps five minutes less. This dish is nicest with mashed potatoes.

Serves 4

1 quantity thick, Béchamel Sauce (see page 19)
4 × 175 g (6 oz) haddock fillets
100 g (4 oz) peeled prawns
100 g (4 oz) button mushrooms, halved
2 tablespoons double cream
Juice of ½ lemon
1 bay leaf

Pre-heat the oven to gas mark 4, 180°C (350°F). Pour one-third of the thick Béchamel Sauce into a gratin or baking dish. Lay the haddock fillets in a single layer on the sauce and sprinkle with the prawns and button mushrooms. Mix the cream and lemon juice into the remaining sauce and pour over the fish and mushrooms. Tuck in the bay leaf and bake in the oven for 25 to 30 minutes until the top is just golden and bubbling. The fish will cook in the sauce and the flavours will have intermingled beautifully.

WINE tip **Haddock in general needs a soft and approachable wine – how about an Italian Orvieto, or a Pinot Blanc? With the Dieppoise sauce try a white Graves, an oak-aged Sauvignon Blanc or an Australian Semillon.**

3. Grilling fish

Always use foil to line your grill pan as it saves on washing up and can help cook the fish that little bit quicker by reflecting heat. Always pre-heat the grill for at least 10 minutes before you use it – that way you achieve the maximum temperature. Also, position the fish as close to the grill as you reasonably can. Chicken has to be cooked quite slowly to make sure the flesh is completely penetrated by the heat, but fish cooks so quickly that the closer it gets to the heat without burning the better.

Grilled Italian monkfish

Monkfish is a very dense, solid fish with no conventional bones at all – an ideal way to introduce those people who 'don't like fish' to its delights. Although expensive, it is worth cooking, especially in this Italian style which makes best use of its robust almost lobster-like flavour and texture. This is nicest served with sautéed potatoes and a pepper and tomato salad.

Serves 4

675 g (1½ lb) monkfish tail
2 cloves garlic
¼ teaspoon salt
4 teaspoons olive oil
Juice of 1 small lemon
4 small sprigs fresh rosemary

Pre-heat the grill and line it with kitchen foil.

Cut the monkfish closely along the central bone to remove the fillet. Cut the two pieces into four equal portions. It should be semi-circular in section rather like four pieces of parsnip that have been cut in half. Without cutting right the way through, split along the length of each piece so that it opens out slightly. Crush the garlic with the salt and mix with the olive oil and lemon juice. Brush the fish with this mixture and lay a sprig of rosemary into the slit cut along the top of each piece of fish. Cook under a hot grill with the top of the fish at least 5 cm (2 inches) away from the grill for about 6 to 8 minutes. If the fish is very thick you may need to turn it to finish grilling, otherwise turn the grill down and continue to cook for a further 2 to 3 minutes until the fish is opaque and cooked all the way through. The top should have a crisp browned appearance and the rosemary should not have turned into a cinder.

Cut the monkfish closely along the central bone to remove the fillet

Cut into four equal portions.

Without cutting right the way through, split along the length of each piece of fish so that it opens up slightly

33
....

Brush each piece with the mixture of garlic, salt, olive oil and lemon juice and lay a piece of rosemary into the slit cut along the top of each piece

WINE *tip* **Quite a solid, meaty fish which can easily take red wine. Try something light and fruity such as Italian Bardolino or Dolcetto or a Gamay.**

Mackerel with gooseberry sauce

Mackerel with gooseberry sauce

Britain's classic accompaniment to the very rich flesh of mackerel has for centuries been green gooseberry sauce. It may seem an unlikely combination but we eat fruit sauces with meat. Bread and butter is good with this dish, preferably granary or wholemeal, but you can serve boiled potatoes with it as well if you like.

Serves 4

4 medium-sized fresh mackerel
175 g (6 oz) gooseberries, topped and tailed
1 tablespoon water
50 g (2 oz) sugar
25 g (1 oz) butter

Pre-heat the grill and line it with kitchen foil.

Trim the cleaned mackerel and place on a grid on a grill pan. They do not need oiling as they are already rich in oil. Grill for 5 minutes on each side until the skin blisters and the flesh is cooked. If the mackerel are very fat, it might be worth slashing each of them across the fattest part with a very sharp knife to allow the heat to penetrate.

Meanwhile, put the gooseberries, water and sugar into a non-stick pan and simmer until the gooseberries have pulped. This can be done well in advance if you prefer. When the gooseberries are thoroughly cooked, add the butter and stir it into the sauce. Serve the sauce warm with the grilled mackerel.

Sole with lime butter

This is originally a recipe for Dover sole but as Lemon or Wytch sole are more widely available (and much cheaper) they make a good alternative. The lime flavour in the butter adds just the right note of sharpness to the fish's quite sweet flesh.

34

Serves 4

40 g (1½ oz) butter, softened
Grated rind and juice of 1 lime
1 tablespoon chopped fresh parsley
4 × 100–175 g (4–6 oz) sole fillets

Pre-heat the grill and line it with kitchen foil.

Mash the butter, lime rind and juice, and parsley together until it forms a coherent mass. Form into a little sausage roll and divide into 4. Cut each section in half and put 2 on the skin side of the fillets of sole (if they are not skinned), spreading them as if you were buttering bread. Grill for 3 to 4 minutes then turn the fillets over. Spoon the melted butter over the fish and grill for another 2 to 3 minutes before serving. As you serve, put the reserved butter on the fish to melt, and discard the grilling juices.

WINE *tip* A delicate fish, Alsace Pinot Blanc which adds a little creaminess.

WINE *tip* Oily fish and sharp sauce need something crisp and delicate with refreshing acidity – try French Ménétou-Salon (a Loire Sauvignon Blanc) or Vin de Pays des Côtes de Gascogne.

Halibut with nutmeg and orange

Herrings with oatmeal

4. Sautéeing fish

Sautéeing (shallow frying) is a very quick way of cooking fish. None of these dishes takes more than ten minutes from putting the fish in the pan to serving it on the plate – ideal for entertaining in these busy times.

Halibut with nutmeg and orange

Halibut is a very dense-textured fish with a strong, meaty flavour and very few of the dreaded bones. The flavourings may sound unusual but are delicious. Serve with new potatoes or tagliatelle.

Serves 4

50 g (2 oz) plain flour
½ teaspoon freshly grated nutmeg
4 × 100–175 g (4–6 oz) halibut steaks
25 g (1 oz) butter
1 tablespoon cooking oil
175 ml (6 fl oz) fresh orange juice
Juice of ½ lemon
1 tablespoon Worcestershire sauce

Mix together the flour and nutmeg and use to dust the fish. Heat the butter and oil in a frying pan big enough to take all the fillets in a single layer. Sauté them gently on both sides for 3 to 4 minutes. Turn up the heat, add the orange juice, lemon juice and Worcestershire sauce and bring to a rapid boil, spooning the sauce over the fish. It will thicken and glaze in a matter of 1 or 2 minutes. Do not cook for longer than this.

Herrings with oatmeal

Herrings and oatmeal are the classic Scottish combination. Herrings are now widely available again, having been banned from being fished for a while because their stocks had been so depleted. This dish is beautiful in its simplicity – it should be eaten with nothing except wholemeal or, better still, scoffa or oatmeal, bread and butter. And to drink? Buttermilk or tea.

Serves 4

2 teaspoons sea or coarse salt
4 medium-sized fresh herrings, gutted and trimmed
2 tablespoons oatmeal
1 lemon, quartered

Sprinkle the salt in a very solid frying pan with a non-stick or well seasoned surface. Heat the pan without any oil until the salt is just beginning to brown. Put in the herrings and cook over a medium heat for 4 to 5 minutes on each side. The herrings will grease the pan quite adequately with fish oil drawn out by the salt. After you've cooked them on the second side, sprinkle in the oatmeal which will crisp in the pan with the herrings. When it is nutty in texture and colour, serve the herrings sprinkled with the oatmeal and a quarter of lemon to squeeze over.

Trout with almonds and cucumber batons

Farm trout is now one of the easiest to obtain and best value of all fish. While it does have a few bones, they're easily removed and the flavour of well-fed fish, both mild and rich, is liked by almost everyone. This recipe is best served simply with new potatoes and no other vegetable dish.

Serves 4

1 tablespoon oil
4 × 175–225 g (6–8 oz) trout, gutted and trimmed
15 cm (6 inch) piece of cucumber
2 tablespoons butter
50 g (2 oz) slivered almonds

Heat the oil in a large frying pan into which all the trout will fit in one layer. Add the trout and sauté gently for 3 minutes. Split the cucumber lengthways, scoop out the seeds and cut across into slim half moons about 3 mm (⅛ inch) thick. Turn the trout and sauté for a further 3 to 4 minutes on the second side. Add the butter and turn the heat up until it foams. Add the cucumber, spread around the pan, and then the almonds and sauté carefully until the almonds start to turn golden. Serve the trout with a good measure of cucumber and almonds for each serving.

36

Plaice fillets with Parmesan

This is great with spinach and sautéed potatoes, but you can serve it with a wide variety of vegetables.

Serves 4

1 tablespoon oil
1 tablespoon butter
4 × 175 g (6 oz) plaice fillets
2 tablespoons grated Parmesan cheese
1 tablespoon chopped fresh parsley
½ teaspoon garlic salt

Place the oil and butter in a large frying pan into which all the plaice will fit in one layer and heat until the butter has ceased to sizzle. Put in the fish skin side up, sauté for 1 minute, turn over and sauté for another 2 to 3 minutes until just cooked through. Sprinkle with the Parmesan, parsley and garlic salt, covering the fish as much as possible. Put under a pre-heated grill for just 1 minute to allow the Parmesan to colour, then serve immediately, pouring any pan juices over the fish.

WINE tip **Plaice is delicate on its own so try a soft wine which will not overpower it – such as South African Colombar. But to cope with the Parmesan, a good weighty Italian white like the fuller, richer Verdicchio, or even a French red such as Côtes de St Mont or vin de pays des Côtes de Gascogne rouge.**

5. Pickling fish

Here are two simple recipes for two fish which have been traditionally pickled in Britain – mackerel and herring. Both recipes use methods which are slightly less vigorous than the historical British sousing systems.

French pickled mackerel

This is similar to the *Maquereau au Vin Blanc* which appeared for decades on almost every French *table d'hôte* menu. It's easy to make and will keep well covered in a fridge for three or four days. It makes a super starter and is delicate enough to be eaten with salad as a main course for a light lunch.

Serves 4 as a main course or 8 as a starter

8 mackerel fillets
300 ml (10 fl oz) water
Juice of 1 lemon
2 bay leaves
6 tablespoons white wine vinegar
1 teaspoon cracked black peppercorns (or coarsely ground black pepper)
1 teaspoon sea or coarse salt
1 onion, peeled and thinly sliced

Pre-heat the oven to gas mark 4, 180°C (350°F).
   Put the water, lemon juice, bay leaves, white wine vinegar, pepper and salt into a non-aluminum pan. Bring to the boil and simmer for 5 minutes. Add the onion and simmer for another 3 to 4 minutes until the onion is translucent. Place the mackerel in a baking dish, pour the hot marinade over them and bake in the oven for 20 minutes. Remove from the oven, turn the fish over and allow the dish to cool. Cover and keep in the fridge for 3 to 4 days before eating.

Scandinavian pickled herrings

The Scandinavians have a wide variety of pickled herring dishes. This is a very simple and delicious one that will keep for up to three weeks in the fridge. It is wonderful served with hot new potatoes and a cucumber salad.

Serves 4 to 8

8 herring fillets, skinned if possible
2 tablespoons sea or coarse salt
300 ml (10 fl oz) cider vinegar
300 ml (10 fl oz) boiled water
50 g (2 oz) caster sugar
2 bay leaves
4 sprigs fresh dill or 1 tablespoon freeze dried dill

Rub the fillets all over with salt and leave in a china or glass bowl for 1 hour. Rinse thoroughly in cold water and lay in a glass or china dish which will take them in 2 even layers. Mix the cider vinegar, cooled boiled water and sugar and stir until the sugar has dissolved. Add the bay leaves to the fish and the dill sprigs and pour over the marinade. It should cover the herrings. If it does not, you will need to turn the herrings every day. Cover the dish and keep in the fridge for 1 week before eating. The herrings will last 3 weeks if kept covered in the fridge.

37

Pickled fish won't easily take a wine. Try Aquavit, Schnapps or, less exotically, lager.

Three fabulous pâtés

Here are three crafty fish pâtés, two cold and one hot, which should satisfy almost every culinary need. The smoked mackerel pâté makes the most delicious picnic food, carried in a plastic container and spread 'on site' on crusty French bread.

Smoked mackerel pâté

Smoked mackerel can be obtained in a variety of flavours. Make sure you buy hot-smoked and not 'kippered' mackerel. Choose fish according to the flavour that most excites you – original, with garlic, with pepper or with herbs – surprisingly the flavourings make only a small difference to the flavour of the finished pâté, which is great with toast or crusty French bread.

Serves 4 to 8

1 slice white bread, crusts removed
2 tablespoons milk
225 g (8 oz) smoked mackerel fillets, skinned
120 ml (4 fl oz) fromage frais or Greek-style yoghurt
Juice of 1 lemon
1 tablespoon melted butter (optional)

38

Put the bread into a liquidizer or processor with the milk and mix to a smooth purée. Add the other ingredients except the butter, and blend to a smooth purée. If you're using the butter it does add richness. Melt it in a pan and pour it in once the pâté is smooth. Pack into a small soufflé dish or suitable china or glass mould and chill for at least 4 hours before using. For long-term (up to a week) storage, cover with a thin layer of melted butter and a piece of tightly drawn cling film.

 Something lively to cope with smoked fish – sparkling French Saumur or the 'pétillant' Vinho Verde.

Salmon and dill moulds

This is an extremely simple but very spectacular first course. It's best served hot, but you can also use it as a cold salmon pâté.

Serves 4

225 g (8 oz) salmon fillet, skinned
3 tablespoons fromage frais
1 tablespoon sunflower oil
2 eggs
1 tablespoon chopped fresh dill or ½ tablespoon freeze-dried dill
Salt and freshly ground black pepper

Cut the salmon fillet into 1 cm (½ inch) chunks and place in a food processor with all the other ingredients. Process for 10 seconds, scrape down and process for another 10 to 15 seconds until it's a smooth purée. Line 4 dariole moulds or small teacups with a little oiled cling film. Divide the pâté mixture between the cups, tap down till the surface is reasonably smooth and place in a frying pan with 2.5 cm (1 inch) of boiling water in it. Make sure that the water does not come near the top of the moulds or cups. Cover with a lid and simmer for 12 to 15 minutes until the pâtés are thoroughly cooked. Invert them carefully on to a plate to serve and remove the cling film. They're very nice on individual plates spread with 2 tablespoons of Tomato Coulis (see page 21).

 This classy dish needs a fullish wine, steely enough to cut through the richness – Chardonnay Vin de Pays d'Oc, or Chablis.

Neapolitan terrine

The trick is to make this in a loaf tin, to turn it out when it's cooked and chilled, and to slice it so that all the different layers are revealed. Serve with a fromage frais and herb sauce, one of the flavoured mayonnaises on pages 23–4 or a cold version of Arrabbiata Sauce (see page 22).

Serves 8

675 g (1½ lb) white fish fillets, cod or whiting
350 g (12 oz) salmon fillet, skinned
3 eggs
120 ml (4 fl oz) fromage frais
1 lemon
2 tablespoons oil
Salt and freshly ground black pepper
2 tablespoons chopped fresh parsley
*1 tablespoon chopped fresh dill or ½ tablespoon freeze-
 dried dill*
175 g (6 oz) carrots
175 g (6 oz) green French beans, topped and tailed

Pre-heat the oven to gas mark 4, 180°C (350°F), and line an oiled loaf tin with cling film or greaseproof paper.

Skin the white fish and salmon and cut them into 2.5 cm (1 inch) cubes. Place the white fish in a food processor with 2 eggs, 2 tablespoons of fromage frais, the juice of ½ the lemon, half the oil, salt and pepper, and process to a smooth purée, scraping the bowl down once during the process. Use half the mixture to fill the bottom of the loaf tin.

Add the herbs to the remaining white fish purée and process again until it turns green. Reserve this in a separate bowl. Rinse the processor then add the salmon cubes, the remaining egg, oil, lemon juice, fromage frais and seasoning. Process until smooth; reserve.

Peel the carrots, split them lengthways then cut those slices into 3. Cook the carrot and beans in boiling water for 5 minutes then drain. Put a layer of carrots on top of the white fish purée then add the green fish purée. Put a layer of green beans on top of that and then add the salmon purée. Tap the mould to make sure that the layers have settled down, place in a roasting tin filled with 2.5 cm (1 inch) of water and cover with a butter paper or piece of oiled kitchen foil. Bake in the oven for 45 to 50 minutes until the mousse is cooked through and has shrunk slightly from the sides of the tin. Remove from the water and allow to cool before chilling for at least 12 hours. Turn out, remove the cling film or greaseproof paper, and slice into 1 cm (½ inch) slices to serve.

WINE tip Something dry but not too lean to offset the carrot but with enough body for salmon and herbs – lightly oaked Spanish white Rioja or an oaked white from Valdepeñas in Spain.

FISH SKINNING IN FOUR EASY STEPS

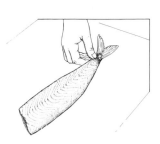

● Fillet the fish or get a fishmonger to do it for you. Put it on a board skin side down with the thin end towards you.

39

● Sprinkle the tail with salt and seize it firmly.

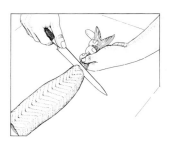

● Holding a very sharp knife in your other hand, cut at 45 degrees away from you until you reach the skin.

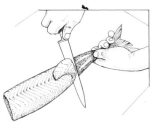

● Turn the knife parallel to the board, make a slight sawing action with it and pull the fish skin towards you by the tail. The fillet will lift off the skin.

CHAPTER FOUR

While in Europe, shellfish are regarded as a delicacy and cooked with understanding and style, the British tend to be rather wary and miss out on the delicate and sumptuous flavours they offer.

shellfish

Eight crucial crustaceans and two key facts about each of them

1. Prawns

These come in a variety of sizes up to and including the gigantic Mediterranean prawns or *gambas*. But here we are talking about North Atlantic prawns that never in their wildest dreams exceed the size of your little finger, and almost inevitably arrive ready-cooked and bright pink.

- **Fresh** It is possible occasionally to buy fresh, cooked prawns with or without their shells. But make sure you're not paying the fresh premium for the frozen product. Reputable fishmongers and supermarkets should play fair.

- **Frozen** Frozen prawns are fine and come in several forms. Some have an ice shell (these should be cheaper because ice doesn't cost as much as prawns), others are 'blast frozen' (chilled very quickly) and these have the best flavour. You can also buy uncooked frozen prawns in some fishmongers and supermarkets, which need cooking until they turn pink. (There are also prawns in brine – fine for a garnish but not for serious eating.)

TWO HOT DISHES WITH PRAWNS

Cooked prawns should be cooked as little as possible. Any more than two or three minutes heat will turn them rubbery.

**Above: *Melon, prawn and yoghurt salad* (page 43).
Below: *Dressed crab* (page 45).**

Prawn and fennel gratin

A creamy dish with a hint of Italian flavour from the fennel. This is good served with crusty bread, with rice as a main course, or as a starter.

Serves 4

*1 × 225–275 g (8–10 oz) head fennel
1 tablespoon olive oil
1 tablespoon butter
300 ml (10 fl oz) Béchamel Sauce (see page 19), hot
175 g (6 oz) cooked, peeled prawns
Juice of ½ lemon
Salt and freshly ground black pepper
4 tablespoons grated Parmesan cheese*

Pre-heat the grill.
   Trim the fennel, saving the green, feathery bits for garnish. Chop the leaves and cut the fennel bulb into 5 mm (¼ inch) dice. Heat the oil and butter until the butter melts. Add the cubes of fennel and cook for 5 to 6 minutes until pale golden and succulent. Stir it into the hot Béchamel Sauce and add the prawns and lemon juice, checking the whole mixture for seasoning. Pour into a flameproof gratin or baking dish and top with the grated Parmesan cheese. Place under the hot grill for 3 to 4 minutes until the top is bubbling and golden. Sprinkle the finely chopped fennel leaves over the gratin dish and serve immediately.

WINE tip **Needs positive flavour with enough character to match the spice – the crisp, almost green Torres Viña Sol from the Barcelona area of Spain is a suggestion, or an inexpensive oaked Spanish wine from Navarra.**

Stir-fried prawns with cashew nuts and mangetout

A slightly Westernized version of a Chinese technique. This can also be made with uncooked prawns which require five minutes extra in the pan. It's fine as a light main course served with plain boiled rice or it can be served with other Chinese-style dishes.

Serves 4

2 tablespoons orange juice
2 tablespoons soy sauce
1 teaspoon lemon juice
1 tablespoon oil
1 clove garlic, peeled and crushed
1 teaspoon peeled and chopped fresh ginger root
225 g (8 oz) mangetout
75 g (3 oz) lightly salted cashew nuts
225 g (8 oz) cooked, peeled prawns
1 teaspoon cornflour (optional)

42

Mix together the orange juice, soy sauce and lemon juice. Heat the oil in a large frying pan or wok, add the garlic and ginger and stir-fry for 30 seconds. Add the mangetout and turn and stir until bright emerald green. Add the cashew nuts and stir-fry for 30 seconds then add the prawns and stir-fry for 30 seconds. Add the sauce ingredients and cook for 1 minute over a high heat, tossing and stirring to make sure everything is coated. You may, if you wish, thicken the sauce by stirring the cornflour into the sauce mixture before adding it to the pan.

These hot oriental flavours cry out for a good lager such as Czechoslovakian Budweiser. Or try a marvellous, clove-scented Wheat Beer from Germany.

TWO COLD DISHES WITH PRAWNS

Perfect prawn cocktail

This much-maligned dish is delicious when properly made. You need fresh Mayonnaise (see page 23) and really good prawns.

Serves 4

1 small crisp head lettuce
Grated rind and juice of 1 lime
1 tablespoon tomato purée
100 g (4 oz) home-made Mayonnaise (see page 23)
225 g (8 oz) cooked, peeled prawns
Piece of celery stalk from the centre of the head, leaves removed and finely chopped
1 tablespoon chopped fresh parsley

Wash the lettuce, dry it thoroughly and slice it into 5 mm (¼ inch) ribbons. Use these to line the base of 4 individual bowls or serving glasses. Mix together the lime juice, tomato purée and mayonnaise. Add the prawns and celery. Pile on to the lettuce ribbons, sprinkle over a little parsley and serve not more than 30 minutes later.

WINE tip **A grapey wine with slight sweetness and softness – a lightly alcoholic Moscato from Piedmont in Italy would be delicious.**

Melon, prawn and yoghurt salad

A light, low fat alternative to the Prawn Cocktail.

Serves 4

1 small Galia melon
100 g (4 oz) seedless grapes
225 g (8 oz) cooked, peeled prawns
120 ml (4 fl oz) Greek yoghurt
1 tablespoon finely chopped fresh parsley

Cut the melon in half, remove the seeds and scoop out the flesh using a melon baller or small soup spoon to produce round-shaped pieces. Mix these thoroughly with the washed and de-stalked grapes, the prawns and the yoghurt. Pile into tall wine glasses or serving bowls and sprinkle with the parsley. The flavours improve with up to an hour in the fridge.

2. Shrimps

- **Size** Shrimp in this context means the tiny crustaceans that come from places like Morecambe Bay, in Britain. In other parts of the world, shrimp can mean shellfish of a wide variety or size, including the giant shrimp of the Gulf Coast of America, nearer the size of your thumb than a fingernail. For our purposes, however, they are small and come either pink or grey – a little brother to prawns.

- **Picking** How many of the bits of the shrimp should you get rid of before you eat it? Faced with a bowlful and some mayonnaise to dip them in, some people get rid of the heads but eat the tails and remaining bits of leg. Some people eat them all and others pick the head, legs and tiny tail out of each one. This is what you should do if you're going to pot them, though it's a fiddly business and takes a lot of time.

  If you have picked them clean and want to pot them this is the method.

Potted shrimps

Serve this as a starter with crusty wholemeal toast.

225 g (8 oz) fine butter
450 g (1 lb) cleaned shrimp
2 teaspoons paprika
Juice of 2 lemons
1 teaspoon salt
½ teaspoon ground mace
Freshly ground black pepper

Clarify the butter by melting it in a non-stick saucepan and, when it is completely liquid, pouring it off carefully, leaving the white residues behind. Put two-thirds of the clarified butter, the shrimps, paprika, lemon juice, mace, salt and a good seasoning of black pepper in a clean saucepan. Bring to the boil, remove from the heat immediately and leave to stand for 5 minutes. Pour into individual soufflé dishes. Allow the potted shrimp to settle and then seal with the final layer of butter. Cover with cling film and keep in the fridge for up to 5 to 6 days, but they are at their best eaten after about 3 days.

43
....

 SHELLFISH AND FOOD POISONING
Many shellfish are 'filter feeders' and they can harbour both bacteria and viruses: hence their reputation for food poisoning. Many companies that sell shellfish now test them first and often only buy them from carefully controlled farms or unpolluted seas (Britain's seas can still be very polluted). The best advice is never eat raw shellfish unless you are confident about its source. Well-cooked shellfish are safe.

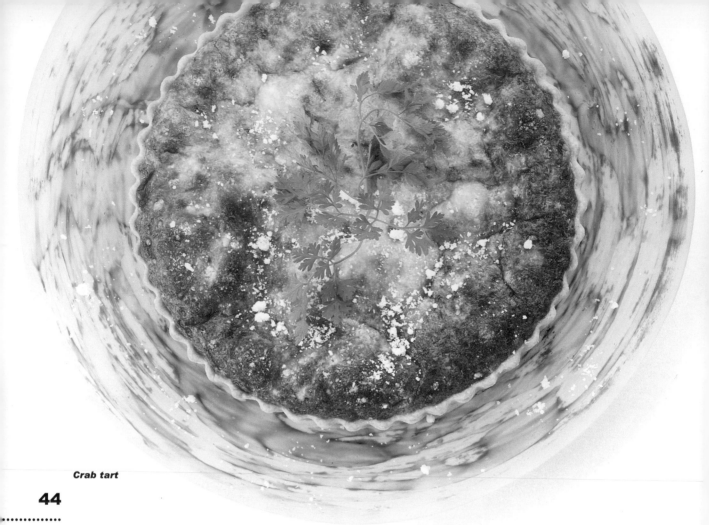

Crab tart

3. Crab

Choose a heavy, live crab which does not make a sloshing noise when you shake it. If you are buying a cooked crab, move on to 'Dismembering' below.

- **Humane killing** Crabs, like lobsters, can and should be humanely killed. To achieve this with a crab, turn it on to its back, avoiding its claws, and with the back of a heavy knife or chopper, hit it firmly across the underside of the body on a central line running from front to back. One good bang and the crab will be dead. It should then be immediately boiled for 20 minutes.

- **Dismembering** Allow the crab to cool slightly, pull the shell open from the back – you may need to prise it open with a knife point – and remove the spongy 'dead man's fingers' and the sac of gritty stuff immediately behind the mouth parts. The rest of the crab is edible although you will need patience to remove some of the white flesh from the body cavities of the central part of the crab.

To kill a crab humanely turn it on its back and hit it firmly across the underside of the body on the central line running from front to back

Pull the shell open from the back. You may need to prise it open with a knife point

Remove the spongy 'dead man's fingers' and the sac of gritty stuff behind the mouth parts

Potted shrimps (page 43)

Dressed crab

The basic cold crab dish. Freshly cooked there is nothing better.

Serves 4

1 × 900 g (2 lb) crab, cooked and cooled
Grated rind and juice of 1 lemon
2 tablespoons chopped fresh parsley
4 tablespoons Mayonnaise (see page 23)
4 tablespoons brown breadcrumbs
2 teaspoons Dijon mustard

Crack the crab claws and remove and reserve the flesh, keeping it as intact as possible. Put all the rest of the white meat from the claw arms, the legs and body of the crab into a bowl. Season with the grated lemon rind and half the juice. Add a tablespoon of chopped parsley and 3 tablespoons of the mayonnaise and stir lightly. Put the breadcrumbs, mustard, remaining mayonnaise and lemon juice, in a separate bowl and mix thoroughly with the brown meat from the crab, scooping it right out from inside the shell. Wash the shell and dry it. Use the brown meat mixture to fill the two sides of the shell. Pack the white meat into the central area. Arrange the claws attractively on top and spread a little parsley in a line down the middle.

To serve, make sure each person gets a portion of white and brown meat to eat with plenty of thinly cut wholemeal bread and butter.

WINE tip Rich but delicate meat so a wine not too full of flavour but with just enough body to go with mayonnaise – French Bourgogne-Aligoté or non-oaked Chardonnay either from southern France or northern Italy.

Crab tart

This can be made in individual-sized tart tins or a 20 cm (8 inch) tart ring or baked without the benefit of any pastry in individual ramekin dishes.

45
············

Serves 4

White and brown meat from 1 × 675–900 g (1½–2 lb) cooked crab
Juice of ½ lemon
1 teaspoon Dijon mustard
Shortcrust pastry to line 1 × 20 cm (8 inch) or 4 × 7.5 cm (3 inch) shells
150 ml (5 fl oz) double cream
1 heaped teaspoon cornflour
½ teaspoon salt
Freshly ground black pepper
2 eggs
50 g (2 oz) Parmesan cheese, grated

Pre-heat the oven to gas mark 4, 180°C (350°F).

Mix the brown crab meat with the lemon juice and mustard and use it to fill the base of the pastry (or soufflé dishes). Put the cream in a small non-stick saucepan, whisk in the cornflour and bring gently to the boil, stirring until thickened. Add the white crab meat and season generously with salt and pepper. Remove from the heat, beat in the eggs and pour the mixture into the pie casings or soufflé dishes. Sprinkle with the Parmesan cheese and bake in the oven for 25 minutes until the filling is cooked and golden and the pastry browned throughout.

Crab cakes

A recipe originally from the southern states of America, this is a marvellous way of making a little crab go a long way. Superb eaten at brunch, very good as a first course for a dinner party and, if it's your inclination, fantastic at high tea.

Serves 4

White and brown meat from a 675 g (1½ lb) cooked crab
175 g (6 oz) white breadcrumbs
50 g (2 oz) Cheddar or Gruyère cheese, grated
Juice of ½ lemon
½ teaspoon tabasco or chilli sauce
4 spring onions, finely chopped
2 eggs

Mix the white and brown crab meat with the breadcrumbs, cheese, lemon juice, chilli sauce and chopped spring onions. Separate one of the eggs and use the 2 yolks and 1 white to bind the mixture. Shape into 12 balls and flatten them into the shape of miniature hamburgers.

Whisk the remaining egg white until thick. Dip the crab cakes in the egg white then leave to set, out of the fridge, for about 20 to 30 minutes. When ready to eat, you can either deep-fry them for 4 to 5 minutes or shallow fry them in hot oil for about 5 minutes each side. They should be served hot.

46

4. Lobster

The most luxurious shellfish of all, lobster is widely available if you can afford it. It is black or dark blue when still alive, which is how you should plan to buy it. By the way, it's a lobster if it has claws – if it has long feelers instead, it's a warm-water cousin called a crayfish.

● **Humane killing** There is a tradition of putting live lobsters into boiling water or even, in France and Japan, splitting them in half while still alive and then cooking them. The humane method is to hold the lobster carefully down on a surface with its head (and claws!) pointing to the left – if you are right-handed. Insert a knife point in the top of the third segment, from the left of its shell, and cut down about 2.5 cm (1 inch). The lobster will die immediately. You can tell this because it will go limp. You can then put it into boiling water or cut it in half and grill it with no loss of flavour.

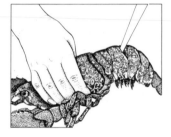

The best way to kill a lobster (see above)

● **Dismembering** This should be done after the lobster has been cooked in boiling water, about 20 minutes for an average-sized lobster. Remove the claws and split the body in half vertically from front to back. Remove and discard the grey, flat, feathery bits in the head and the long dark 'vein' running the length of the tail. Everything else in the lobster, including the green and orange bits, is edible. Crack the claws to extract the meat – connoisseurs crack the legs and extract the meat from those, too.

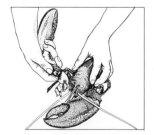

Remove the claws

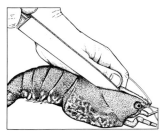

Split the body in half vertically from front to back

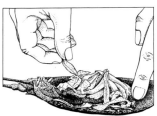

Remove and discard the grey, flat feathery bits in the head

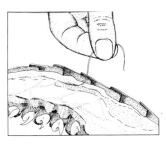

Also remove the long dark 'vein' running the length of the tail

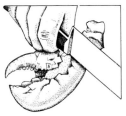

Crack the claws to extract the meat

TWO SCRUMPTIOUS LOBSTER RECIPES

Lobster with lemon-drawn butter

This is strictly for serious eaters.

Serves 2

75 g (3 oz) fine butter
Juice of 1 lemon
1 × 675–900 g (1½–2 lb) lobster, cooked and split as on
page 46

Pre-heat the grill and line it with kitchen foil.
Melt the butter in a non-stick pan and when fully liquid but not boiling, pour out, discarding the white sediment in the bottom. Add the lemon juice to the clarified butter. Spread some of this on the cut sides and cracked claws of the lobster and place under a grill for 5 to 6 minutes until brown and sizzling. Pour some more lemon butter over the lobster and serve with napkins, finger bowls and the remaining butter to act as a dip.

Lobster thermidor

Named after the month of August in the Revolutionary calendar in France, this highly flavoured dish reflects how high feelings ran at that time. Serve it with a saffron pilau or mashed potatoes and plenty of crusty French bread. A salad should follow, not accompany it.

Serves 4

1 × 900 g (2 lb) lobster, cooked and split as on page 46
1 tablespoon Bordeaux or Dijon mustard
300 ml (10 fl oz) thick Béchamel Sauce (see page 19)
Salt and freshly ground black pepper
100 g (4 oz) Gruyère cheese

Pre-heat the grill.
Remove all the flesh from the lobster, leaving the body and tail sections intact to act as receptacles, and cut the meat into 5 mm (½ inch) dice. Stir the mustard into the Béchamel Sauce, season generously, then stir in the lobster meat until well coated. Pile into the shells (or a gratin dish if you prefer), sprinkle with the Gruyère cheese and grill for 4 to 5 minutes until the cheese has melted and the sauce is bubbling.

5. Mussels

Mussels are the most widely available and cheapest of all hard-shell shellfish. They now come in packs that need minimal cleaning.

- **Cleaning and safety** Wash all the mussels thoroughly in plenty of water. Discard any with a cracked shell or a shell that stays open after you've tapped it a couple of times. Remove any obvious encrustations and the beard with a sharp knife. Put back into salted cold water to keep or cook immediately.

- **Basic cooking** This is the standard first stage for almost all mussel recipes. Get a large saucepan into which all the mussels will fit at once. For 1.2 litres (2 pints) of mussels (enough for four people for a first or two for a main course), put in a wine glass of apple juice (cider or white wine are alternatives), a chopped clove of garlic and a teaspoon of salt. Bring it to the boil, add all the mussels, put a well-fitting lid on the pan and cook for 4 or 5 minutes over maximum heat, shaking the pan two or three times. Take it off the heat and remove the mussels. Any that have not opened at this point should be discarded. This is basic Moule Marinière, with a tablespoon of chopped fresh parsley sprinkled over the top.

- **Moules à la crème** Cook the mussels as above and transfer them to a warm serving dish. Strain the liquid (there's usually some sand in the bottom) and return it to the pan. Mix 150 ml (5 fl oz) of double cream and 2 teaspoons of cornflour to a smooth paste, add it to the pan and bring to the boil. Add a tablespoon of chopped fresh parsley and pour over for Moules à la Crème.

- **Mussels with garlic butter** Cook the mussels as above and discard the liquid. Take half the shell off each mussel and place the mussels, fish up, on a baking tray. Mix 50 g (2 oz) of butter with a chopped, crushed clove of garlic, the juice of half a lemon and 2 tablespoons of chopped fresh parsley. Dot each of the open mussels with a blob (about half a teaspoon) of the mixture and flash under a hot grill for 1½ minutes.

WINE *tip* A thrusting white wine to cut through garlic but with rustic fruit and body – French Saumur Blanc, the rosé Cabernet d'Anjou, or a rosé from the south of France such as Tavel or Minervois.

6. Oysters

Oysters are the most expensive shellfish in Britain although they're now, by and large, farmed. You can get them in most supermarkets and fishmongers, especially if you order them in advance, and they are available from one or two very reliable sources by mail (see page 50). The native oysters are making a slow come-back in both Whitstable and Colchester. They're much more expensive than the farmed ones but are extraordinarily good if you can get them.

● **How to open oysters** You need a blunt-pointed, sharp-bladed and very strong knife and something to protect your oyster-holding hand with – this is not only from the rough shell of the oyster but from the knife should it slip. A heavy oven glove or a very carefully wrapped tea towel is crucial. Hold the oyster flat side down on something firm like a chopping board. Put the point of the knife into the gap between upper and lower shell, half way along the side. Drive it in firmly and swivel it round to cut the hinge at the narrow end of the oyster. The oyster should then open slightly. Try and conserve as much of the juice as possible.

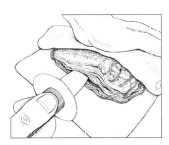

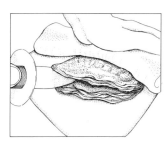

Opening an oyster (see above)

● **To eat oysters raw** Remove the top shell entirely, trim the black, fringy beard away from the main body of the oyster, squeeze a piece of lemon over them, and swallow with delight.

If raw oysters worry you, try cooking them in one of these two delicious ways.

● **Oysters mornay** Three oysters per person is plenty for this dish. Put the oysters into their deep half shell and place them on a baking tray so that they remain fairly level. A handful of rock salt may help provide the base for this. Prepare a Mornay Sauce (see page 20). Put a tablespoon of this over each oyster and add a teaspoon of grated Parmesan cheese to each one. Bake under a hot grill for 5 minutes.

WINE tip | Something dry but softly rounded with approachable fruit – French Entre-deux-Mers or Italian Pinot Bianco.

● **Tomato and basil oysters** Prepare the oysters as above. Put 200 g (7 oz) tinned, chopped Italian tomatoes into a pan with a little olive oil, a pinch of sugar and salt, and a couple of drops of tabasco or chilli sauce. Stir and bring to the boil then simmer until reduced a little. Stir in a tablespoon of pesto (basil, garlic and Parmesan paste, available in all supermarkets), and put a tablespoon of the mixture on each oyster. Grill for 3 to 4 minutes until thoroughly hot.

49

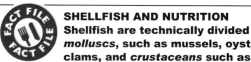

SHELLFISH AND NUTRITION
Shellfish are technically divided into *molluscs*, such as mussels, oysters or clams, and *crustaceans* such as prawns, shrimps, crabs and lobsters. All are good sources of protein, vitamin B_{12} and trace elements. The soft shells and tails are very high in calcium.

  Now an important question – are oysters an aphrodisiac? There is no solid medical evidence for this but if it works for you . . .

7. Clams

Clams are a most neglected shellfish in Britain. In America, Italy, France and Spain, they are a favourite. The edible ones come in all sizes from a thumbnail to a handspan. Although clams can be eaten raw, they are much better cooked.

- **Buying clams** Most supermarkets and fishmongers will get them (if they haven't got them already) if you ask them. They are also available by post.

- **Opening clams** The big ones, the size of the palm of your hand – the kind that can be made into chowder – can be opened in a manner similar to oysters, though they need to be surprised. If they know the knife's coming they clamp so tightly shut it's impossible to get the blade in. The simplest method, though, is to pop them into the freezer for about 10 minutes; this renders them unconscious and the shells open without difficulty. You can cut the hinge open and proceed. Little ones don't usually need opening before you cook them, but you can freeze them as above.

50

FACT FILE

SHELLFISH BY POST
You can order oysters – both Pacific and native (when in season) – by post. Clams are also available from Seasalter Shellfish. Here are some addresses:

Colchester Oyster Fishery
Pyefleet Quay, East Mersea, Colchester, Essex.
(Tel: 0206 384141).

Loch Fyne Oysters (Pacific only)
Clachan Farm, Ardkinglas, Cairndow, Argyll PA26 8BH. (Tel: 0499 6217)

Seasalter Shellfish (Whitstable) Ltd
The Harbour, Whitstable, Kent CT5 1AB.
(Tel: 0227 272003)

TWO CLAM RECIPES

Clam chowder

A great, classic recipe from New England. It can be made with tinned or frozen clams if you can't get the fresh article.

Serves 4

225 g (8 oz) clam meat
450 g (1 lb) new potatoes, peeled
1 bunch spring onions
600 ml (1 pint) milk
Salt and freshly ground black pepper
150 ml (5 fl oz) single cream
2 teaspoons cornflour
1 tablespoon chopped fresh parsley (optional)
4 cream crackers or water biscuits (optional)

Dice the clam meat and potatoes into 1 cm (½ inch) pieces. Cut the onions into 5 mm (¼ inch) lengths. Put the potatoes and onions into the milk, bring to the boil and simmer for about 5 to 6 minutes until almost tender. Add the clam meat and simmer for another 4 to 5 minutes. Season generously. Mix together the cream and cornflour, and stir it into the pan. Bring gently to the boil, stirring until the mixture thickens. Serve immediately in individual bowls, sprinkled with parsley and the crushed crackers or biscuits, if liked.

WINE tip **Fairly robust flavours, so not a fine wine. Needs French country wine with an appley character – Vin de Pays d'Oc Chardonnay or Gaillac.**

Above: *Lobster with lemon-drawn butter* **(page 47)**
Below: *Moules à la crème* **(page 48)**

Spaghetti alle vongole

The classic Italian way with clams is to serve them with the most traditional of pasta. Use only half a teaspoon of each of the herbs if you are using freeze-dried. It is not traditional to eat Parmesan cheese with fish pasta dishes, but tradition does not always have to be obeyed.

Serves 4

4 tablespoons olive oil
1 clove garlic, peeled and finely chopped
1 medium onion, peeled and finely chopped
1 × 400 g (14 oz) tin chopped Italian tomatoes
1 tablespoon tomato purée
1 teaspoon chopped fresh thyme
1 teaspoon chopped fresh oregano
1 teaspoon chopped fresh basil
Salt and freshly ground black pepper
1 kg (2¼ lb) small clams, approximately 2.5 cm
*   (1 inch) across, in shell, washed*
350 g (12 oz) cooked spaghetti, drained and tossed in
*   butter*

52

Heat the oil and fry the garlic and onion for 2 to 3 minutes. Add the tomatoes and the tomato purée, stir well then simmer for 15 minutes. Add the herbs, season generously and add the unopened clams. Put a lid on the saucepan, shake vigorously and cook over a high heat for 4 to 5 minutes. The clams will open and give off some juice. Put some hot spaghetti into 4 soup bowls and pour the sauce over the top.

WINE *tip* A mouthful of flavours, so choose a white wine with plenty to say for itself such as Pinot Grigio from northern Italy or Tuscan Galestro.

8. Squid

The thought of eating squid puts a lot of people off, but the actuality – delicate, pure white, boneless and succulent flesh – soon converts all but the most obdurate. If you think they're rubbery, then you've never had them properly cooked. Technically, squid is not a shellfish but is placed here for convenience

- **Cleaning** A fishmonger will do this for you, but if you are into DIY . . . Place the squid in a bowl of cold water and you will find that the purpley outer skin rubs off with virtually no effort, leaving the milky white flesh. Pull the tentacle part out of the end of the squid and empty the contents of the body sac into a plastic bag or a rubbish bin, pulling out the transparent quill-pen-shaped cartilage as well. If you want to, you can dispose of the tentacles, or you can cut them off and use them as well. Rinse the fish carefully and it's ready to cook; 450 g (1 lb) should take no more than 5 minutes to prepare in this effortless manner.

- **Cooking** Cut the squid up into rings across the body and you're ready to proceed with a number of different recipes.

- **Crisp-fried squid** Dry the squid rings, dip them in a little beaten egg and then in some breadcrumbs and deep or shallow-fry. If deep-frying, it takes about 4 to 5 minutes; if shallow-frying, about 5 minutes a side. Serve with tartare sauce while they're hot.

WINE *tip* Good, honest plonk is needed for this! Portuguese red Vinho Verde would be great but French Gamay de Touraine is a good alternative.

PREPARING SQUID

Place the squid in a bowl of cold water and rub off the purpley outer skin

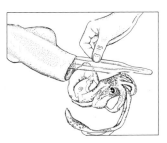

Pull the tentacle part out of the end of the squid

Pull out the transparent quill-pen-shaped cartilage as well

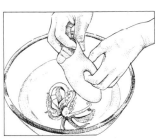

Either cut the tentacles off and use them as well, or dispose of them

Rinse the fish carefully

Stir-fried squid with red and green peppers

Serve this delicious stir-fry with boiled rice and, for a meal for six or eight, with two or three other oriental dishes. [Stir-fry mangetout (page 126), Rich turkey stir-fry (page 89), Far Eastern rice (page 150) and Tom yam kung soup (page 16)]

Serves 4

450 g (1 lb) squid, cleaned and prepared
4 spring onions
1 tablespoon oil
1 teaspoon chopped garlic
1 teaspoon chopped fresh ginger root
1 red pepper, de-seeded and thinly sliced
1 green pepper, de-seeded and thinly sliced
2 tablespoons soy sauce
1 teaspoon lime juice

Slice the cleaned squid into very thin rings. Trim and cut the spring onions into 2.5 cm (1 inch) lengths. Heat the oil in a wok or large frying pan, add the garlic and ginger and stir for 30 seconds. Add the squid and cook, stirring and turning, for 3 to 4 minutes. Add the green and red peppers, spring onions, soy sauce and lime juice, turn the heat to maximum and stir-fry for 3 to 4 minutes until the peppers are still crisp but hot right through.

53

DRINKS TIP

Big flavours, so sparkling water would probably be best, or delicately weak jasmine tea.

CHAPTER FIVE

· ·

We eat 28 million eggs a day in Britain and they are the most versatile of all our cooking ingredients. Yet we often tend to take them for granted rather than using them as a star turn.

eggs

Five key choices to make about eggs

The EC has agreed the following five categories for egg production.

- **Farmyard** Eggs produced by chickens genuinely living in farmyard conditions.

- **Traditional free range** Eggs produced by chickens with access to large areas of open ground, usually fed on an exclusively grain diet.

- **Free range** These comply with the EC regulations for space for the birds, approximately 1 square metre (39 square inches) per chicken, with access to fresh air.

- **Barn or perchery** Percheries leave hens unconstrained inside large open buildings. They sometimes have access to fresh air, with the birds able to perch in a variety of locations.

- **Battery or intensive** The traditional factory-farmed egg, produced by birds physically constrained and fed with a view to their maximum production.

You can also buy organic eggs. The hens are reared to Soil Association organic standards.

There is also a move to go back to old breeds of chicken to produce eggs with better flavour. Some of these are marketed widely under the Speckledy Hen label and really do seem to taste better.

EGGS AND SALMONELLA
It is not known what proportion of eggs is, or ever was, contaminated by the salmonella food poisoning bacterium. But eggs (cooked or raw) remain a great breeding ground for salmonella once cross-contaminated. So basic hygiene is crucial:

● **Cross-contamination:** Avoid all cross-contamination by treating eggs like raw poultry in the kitchen (see rules for poultry on page 66).
● **Storage:** Keep eggs in the fridge until required.
● **Raw egg dishes:** Cooking eggs thoroughly kills salmonella if it is present. Hence official government advice is still to avoid eating raw egg dishes such as ice-cream and mayonnaise. It is certainly sensible not to give raw egg dishes to vulnerable people such as the sick, the elderly, the very young and pregnant women. But since the risk of poisoning is still very small the rest of us may decide to take our chances. Despite all the scares about eggs contaminated at source it is a fact that food poisoning cases would fall dramatically if we all obeyed proper food hygiene practice in the kitchen.

55
· · · · · · · · · · ·

Soufflé (page 60)

Four kinds of omelettes

1. French omelettes

This is the classic, folded omelette, often with a filling and usually flavoured. You need only worry about four things.

Break the eggs into a bowl and beat lightly with a fork

- **Choice of pan** Choose a pan smaller than you think you'll need. Good French omelettes are made thicker than you would expect and a 13 cm (5 inch) pan is quite enough for 3 eggs, an 18 cm (7 inch) for 6, and a 25 cm (10 inch) for 10 eggs. You need 2 or 3 eggs for each person. You can make individual omelettes or a large omelette and divide it up after it has been rolled. Both methods are traditional in France.

Melt a little butter in a pan, add the eggs and scramble with a fork. Allow the bottom to set and add the appropriate flavouring

- **Beating** Break the eggs into a bowl and beat them lightly with a fork. Don't use a whisk and don't beat them to a froth. You can add a little water if you like for a lighter omelette, but never milk or cream.

When fully cooked, use a spatula or a fork to fold it in half, away from the handle

56
....

- **Cooking** Melt a knob of butter the size of half a walnut for each set of 3 eggs in the pan. Let it heat until the butter is completely melted and has stopped sizzling. Add the eggs and scramble with a fork for a minute or so over maximum heat until all the eggs curdle. Allow the bottom to set and add the appropriate flavouring.

    When the omelette is fully cooked (after no more than 2 minutes) use a spatula or a fork to fold it in half, away from the handle. Then tip the pan away from you so that the omelette rolls over on to a warmed plate. It should form an oval with the centre still moist and the outside crisp and browned in patches.

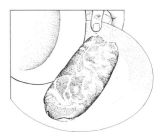

Tip the pan away from you so that the omelette rolls over on a warmed plate

Fillings These can be almost anything you please but some particularly good ones are:

- 2 tablespoons of grated Gruyère or other strong, hard cheese, added before folding;
- 1 tablespoon per serving of chopped fresh herbs – parsley, chives and marjoram are tasty;
- croûtons – tiny 5 mm (¼ inch) cubes of bread quickly fried in butter or oil before you start making the omelette, then add a tablespoon per serving as a filling;
- mushrooms, sliced and tossed quickly in a little butter for a minute before you make the omelette;
- cooked, hot, buttered spinach, about a tablespoon or so spread over the omelette before folding.

WINE tip **Eggs tend to coat the mouth and detract from the flavour of wine, so don't buy anything too special. With the refined flavour of Gruyère, a light red such as young Chianti or Valpolicella from Italy or French Beaujolais.**

2. Spanish omelettes (tortillas)

Very different from the French style, this is served as a flat cake with a lot of vegetable bound with the egg rather than folded in.

- **Pan** The pan should be at least 2.5 cm (1 inch) deep and 18 cm (7 inches) across for two people, 25 cm (10 inches) for four, and 30 cm (12 inches) for six.

- **Fillings** The classic filling is a mixture of Spanish onion and cooked potato in equal quantities. Variations include: sausage, tomatoes, finely sliced cold meats, anchovies, prawns, cheese or herbs. Please note: not all of these are included at the same time.

Tortilla

Serves 2 as a main course

2 tablespoons olive oil
175 g (6 oz) onions, peeled and sliced
175 g (6 oz) cooked potatoes, peeled and cubed
6 eggs
½ tablespoon chopped fresh herbs

Pre-heat the grill.

Heat the oil in the pan until hot. Fry the onions for 3 to 4 minutes until translucent. Add the potatoes and stir with the onions until lightly browned. Beat the eggs in a bowl until well mixed but not frothy. Pour over the onion and potato mixture and turn till the whole is amalgamated. Allow the bottom to set. Add herbs and any or two of the suggested additional ingredients. When the bottom is set, place under a hot grill for 1 to 1½ minutes until the top is browned and bubbling. Serve in slices like a cake directly from the pan.

WINE tip **Light oak-aged white would be traditional – you could try the ever-popular Don Darius Bianco or a Navarra white, both from Spain.**

3. Italian omelettes (fritatta)

A thinner, more pancake-like omelette that is served flat. Often made in individual-sized servings, it has a variety of possible ingredients (as well as the eggs!).

- **Pan** A shallow frying pan is ideal for this.

- **Fillings** These are usually vegetable: sliced courgettes; a couple of tablespoons of nutmeg-flavoured spinach; finely chopped green and red peppers; thickly sliced fresh plum tomatoes; broccoli florets the size of half a walnut. These should be used separately, not in mixtures.

- **Cooking** For an individual omelette, heat a tablespoon of olive oil in the pan and cook 25–50 g (1–2 oz) of the chosen vegetable until hot right through but still crisp. Beat 2 eggs very thoroughly, pour around the vegetable, and shake the pan so that the egg is spread evenly over the base. It should be like a thick pancake with the vegetables proud in the middle. Cook for about 1 to 1½ minutes until the egg is completely set. Season generously – it can be dusted with grated Parmesan cheese at this point – and serve flat on to a hot plate.

WINE
tip
Light Italian reds like Dolcetto d'Alba or Teroldego Rotaliano.

4. Soufflé omelettes

These are a fancy form of omelette – easy to do but spectacular. They can be made savoury or sweet. The simpler the filling, the more the impact.

- **Sweet omelette fillings** A tablespoon per portion of good French-style conserve or jam with or without a teaspoon of toasted, slivered almonds.

- **Savoury omelette fillings** These benefit from a tablespoon of flaked, cooked, smoked haddock mixed with cream, or white crab meat, or finely grated fresh Parmesan or Gruyère cheese.

Soufflé omelette

These have to be made in individual-sized portions unless you're a master craftsman. A 13–15 cm (5–6 inch), preferably non-stick pan, is ideal.

Serves 1

2 eggs, separated
Butter
1 tablespoon appropriate filling
1 teaspoon icing sugar or grated cheese, depending on sweet or savoury

Pre-heat the grill.
   Beat the egg yolks. In a separate bowl beat the whites until stiff. Fold them into the yolks. Heat a frying pan until very hot. Add half a walnut-sized portion of butter. When it stops sizzling, add the omelette mixture and cook over a high heat. It will puff up and the bottom will set. Flash it under the hot grill for about 30 seconds to set the top. Spread the filling over half the omelette, fold over gently and sprinkle over with the sugar or cheese. Serve immediately on a warm plate. It should look like a half-closed cushion.

Five other ways to enjoy eggs

1. Boiled eggs

A few simple elementary rules make life much easier:

- Never cook eggs straight out of the fridge. Allow them to come to room temperature first if possible.

- Pierce the end with a needle or sharp pin. This will help prevent the shell cracking.

- Soft-boiled eggs, sizes 1 or 2, need 3½ to 4 minutes cooking only. Remove from the water and break the blunt end of the shell with a spoon to stop the cooking going on before you eat it.

- **Eggs mollet** These are eggs boiled for 5 minutes and then dipped in cold water before carefully shelling. The whites will be completely set and the yolks still soft, which makes them perfect as centrepieces for individual gratins or special soufflés.

- Hard-boiled eggs require 8 minutes and should be dipped immediately in cold water to prevent the nasty grey lining to the yolk appearing. Try hot hard-boiled eggs dipped Roman-fashion in a mixture of good salt and freshly ground black pepper as a rustic first course or eat them cooled and halved coated with one of the flavoured mayonnaises on pages 23–4.

2. Scrambled eggs

The great secret with scrambled eggs is to add the eggs unbeaten to the pan in which a tablespoon of water has cushioned the melting of a good knob of butter. Add the eggs before the butter is completely melted. The proportion is 2 or 3 eggs per person to half a walnut-sized piece of butter. A non-stick pan helps, particularly with the washing up. Scramble with a wooden spoon, stirring gently but constantly over a medium heat until the eggs have all granulated but are still soft. They will go on cooking when you serve them. If you cook them till they're hard in the pan they will be rubbery on the plate.

Try adding a finely chopped clove of garlic to the butter and water mixture before you scramble the eggs and a tablespoon of lemon juice just before they set. Or try adding a tablespoon or two of flaked, smoked fish – haddock, or, best of all, smoked salmon – just before the eggs finish setting.

3. Baked eggs

59

One of the great tricks of French cuisine, the method for these is simple. Individual-sized dishes are crucial – most kitchen shops sell a variety of shapes, some like miniature frying pans, some like miniature soufflé dishes. In fact, good teacups work very well and are easy to lift out of the pan when cooked. Butter your dish carefully, break a good, large egg into it, add another knob of butter to the top and a tablespoon of cream. Season generously. Place the cups in a frying pan with 2.5 cm (1 inch) of water in it and a good lid. Bring to the boil, cover, and cook over medium heat for 4 minutes. The yolks should still be soft and the whites set. Eat immediately with plenty of French bread and butter. You can put a tablespoon of filling in the bottom of the dish before breaking in the egg – crab meat, cheese, cooked spinach, or chopped, buttered mushrooms are all goodies.

WINE tip A great breakfast dish demands Bucks Fizz or a dry sparkling wine – lively high acidity to cope with smoked fish.

WINE tip Baked eggs with cream – Vin de Pays des Côtes de Gascogne or Côtes de Saint Mont blanc. With seafood – Chilean Chardonnay.

Crème caramel

Make a little caramel by melting 2 tablespoons of sugar and 1 tablespoon of water in a non-stick saucepan until pale gold. Do not let it cook any more than that. Pour the hot caramel into a 600 ml (1 pint) soufflé dish or four individual crème caramel-sized moulds.

Serves 4

2 tablespoons caster sugar
150 ml (5 fl oz) milk
150 ml (5 fl oz) single cream
1 teaspoon real vanilla essence
3 egg yolks
2 egg whites

Pre-heat the oven to gas mark 4–5, 180–190°C (350–375°F).

Heat the sugar in the milk until dissolved, then add the cream and vanilla essence. Beat the egg yolks and whites and pour through a sieve into the cream mixture. Stir thoroughly and pour carefully over the caramel in the dishes. Place in a baking tray with 2.5 cm (1 inch) of water and bake in the oven for 35 to 40 minutes until set. Chill and tip upside down on a deep plate to serve.

Vanilla custard

This is a basic pouring custard. It can be flavoured in a variety of ways. Favourite flavourings include melted chocolate, very strong coffee or citrus juices – orange or lemon. If using the latter, you may need to add a tablespoon more sugar to the custard when you're making it.

Serves 4

50 g (2 oz) sugar
300 ml (10 fl oz) milk or cream
½ teaspoon vanilla essence
2 teaspoons cornflour
2 egg yolks
1 egg white

Mix the sugar with the milk or cream and heat gently until dissolved. Add the vanilla essence. Slake the cornflour with a couple of tablespoons of milk and stir gently in, whisking thoroughly over the heat until it begins to thicken. Before it boils, whisk the egg yolks and white thoroughly and pour through a sieve into the cream mixture, whisking as you go. Bring gently to the boil then stop cooking immediately.

Variation

- **Crème brulée** Make the custard with double cream and pour into individual-sized soufflé dishes or custard cups and leave to cool then chill in the fridge for at least an hour. Make caramel in a non-stick saucepan with 4 tablespoons of caster sugar and 2 tablespoons of water. Heat it gently until the mixture goes pale golden brown. Do not cook it beyond this! Pour gently over the chilled, set custard so that the caramel coating covers the custard in each cup. Do not return to the fridge but allow to cool and harden in a cool place. When the caramel sets it may be served anytime up to about 12 hours, after which it will begin to soften. This is also known as Burnt Cream – an older and less crafty way of producing a caramel coating.

From top: *Egg custard* (page 61); *Pouring custard* (page 61); *Crème caramel*

CHAPTER SIX

The best buying advice, the simplest preparation and a whole host of recipes for five key types of poultry.

poultry

Five key types of poultry

1. Chicken

The most widely eaten meat in Britain today is chicken. There are lots of different grades (see below), but what they all have is chicken's versatility and lightness. If you don't eat the skin, chicken is a very low fat meat with a high proportion of flesh to bone. It's usually mild in flavour but a very good carrier of other flavours, from delicate cream sauces to spicy curries. It's also the one bird that's common to all meat-eating cuisines anywhere in the world.

2. Duck

A rich and quite fat bird, duck is a more expensive proposition because a standard 2.25 kg (5 lb) duck will barely feed four people, the ratio of bone to flesh being quite high. It is, however, widely regarded as a special treat across a range of cuisines from China to France. Always succulent, the flesh has a natural affinity for a range of sweet and savoury flavourings that make it good for celebrations.

3. Turkey

Coming from the New World 400 years ago, turkey has conquered our great festive feasts, being the required bird for Christmas and often Easter. It is now sold in portions for eating during the rest of the year as well. It

English roast chicken (page 68)

contains less fat than any other domestic meat, although it has a tendency to dryness. It makes an admirable substitute for veal.

4. Goose

Goose has only recently come back into favour. It's often regarded as a large duck, being rich and quite fatty. But for more sophisticated festive gatherings, especially around Christmas, it is often the first choice. It's also a prime ingredient for the classic French bean dish, Cassoulet, and even occasionally appears in portion-sized pieces.

THE LOW-DOWN ON FAT
- Turkey is 3 per cent fat.
- Chicken is around 5 per cent fat.
- Goose is around 20 per cent fat.
- Duck is around 30 per cent fat (wild duck is lower, see page 80).

The white meat is lower in fat than the dark leg meat. The best way to avoid the fat in chicken is to discard the skin, although it is best to do this after cooking since the small amounts of fat in the skin are important for flavour. But don't become obsessed by poultry fat – the skin is delicious.

5. Guinea fowl

This half-way house between poultry and game has long been more popular in France than it has in Britain. But recently a number of specialist producers have begun to supply supermarkets. It's excellent if you fancy a slightly richer-tasting bird than chicken and is particularly attractive in casseroles.

HOW TO AVOID SALMONELLA POISONING

Chicken is the commonest source of the salmonella bacterium. Observe these simple rules and you will not suffer food poisoning as a result:

● Store poultry in the fridge separate from and below cooked foods, ideally at no more than 5°C (11°F).
● Always defrost frozen poultry thoroughly (see table below).
● Cook thoroughly – to at least 75°C (167°F) if you are using a meat thermometer. When pierced with a skewer, clear liquid, not blood, should flow out.
● Barbecues are a great source of food poisoning – make doubly sure that barbecued poultry is cooked right through.
● Avoid spreading salmonella bacteria to other 'hosts' by cross-contamination – never re-use equipment or surfaces on which raw poultry has been prepared without thorough washing with hot water and detergent or an anti-bacterial spray.
● Plastic boards are easier to clean than wooden and can be dedicated to poultry if you wish.
● Observe good personal hygiene at all times.

THAWING TIMES FOR FROZEN POULTRY

Frozen poultry must be thawed thoroughly so that it cooks properly. It is best done slowly in the fridge but can be done in cold water. Doing it at room temperature is inadvisable but if you must, make it a cool room.

Weight	Thawing time	
	In the fridge (4°C (40°F))	In cold water (hours)
1.4 kg (3 lb)	24 hours	8
1.8 kg (4 lb)	36 hours	11
2.25 kg (5 lb)	42 hours	13
2.7–3.5 kg (6–8 lb)	2–2½ days	16–18
3.5–4.5 kg (8–10 lb)	2½–2¾ days	18–20
4.5–5.4 kg (10–12 lb)	2¾–3 days	20–22
5.4–6.4 kg (12–14 lb)	3–3½ days	22–24
6.4 kg–7.3 kg (14–16 lb)	3½–3¾ days	24–26
7.3–8.2 kg (16–18 lb)	3¾–4 days	26–28
8.2–9 kg (18–20 lb)	4–4½ days	28–30

Chicken

SEVEN CHOICES OF CHICKEN

● **Farmyard** Theoretically reared with a minimum of domestication in a 'farmyard' with completely free access to the open air and pecking places.

● **Traditional free range** Specially designated and reared on a range of farms under strict conditions with good access to open air and land and quite careful conservation and feeding techniques.

● **Free range** Designated under EC regulations which are subject to amendment. By and large it means that the bird has access to the open air and to some pecking space. Usually this is less than one might expect, at around 1 square metre (39 square inches) per bird.

● **Corn fed** This describes the chicken's diet, meaning that it's been fed on a diet with a high proportion of maize. It produces a golden-coloured skin and (it is claimed) more delicate flesh.

● **Premium** A designation given to chickens of a supposedly high quality, many of which have been fed on a grain-only diet. It's an arbitrary distinction with no formal qualification.

● **Organic** Chickens are fed on vegetarian food products grown to organic standards and no preventative or growth-promoting drugs have been used. Rare and expensive.

● **Battery** All other chickens – usually raised in confined conditions and fed a diet often containing a significant proportion of prophylactic drugs. They are the basis of almost all frozen chicken and of the lower-priced fresh or chilled birds available.

Twelve key cuts to perfect chicken portions

There is a simple way to portion a chicken yourself if you wish to buy it whole and use only part of it. This is by far the most economical way of buying chicken portions, except for wings which are always sold below their nominal value as there is a low demand for them.

You need a good sharp knife not more than 23 cm (9 inches) long and a safe, stable cutting board. The technique is simple and once mastered can be carried out at a very rapid and efficient speed.

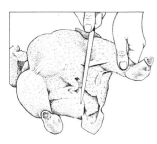

Cut 1. Pull one leg away from the body and cut through the skin that is stretched between the thigh and body. Continue to cut through the joint of the thigh until the whole leg is released

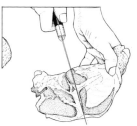

Cut 2. Sever the drumstick from the separated thigh at the joint, following a line of fat inside the leg

Cuts 3 and 4. Repeat cuts 1 and 2 for the other leg

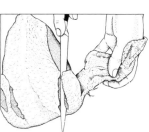

Cut 5. Circle around the base of the wing with a sharp knife, cutting through to the bone. Twist the wing and sever through the joint thus revealed

Cut 6. Separate the other wing as in cut 5

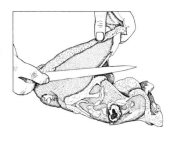

Cut 7 and 8. Down each side of the chicken there is a line of fat running just below the meat of the breast. Cut along it from the vent end towards the neck on each side, separating the breast from the backbone and ribs

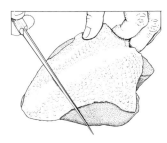

Cut 9. Place the breast section flat on the chopping board. Cut across the pointed end a third of the way along to produce one breast section

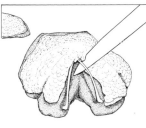

Cuts 10 and 11. Remove the wishbone by severing its ends and pulling away

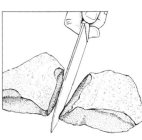

Cut 12. Split the remaining breast in half right down the flesh and bone to give you nine partially-boned, perfectly proportioned portions!

67

THREE WAYS OF ROASTING CHICKEN

All chickens can be roasted to advantage. They should be roasted for approximately 20 minutes per 450 g (1 lb) at gas mark 5, 190°C (375°F), then left to stand for another 10 to 15 minutes afterwards in a warm place to finish cooking. Always check that a chicken is cooked through, regardless of any timings, by inserting a sharp blade or skewer into the thigh. If the juices run clear it is cooked; if they run pink it requires further cooking until the test produces clear juices. Different ovens, chicken starting at different temperatures, different densities of stuffings, and a wide variety of other factors can affect the cooking. Always check with the thigh method.

English roast chicken

English roasting generally uses a stuffing placed in the cavity of the bird.

Serves 4

50 g (2 oz) coarse, fresh breadcrumbs
½ onion, peeled and chopped
Grated rind and juice of ½ lemon
1 tablespoon chopped fresh parsley
1 teaspoon freeze-dried thyme
1 tablespoon butter
1 small egg, beaten
1 medium chicken
1 bread crust
Salt and freshly ground black pepper

Pre-heat the oven to gas mark 5, 190°C (375°F).
   Mix the stuffing ingredients, binding with the beaten egg. Place in the cavity, fill the gap with a crust of bread, and put a skewer across the back to seal it. Salt and pepper the chicken and roast on a rack in the oven for 20 minutes per 450 g (1 lb) (weighed after stuffing) plus 15 minutes resting time.
   This is traditionally served with gravy made from thickening the juices in the pan with cornflour and vegetable water. Serve with bread sauce or cover the breast of the chicken with buttered papers before roasting.

WINE *tip* California Pinot Noir is excellent for chicken; or Pinot Noir from Romania which is reasonably priced, or try the light, fruity German Dornfelder.

68

French roast chicken

The French don't usually put stuffing in their chickens when they're roasting them. What they do is put half a lemon into the chicken and squeeze the other half over it. They then cook it in a shallow, oval gratin-type dish with at least a tablespoon or two of butter in the dish and turn the chicken three times as they roast it, starting on one breast, then on the second breast, and then breast up for the final period. Cooking time is 20 minutes per 450 g (1 lb) plus 10 minutes resting time. They're likely to add a little cream and herbs to the cooking juices with perhaps a little water to thin them down, bring the mixture to the boil and serve it with the roast chicken.

WINE *tip* Beaujolais, what else? A light, fruity French red.

Crafty roast chicken

This is an adaptation of the French style. The chicken is again stuffed with only half a lemon but as well as having the other half lemon squeezed over it, it is sprinkled with a teaspoon each of garlic salt and paprika and half a teaspoon of ground bay leaves. The breast, body and legs are covered with two or three butter papers (save these in the freezer) and it is roasted on a rack over a roasting pan in which 600 ml (1 pint) of warm water has been placed. Roast at a slightly higher temperature of gas mark 6, 200°C (400°F). Once again, 20 minutes per 450 g (1 lb) plus 15 minutes resting is ideal. The crafty system has the juices from the chicken falling into the liquid which makes a gravy in its own right. This can be thickened, coloured or flavoured if you wish with herbs or other liquids. It also makes the washing up much easier.

WINE *tip* Try a light fruity young red wine – St-Chinian from France, or a Bulgarian country red.

Above: *Sauté chicken with cream and chives* (page 72).
Below: *Sauté chicken peperonata* (page 73)

THREE KEY POINTS FOR FRIED CHICKEN

Crucial points for Colonel Sanders to note

- **Coatings** The classic southern-fried chicken (and I do know that Maryland and Kentucky have alternative methods) used flour, not breadcrumbs. Dip the chicken in a little lemon juice and then in flour and shake it dry. In some parts of the south they add a teaspoon of ground cinnamon, the same of garlic salt, and half a teaspoon of ground bay leaves to the flour before they shake the chicken in it. A plastic or paper bag with the flour in it and the chicken added is the easiest way to do this.

- **Frying** Fry in shallow not deep fat. The depth of the oil should be 5 mm (¼ inch) (vegetable oil like soya or sunflower is best) in a large frying pan with a lid. Heat the oil until it's hot but not smoking. Place the chicken in it carefully and allow to fry for 5 minutes until golden. Turn over, allow to fry for 2 or 3 minutes more and then cover.

70
- **Covering** The lid is crucial. It helps the chicken steam as well as fry so that it's cooked right through after 20 minutes on a medium heat. It also remains moist and succulent and not hard and stringy.

Now you have the perfect fried chicken to eat hot or cold. If you're eating it hot, the three great 'fixings' are Corn Fritters, Sauté Bananas and Red-Eye Gravy.

Corn fritters

Serves 4

100 g (4 oz) plain flour
1 small egg
250 ml (8 fl oz) of milk
1 × 175 g (6 oz) tin sweetcorn, drained
Salt and freshly ground black pepper

Blend the flour with the egg and the milk to make a smooth batter then leave to stand for 20 minutes. Add the sweetcorn, season and stir with salt and pepper – it should be the consistency of thick double cream. To cook, pour tablespoons at a time into the fat in which you've fried the chicken, turning after 1 or 2 minutes with a fish slice. They should be golden and speckled with brown when they're ready.

Sauté bananas

Choose under-ripe bananas with a hint of green still in the skin. Peel them and split them lengthways. Dust them with the same flour you use for the chicken and sauté one or two strips per person in the same oil that you cook the chicken.

Red-eye gravy

This is real Louisiana country gravy. It's not obligatory but it is an eye-opener in both senses of the word.

Take a tablespoon of the oil which you've used to cook the chicken, fritters and bananas. Stir a tablespoon of flour into that and add a cup of strong black coffee. Stir until you have a smooth sauce. Add an equivalent-sized cup of single cream and simmer for a couple of minutes until the mixture is thoroughly blended. Serve this with the chicken, the fixings and plenty of mashed potatoes.

Above: Red-eye gravy. Below: Southern-fried chicken with corn fritters and Sauté bananas

THREE SMASHING CHICKEN SAUTÉS

The method for chicken sauté dishes is the same whatever the flavourings. This is simple, elegant and effortless cooking.

Sauté chicken with cream and chives

Serves 4

1 tablespoon sunflower oil
1 tablespoon butter
4 chicken breasts
Salt and freshly ground black pepper
150 ml (5 fl oz) double cream
2 tablespoons snipped fresh chives

Heat the oil and butter in a frying pan into which all the chicken breasts will fit. When the sizzling stops, add the breasts, skin side down, and sauté for 5 minutes. Turn over and sauté for another 10 to 15 minutes over a low heat. You may wish to use a lid to help this along. When the chicken is cooked through, season generously and pour the cream over the chicken in one single action. Stir so all the bits in the pan are absorbed into the sauce and allow the cream to come briefly to the boil. Add the chopped chives, turn the chicken breasts in the sauce, and serve immediately.

72

Sauté chicken with mushrooms and garlic

Serves 4

1 tablespoon sunflower oil
1 tablespoon butter
4 chicken breasts
1 clove garlic, peeled and crushed
250 ml (8 fl oz) chicken stock
225 g (8 oz) button mushrooms
Salt and freshly ground black pepper
2 teaspoons arrowroot or cornflour
1 tablespoon chopped fresh parsley

Heat the oil and butter and sauté the chicken, skin side down, for 5 minutes. Turn and sauté for a further 5 minutes, adding the garlic for the last minute. Add the chicken stock and simmer gently for about 15 minutes until the chicken is cooked through. Wash the mushrooms under boiling water and slice vertically into 5 mm (¼ inch) slices. When the chicken is cooked, season it generously. Slake the arrowroot or cornflour in a little water, stir into the liquid in the pan and bring gently to the boil until thickened and, if using arrowroot, clear. Add the mushrooms and simmer for 2 minutes. Serve sprinkled generously with parsley.

Sauté chicken peperonata

Serve this dish with fine, fresh pasta.

Serves 4

2 tablespoons olive oil
4 chicken breasts
1 clove garlic, peeled and finely chopped
½ Spanish onion, peeled and finely chopped
225 ml (8 fl oz) chopped Italian tomatoes
½ red pepper, de-seeded and thinly sliced
½ green pepper, de-seeded and thinly sliced
½ yellow pepper, de-seeded and thinly sliced
½ teaspoon chopped fresh basil
½ teaspoon chopped fresh oregano
Salt

Heat the oil and sauté the chicken, skin-side down, for 5 minutes. Turn and sauté for another 10 minutes, using a lid if available. Add the garlic, onion and tomatoes and simmer for 2 to 3 minutes. Add the peppers and herbs and a generous pinch of salt and cook for a further 5 to 6 minutes until the peppers are softened but not broken up. A lid certainly helps while you're doing this. After 20 minutes cooking, the chicken should be fully cooked and the peppers should still have some texture left in them.

WINE *tip* Chicken is a very forgiving bird which goes well with red or white. With these sautés, try the wines recommended elsewhere in this chapter – from white Sauvignon to red Burgundy.

THREE SCRUMPTIOUS CHICKEN CASSEROLES

Cockaleekie

A Scottish dish which can be eaten either as a slightly liquid casserole or in the Scottish tradition as a clear soup followed by the chicken and its companion prunes and leeks. An extraordinary combination but it works extremely well.

Serves 4 to 6, depending on chicken size

1 tablespoon butter
1 chicken, cut into 9 portions (see page 67)
450 g (1 lb) leeks
Salt and freshly ground black pepper
175 g (6 oz) prunes
1 bay leaf
900 ml (1½ pints) chicken stock or water
1 tablespoon chopped fresh parsley

In a generous-sized saucepan or flameproof casserole, melt the butter and lightly brown the chicken on all sides. Split the leeks lengthways and wash them thoroughly free of grit. Put half of them into the pan with the chicken, season generously, add the prunes and bay leaf and cover with stock or water. Simmer for 25 minutes without a lid. Leave to stand for a moment then remove and discard the leeks. Cut the remaining leeks into 2.5 cm (1 inch) segments across the grain, add to the casserole and bring to a rapid boil for 5 minutes.

To serve, use a slotted spoon to transfer the chicken, freshly cooked leeks and prunes to a serving dish, add a cup of the liquid and keep warm. Pour the rest of the liquid into a soup tureen, check for seasoning, add the tablespoon of chopped parsley and serve with oatmeal or wholemeal bread. Follow this with the chicken, leeks and prunes, served with new boiled potatoes.

73
....

WINE *tip* Try French Côtes-du-Rhone Villages (a bit better than ordinary Côtes-du-Rhone) or its neighbour, Coteaux du Tricastin.

Chicken forestière

This is French-style hunter's chicken. The variety of mushrooms available these days in most supermarkets and greengrocers can make this a really interesting dish. A packet of mixed wild and domestic mushrooms would make the perfect accompaniment to the chicken, but ordinary old-fashioned, button mushrooms will do very well.

Serves 4 to 6, depending on chicken size

1 chicken, cut into 9 portions
1 tablespoon plain flour
1 tablespoon oil
1 tablespoon butter
1 stalk celery
1 large onion, peeled and diced
2 carrots, diced
300 ml (10 fl oz) chicken stock or water
2 bay leaves
1 teaspoon thyme
225 g (8 oz) mushrooms
Salt and freshly ground black pepper
3 tablespoons double cream or fromage frais

74

Dust the chicken pieces in flour. Heat the oil and butter and sauté the chicken for 5 to 6 minutes until golden brown. Split the celery stalk lengthways and cut across into 5 mm (¼ inch) slices. Add the celery to the chicken with the diced onion and carrots and fry gently for 2 to 3 minutes. Barely cover with stock or water (the amount will vary depending on the pan you use), season generously, add the herbs and simmer for 20 minutes. Trim and wash the mushrooms in hot or boiling water but do not peel them. Cut them into equal-sized pieces, leaving small button mushrooms whole. Add the mushrooms to the casserole which should now have comparatively little liquid left in it. Stir them round and allow them to heat through for 2 to 3 minutes. Check for seasoning, and serve. A few tablespoons of double cream or fromage frais can be stirred into the sauce for extra creaminess at the last minute.

 WINE *tip* **Rich, mouth-filling, plummy, ripe, medium-weight red wines such as Chilean or Central European Merlots, or French St-Emilion.**

Chicken véronique

A lovely summer dish made perfectly with the muscat or seedless grapes that are widely available throughout the summer. Use white, not red, grapes for this dish.

Serves 4

4 chicken breasts
½ onion stuck with 2 cloves
2 bay leaves
2 fresh parsley stalks
275 g (10 oz) unsweetened white grape juice
2 teaspoons cornflour
150 ml (5 fl oz) single cream
Juice of ½ lemon
175 g (6 oz) muscat or seedless white grapes
Salt and freshly ground black pepper

Place the chicken breasts in a small casserole or saucepan. Add the onion and herbs and cover with the grape juice. Cover and simmer for 20 minutes until the chicken is thoroughly cooked. Remove and discard the onion and herbs. Place the chicken breasts on a warm serving dish. Mix the cornflour into the cream and lemon juice. Add to the cooking liquid and whisk over a medium heat until thickened and smooth. Add the grapes (if you have seeded grapes, split in half and remove the seeds). Allow to heat through for 1 to 2 minutes – no more – pour the sauce over the chicken breasts, check for seasoning and pile the warm grapes around the chicken breasts.

Cockaleekie (page 73)

FOUR KEY FACTS FOR PERFECT POACHING

Poached chicken is often neglected. It's a delicate and succulent way of cooking the bird, although the portions often look untidy when finished. The method here gives perfect results for hot or cold dishes and has the added advantage of being as low as possible in fat while high on flavour. Serve plain with buttered vegetables or with a velouté sauce over (see p. 20). Or coat it in a cheese sauce and flash under the grill.

- **Choice of liquid** Water is the least complicated but also the least interesting. Chicken stock helps and fresh herbs, particularly parsley stalks, celery leaf, bay leaf and tarragon, improve the flavour of the chicken. The grated rind of a lemon or the juice of half a lemon add a piquancy and sharpness to the stock and bird.

- **Control of the heat** Poaching liquids should boil once to blend their ingredients' flavours, but once the chicken is in them should do no more than bubble gently. The food will cook almost as fast as at a fierce boil but without being bounced about, damaged, and having its texture turned fibrous and stringy.

- **Keep the shape** Wrap the chicken pieces in cling film to maintain their shape. This trick doesn't affect the speed at which they cook but does make sure that they never go raggedy round the edges or pull into funny shapes.

- **Cooling** If you're going to eat the chicken cold, allow it to cool in its cooking liquid. That way it will remain really juicy and succulent.

76

THREE KEY CHICKEN SALADS

These are an ideal way of using poached chicken or left-over chicken from another recipe.

Waldorf salad

A salad from New York's grandest hotel in its grandest period before the Second World War. The Waldorf (Astoria) salad is simple and rich. It makes a good first course or a splendid light lunch.

Serves 4

225 g (8 oz) cold, poached chicken, off the bone
1 large, ripe eating apple
4 stalks celery
120 ml (4 fl oz) Mayonnaise (see page 23) or 2 tablespoons Mayonnaise and 2 tablespoons fromage frais
A few lettuce leaves
50 g (2 oz) shelled walnuts
1 lemon, quartered

Cut the chicken into pieces the size of a half a walnut. Core the apple but do not peel it. Cut it into 12 segments and cut each segment into 3 pieces (an apple cutter is perfect for this). Trim and wash the celery and cut it into 5 mm (¼ inch) slices. Mix the celery and apple pieces with the mayonnaise and/or fromage frais. Fold in the pieces of chicken and place on lettuce leaf cups or a bed of lettuce if serving as a large, single salad. Sprinkle the walnuts over the salad and serve with quarters of lemon to squeeze over.

WINE *tip* Since the dressing dominates any salad on the flavour spectrum, go carefully with your choice of wine – it could be knocked into oblivion if the dressing is too sharp. For Waldorf Salad, try a Portuguese Madeira Sercial.

Coronation chicken

The original of this recipe was devised to meet a range of culinary requirements for Queen Elizabeth II's coronation banquet in 1952. It's rich, simple and (these days) frequently poorly done. Properly prepared, it's a delicious, sweet and sour confection.

Serves 4

350 g (12 oz) cold, poached chicken in neat slices (preferably breast)
4 tablespoons Mayonnaise (see page 23)
2 tablespoons double cream
2 tablespoons apricot jam, sieved
Salt and freshly ground black pepper
1 tablespoon slivered almonds

For the curry sauce:
2 teaspoons butter
1 teaspoon curry powder
1 tablespoon plain flour
250 ml (8 fl oz) poaching liquid

To make the curry sauce, melt the butter and fry the curry powder gently for a couple of minutes. Stir in the flour then whisk in the poaching liquid from the chicken, stir until the sauce thickens, then simmer for 5 minutes. Leave to cool. Mix the sauce with the mayonnaise, double cream, which you can whip a little for extra lightness, and the apricot jam. The mixture should have the consistency of thick double cream. Check the chicken for seasoning, pour the sauce over and decorate with the slivered almonds.

WINE tip For whites – French dry Gewürztraminer or Chenin Blanc. For reds – chilled young Chianti or red Loires or Portuguese Bairrada.

Bang bang chicken

This is a cold chicken recipe from China, an unusual proposition in itself, but using flavourings unique to China's western Szechuan province.

Serves 4

225 g (8 oz) cold, poached chicken, off the bone
100 g (4 oz) flat chinese noodles, cooked for 5 minutes then cooled and drained
A few lettuce leaves
3 tablespoons peanut butter
1 teaspoon chilli sauce
1 teaspoon brown sugar
1 teaspoon lemon juice
120 ml (4 fl oz) water

Shred the chicken into thick matchstick-sized pieces. Cut the noodles into approximately 15 cm (6 inch) lengths and mix with the chicken. Place these on a bed of lettuce or in individual lettuce cups for separate servings. Put all the remaining ingredients into a non-stick saucepan and bring to the boil, stirring from time to time until the sauce thickens and blends. Allow to cool to room temperature before pouring over the chicken and noodles, and leave to marinate for at least 15 to 20 minutes. A tablespoon of soy sauce can be added to the sauce if you prefer a slightly more aromatic version.

WINE tip Italian Prosecco Frizzante – it's not too dry. Serve well chilled.

77
....

TWO CRUCIAL METHODS WITH CHICKEN LIVERS

Chicken livers are a product in their own right these days and can be bought in tubs from the fresh and frozen meat sections of supermarkets and butchers. If you can still buy your chicken with the livers in it (lucky you!) they're worth storing in a plastic bag in the freezer until you have enough for one of these recipes.

Chicken liver pâté

A simple, delicious and rustic pâté, this will keep well in the fridge for a week or longer and is perfect for summer lunches, dinner parties and picnics.

Serves 6 to 8 as a starter

225 g (8 oz) chicken livers
100 g (4 oz) butter
1 clove garlic, peeled and finely chopped
1 teaspoon freeze-dried or chopped fresh thyme
1 teaspoon freeze-dried or chopped fresh oregano
1 wine glass of apple juice
Salt and freshly ground black pepper

Wash the livers well, removing any green bits. Melt 75 g (3 oz) of the butter in a non-stick frying pan. Add the livers and garlic and sauté over a high heat for 3 to 4 minutes until the livers are brown on the outside but still a tiny bit pink in the centre. Tip the contents of the saucepan into a liquidizer or food processor, add the herbs and apple juice and process until smooth. You may need to scrape the sides of the bowl down at least once during this process. Season generously and tip into a soufflé or other serving dish. Melt the remaining butter in the saucepan and pour the liquid butter carefully over the smoothed-down pâté, leaving the white bits as residue in the saucepan to be discarded. Chill in the fridge for at least 6 hours before eating – 3 days is ideal.

WINE *tip* Good hearty southern French red such as Minervois or Fitou.

Chicken livers sautéed with grapes

A simple, quick dish that can be cooked from a standing start in less than 10 minutes. This is ideal served with fluffy rice or in small servings as a first course with crusty French bread.

Serves 4 as a main course or 8 as a starter

1 tablespoon butter
1 tablespoon olive oil
450 g (1 lb) chicken livers, trimmed
175 ml (6 fl oz) chicken stock
1 teaspoon arrowroot
Salt and freshly ground black pepper
100 g (4 oz) seedless grapes

Melt the butter in the oil in a medium-sized frying pan and sauté the chicken livers briefly. Mix the chicken stock and arrowroot, add to the pan, bring to the boil, and simmer for 3 to 4 minutes. Check for seasoning, add the grapes and serve immediately.

WINE *tip* White with a bit of sweetness to it would be perfect for this – Vouvray demi sec, or a sweet white Ste-Croix-du-Mont from Bordeaux.

Above: Bang bang chicken (page 77). Below: Chicken véronique (page 74)

Duck

Duck is a luxury dish for many of us. It's always been something to eat on a special occasion in Britain and we're only just beginning to realize its possibilities. It's simple to cook and doesn't need to be 'fatty'. The crafty technique will cure all that.

THREE KEY TYPES OF DUCK

- **Aylesbury** The traditional British duck usually sold as 'duckling' at about 1.8–2.25 kg (4–5 lb). It can, at this weight, have a high proportion of fat to meat but is widely available and roasts well.

- **Barbary** This is closer to a wild duck and is often sold in portions, particularly the breast fillets. It's quite gamey in flavour and comparatively low in fat. The breasts, or *magrets*, can be grilled or pan-fried like steaks and served cut into 5 mm (¼ inch) slices across the grain with one of the sweet and sour sauces that go so well with duck, like cherry or cranberry.

- **Gressingham and Khaki** These are rarer breeds of duck which normally come in much larger sizes – 3.2–4 kg (7–9 lb). They have a stronger flavour and a slightly higher meat-to-bone ratio than conventional Aylesbury duckling, but are expensive and often quite difficult to find. Specialist dealers do sell them. Very good roasted – with adjusted times for the larger size.

THE PERFECT WAY TO ROAST DUCK

However you serve it – in the French, English or Chinese way – use the Chinese-inspired crafty duck roasting technique.

- **Step 1** Remove the loose skin around the neck, the scaly bits on the legs, the wing tips and remove any loose fat from its insides.

- **Step 2** Place it in a colander in a sink and pour over it a kettleful of boiling water, turning the duck half-way. This will loosen the skin from the subcutaneous fat and allow the duck to roast less greasily.

- **Step 3** Allow the duck to dry, out of the fridge, for at least 4 hours.

- **Step 4** Place it on a rack in a roasting pan, breast side down, and roast in a pre-heated oven at gas mark 6, 200°C (400°F) for 20 minutes. Turn it over, and for a 1.8–2.25 kg (4–5 lb) duck let it roast for a further 45 to 50 minutes, adding 10 minutes for every extra 450 g (1 lb). It should roast to a mahogany brown, the skin should be crisp and the flesh underneath succulent. There will be a considerable amount of duck fat in the roasting pan which should either be discarded or, if you wish, stored in a jar for future use.

WINE tip Zinfandel red or a generous red such as Australian Cabernet Sauvignon is ideal for roast duck.

THREE METHODS OF SERVING DUCK

- **French** The French serve their duck with bitter fruit sauces, made from Seville oranges or Morello cherries. If you're using oranges, pare the rind from 2 Sevilles and juice the fruit, adding enough fresh orange juice to make 150 ml (5 fl oz). Cut the orange rind into slivers, blanch in boiling water for 2 minutes then drain. Take a tablespoon of the duck fat, add the juice and thicken with 2 teaspoons of cornflour, simmering the sauce for 5 minutes. Add the blanched, slivered orange rind and simmer for a further 5 minutes before serving over the sliced duck.
French bitter cherry sauce Simmer 225 g (8 oz) of Morello cherries with 250 ml (8 fl oz) of water, 120 ml (4 fl oz) sugar and the juice of a lemon until they are cooked but not disintegrated. Thicken the juice with a teaspoon of arrowroot and serve with the duck slices.

- **English** Green peas and apple sauce are the traditional British accompaniments to duck. The apple sauce should be made with cooking apples, a pinch of cinnamon and as much sugar as the apples and your palate require. A good basis is 225 g (8 oz) of apples to a tablespoon of water, and 50 g (2 oz) sugar. The sauce should be thick enough to leave a permanent trail when the spoon is pulled through it. The green peas should be cooked with a little chopped lettuce and a pinch of sugar, whether they're fresh or frozen. If they're fresh they'll need about 10 minutes cooking with the flavourings added at the end. If they're frozen, use minimum water and add the flavourings when you start to cook them.

● **Chinese** There really is no substitute for this way of eating, known as Peking-style.

Peking duck

Duck pancakes and the thick, savoury hoisin sauce are available in all speciality Chinese supermarkets, many health food stores and some conventional supermarkets.

Serves 6

15 cm (6 inch) piece cucumber
1 bunch spring onions
4 tablespoons hoisin sauce
24 pancakes
Duck, roasted the crafty way (p 80)

Split the cucumber lengthways, scoop out the seeds and cut into matchstick-sized slivers. Trim the spring onions and cut into 2.5 cm (1 inch) lengths and split those again lengthways. Pile into separate bowls. Pour the hoisin sauce into another bowl. Steam the pancakes in a colander over boiling water for 5 to 6 minutes until warmed through.

Cut the skin off the duck and dice it into postage stamp-sized pieces. Remove the flesh from the duck and cut into small, neat slivers about 5 cm (2 inches) long and not more than 1 cm (½ inch) wide in any direction. Put these on to warm dishes.

To eat, each diner takes a pancake, smears it with a little of the hoisin sauce, sprinkles it with a pinch of onion and cucumber, and puts 2 or 3 pieces of skin and 2 or 3 slivers of duck meat on the pancake. You roll one turn in from the side, turn the bottom up, and another roll in from the other side and eat the duck envelope. This goes on until the duck, the pancakes or the diners are all finished.

Smear the pancake with a little hoisin sauce, sprinkle with a pinch of onion, cucumber and 2–3 pieces of meat or skin

81

Roll one turn in from the side

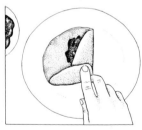

Turn the bottom up

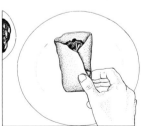

Roll the other side in to form an envelope

TWO RECIPES FOR DUCK PORTIONS

Like turkey and chicken, portions of duck are on sale all year round.

Stir-fry duck with broccoli and bean sprouts

This is an ideal way of using up extra duck from a Peking-style duck, or making two duck breasts, feed four people. Eat with boiled rice and some Chinese-style soup.

Serves 4

225 g (8 oz) duck, off the bone
1 clove garlic, peeled
2.5 cm (1 inch) piece fresh ginger root, peeled and trimmed
2 tablespoons oil (not olive)
225 g (8 oz) broccoli in florets
4 tablespoons soy sauce
275 g (10 oz) bean sprouts
1 teaspoon cornflour
2 tablespoons water

Cut the duck, cooked or raw, into 5 mm (¼ inch) slices across the grain. Chop the garlic and ginger together. Heat the oil in a large frying pan or wok, add the garlic and ginger and fry for 30 seconds. If using raw duck, add that and fry for 4 minutes. Add the broccoli. If using cooked duck, add the duck and vegetable at the same time and cook for 3 minutes. Stir in the soy sauce, then add the bean sprouts, cooking and tossing vigorously for 1 to 1½ minutes. Mix the cornflour and water, add to the sauce and stir, turning and tossing the mixture for about 1 minute until the sauce thickens and goes glossy.

WINE tip A rich white such as Australian Chardonnay or a light aromatic white such as Alsace Muscat.

Duck casserole with apricots and water chestnuts

This is a simple but exotic casserole that's ideal for using up the less glamorous portions of duck like legs and wings. Serve it with a wild rice mixture and a green salad to follow.

Serves 4

175 g (6 oz) dried apricots
250 ml (8 fl oz) orange juice
1 tablespoon cooking oil
4 duck portions on the bone, trimmed
1 onion, peeled and finely chopped
Salt and freshly ground black pepper
8 water chestnuts (tinned are ideal)
225 g (8 oz) button mushrooms
1 tablespoon cornflour

Soak the apricots in the orange juice. Heat the oil and fry the duck portions, skin side down, for 5 minutes. Turn over and fry until browned on both sides. Add the onion and season the duck generously. Add the apricots and enough orange juice just to cover the pieces of poultry. Add a little water if necessary. Bring to the boil and simmer for 20 minutes. Add the water chestnuts and mushrooms and simmer for further 5 minutes. Mix the cornflour with a little water and add to the sauce, stirring over a high heat until it is smooth and glossy. Check for seasoning and serve.

WINE tip Lusty-flavoured reds such as Crozes-Hermitage from France or Australian Shiraz.

Above: Duck casserole with apricots and water chestnuts. Below: Roast duck served the French way (page 80)

Turkey

VARIETIES OF TURKEY

Turkey, like chicken, comes in a variety of grades and qualities. Not of all these are mutually exclusive: some of them refer to the breed and some to the method of rearing.

- **Free range** This usually means free access to fresh air and a substantial area of open ground. They're not common and are quite expensive.

- **Traditional** Reared in sheds with regular access to daylight and fresh air and some open ground, they're normally allowed to come to maturity quite slowly and are hung for tenderness after being slaughtered. Widely available and moderately expensive.

- **Conventional** Not battery-bred but reared more intensively and in larger units than free range or traditional and normally not hung before processing or freezing.

BREEDS OF TURKEY

- **Bronze** A new version of an old-fashioned turkey, this is broad breasted, richly flavoured (some say quite gamey), and black speckled when plucked but not when roasted.

- **White breast** The conventional turkey that we have been used to for some thirty or forty years, very broad breasted and mild in flavour.

- **Norfolk black** An ancient breed producing comparatively narrow-breasted turkeys, lighter in weight than modern breeds and with a strongly flavoured and moist flesh.

FRESH VS CHILLED VS FROZEN

- **Fresh** There is no doubt from the point of view of flavour and quality that a fresh bird, properly hung before being plucked, produces the best results, but it is more difficult to store and transport and, except amongst specialist butchers or direct from the farm, not always easy to come by.

- **Chilled** Chilled birds are widely available and have many of the advantages of fresh ones as they continue to mature in flavour and to tenderize while being chilled.

- **Frozen** Frozen turkeys, while in some ways very convenient, lack the flavour or succulence of fresh ones. They are normally frozen immediately after slaughter and have no time to mature either in flavour or tenderness. They are, however, far cheaper than any of the other kinds and if properly defrosted (see page 66) they are perfectly acceptable.

Turkey polpette in soured cream **(page 89)**

SIX KEY TIPS TO PERFECT QUICK-ROAST TURKEY

- Remove the wishbone using a very sharp knife and cutting carefully to avoid piercing the skin. The method is:
Cut the wishbone at the base end near the wing joints first, cut up along the bone to remove from the flesh and loosen at the top, twisting to remove finally. This will vastly facilitate carving.

- Keep the stuffing separate and cook it in a separate baking dish. If you must stuff the bird itself, only stuff the crop or neck end leaving the cavity empty to help even cooking. Half an onion or a cut-up lemon in the cavity provides flavour and moistness.

- Place the prepared bird on a rack in the roasting pan and put 600 ml (1 pint) of water under the bird. This will catch the drippings, make gravy and keep the turkey moist as it cooks.

- Cover the breast and the legs with butter papers or buttered foil without wrapping it tightly.

- Cook it for 15 minutes per 450 g (1 lb) for a 6.4 kg (14 lb) turkey. Less per 450 g (1 lb) as the bird gets heavier, more as it gets lighter. This weight should be measured after the turkey has been stuffed.

- Temperatures: gas mark 4–5, 180–190°C (350–375°F). Allow the turkey to stand for 20 minutes in a warm place out of the oven before carving.

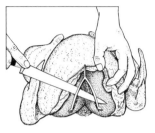

Cut carefully to avoid piercing the skin

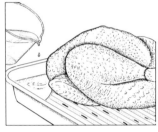

To remove the wishbone, use a sharp knife to cut it at the base end near the wing joints first

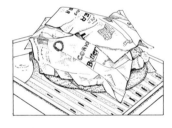

Place the prepared bird on a rack in the roasting pan and put 600 ml (1 pint) of water under the bird

85

Cover the breast and legs with butter papers or buttered foil without wrapping it tightly

Vermont stew (page 88)

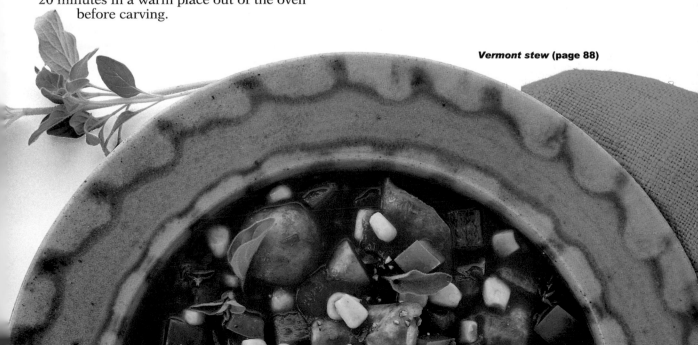

FIVE KEY TIPS TO PERFECT SLOW-ROAST TURKEY

This is an alternative to the conventional roast turkey, cooked over a period of 12 hours or more. Some people believe it makes the cook's life a lot easier on Christmas Day to cook a turkey like this, as all the work is done effectively the day before. An old-fashioned cooker like an Aga with an extremely slow oven is ideal for this, but it can be done at the very lowest settings of modern conventional ovens. A fan oven, however, is not suitable.

- Remove the wishbone, following the instructions on page 85.

- **Stuffing** Slow-roast turkey can be stuffed in the cavity if you wish. Avoid a meat stuffing. Use a mixture of fresh herbs – parsley, spring onions, celery – with breadcrumbs enriched with butter, bound with an egg and flavoured with the juice and grated rind of a lemon. Any other stuffing mixture you care for – cranberries, chestnuts and mushrooms all are popular flavouring ingredients – is fine.

86

- **Wrapping** Wrap the turkey thoroughly but loosely with well-buttered greaseproof paper or foil. Do not seal it tightly as it will steam and not roast.

- **Temperature and oven times** If you have an Aga, the bottom of the simmering oven is the right place. If you have a conventional gas or electric oven, gas mark ½, 120°C (250°F) is the right temperature. The cooking time depends to a certain extent on the size of the turkey but for a 5.4–7.3 kg (12–16 lb) turkey, 12 hours is a reasonable average. A much smaller bird down to about 4–4.5 kg (9–10 lb) may take 9 to 10 hours, and a much larger bird up to 9 kg (20 lb), may take 13 or 14 hours. It can go in usually around midnight and rest quietly in a switched off oven for about 1 hour before carving at lunch.

- The rest of the meal should be cooked in the conventional way at conventional speeds, especially roast potatoes which do not benefit from long, slow cooking.

Either way, make sure the turkey is thoroughly cooked by running a sharp knife or skewer into the thickest part of the thigh where the juices should run absolutely clear. If they don't, the turkey's not cooked yet and needs some more time in the oven. Both these methods produce a very succulent bird which needs to stand for 30 minutes before carving to allow the best texture and moistness to be achieved.

WINE tip Virtually anything goes with roast turkey! If you want further direction, try a Cru Beaujolais (named after a village) such as Fleurie, or a soft friendly German white to suit your bank balance.

SEVEN CUTS OF TURKEY AND THEIR USES

Turkey is now regularly available all year round in joints and pre-prepared form. It's a very economical meat and it's often cheaper than chicken.

It's very lean, having less fat in it than any other domestic meat, and it's very adaptable, coming in a variety of different forms using both breast and dark meat. Here are some of the detailed cuts and some ideas and recipes for cooking them.

1. Turkey breasts

These can come as whole or boned breasts or in slices. The whole boned breasts are fine roasting joints for a family meal or cooked and left to go cold to make ideal picnic or salad food. They should be cooked for about 12 minutes per 450 (1 lb) in a gas mark 5, 190°C (375°F) oven. Season them generously, including some paprika and bay leaf in the seasoning mix, and cover with a well-buttered piece of foil before roasting. If the breast is sliced across the grain into medallions they make excellent quick-cooked dishes in the Italian style, ideal to cook the following.

2. Turkey scaloppine

Brown the medallions in a little oil in a frying pan on both sides, season generously, pour in a wine glass of something you would care to drink – whether it's orange juice, grape juice, or something Jilly would recommend – allow to bubble briefly and add 2 or 3 tablespoons of cream to the sauce. Bring to the boil and serve.

3. Turkey legs

Turkey legs are too substantial to cook like chicken legs and are much better roasted. Allow one medium-sized leg per person. They are good with vigorous and strong tastes like the following recipe.

Spice island turkey drumsticks

Serves 4

4 turkey drumsticks
2 teaspoons French mustard
2 tablespoons tomato ketchup
2 teaspoons soy sauce
2 teaspoons Worcestershire sauce
½ teaspoon chilli sauce
1 teaspoon garlic salt
1 teaspoon freeze-dried tarragon

Mix the sauce ingredients together thoroughly, spread over the drumsticks and allow to marinate for 1 hour.

Pre-heat the oven to gas mark 4, 180°C (350°F).

Roast the turkey in the oven for 45 to 50 minutes until cooked but not shrivelled. The drumsticks can be turned in the sauce 2 or 3 times as they cook.

87

4. Turkey thighs

Turkey thighs can be bought bone in or boneless, although they are usually boned before being sold. They make excellent casserole joints.

If they're not boned, split the thighs in half and discard the bones. Cut the meat into walnut-sized pieces.

Vermont stew

This is a recipe derived from the cuisine that the Indians first demonstrated to the European colonists when they arrived in North America. Turkey itself was one of the foods that they found there as were corn, tomatoes, peppers and potatoes.

Serves 4

1 tablespoon oil
675 g (1½ lb) boneless turkey meat, cut into walnut-sized pieces
1 large onion, peeled and diced
350 g (12 oz) new or waxy potatoes, peeled and cut into 2.5 cm (1 inch) cubes
1 green pepper, de-seeded and diced.
1 × 400 g (14 oz) tin Italian tomatoes, drained
½ teaspoon freeze-dried thyme
½ teaspoon freeze-dried oregano
Salt and freshly ground black pepper
175 g (6 oz) sweetcorn kernels (frozen is probably easiest)

Heat the oil in a flameproof casserole dish and fry the turkey pieces until light brown. Add the onion, potatoes and pepper. Add the tomatoes, breaking them up slightly with a fork as you mix them in, but not attempting to purée them. Add the herbs and enough water just to cover the turkey. Simmer on top of the oven, or in an oven pre-heated to gas mark 4 180°C (350°F) for 45 minutes. Season generously then add the sweetcorn. If the sauce is very thin it can be thickened with a teaspoon of cornflour slaked in a little water, stirred in and brought gently to the boil.

5. Turkey escalopes

These are the centre of the breast cut across the grain and flattened slightly. They can be beaten out thinly and used in the same way as veal escalopes for schnitzel, or holstein-style cooking (egg and breadcrumbed and shallow-fried). They're also tasty grilled.

 WINE tip | **With escalopes try a good, dryish French rosé such as Tavel or a Syrah rosé from Languedoc.**

Escalopes with red pepper sauce

Serves 4

1 clove garlic, peeled and halved
½ teaspoon salt
5 tablespoons olive oil
1 teaspoon freeze-dried basil
4 × 175 g (6 oz) turkey escalopes
2 red peppers, de-seeded and cut into chunks
2 tablespoons tomato purée
½ teaspoon sugar
3–4 tablespoons water

Heat the grill until it's very hot and line the grill pan with a piece of aluminium foil to reflect heat and make the washing up easier.

Chop one half clove of garlic. Crush the other half to a paste with the point of a knife and a pinch of salt. Mix this with 4 tablespoons of olive oil and the basil and spread on the escalopes. Leave to marinate for at least 30 minutes. Heat the remaining olive oil and fry the peppers rapidly until wilted. Add the remaining garlic, the tomato purée, sugar and water, and simmer the sauce for 5 minutes. Pour into a liquidizer or food processor and process until completely smooth. Pour the sauce back in a saucepan and allow to blend over the lowest possible heat for a further 5 minutes while you grill the escalopes for 3 to 4 minutes a side, turning them carefully until you are sure they are cooked through. In modern presentation, the sauce should be placed on the plate first and the escalopes on top, with their grill markings showing as a decoration.

6. Turkey strips

Turkey is sold in many supermarkets in pre-cut stir-fry strips and there seems no reason not to take advantage of these. A robust sauce in a Chinese-style, plenty of rice and a crisp salad made of Chinese leaves (see page 123) are good accompaniments.

Rich turkey stir-fry

Serves 4

1 tablespoon oil
450 g (1 lb) turkey strips
1 bunch of spring onions
1 Spanish onion
175 g (6 oz) tinned bamboo shoots, drained
1 clove garlic, peeled and crushed
2.5 cm (1 inch) piece fresh ginger root, peeled and crushed
Pinch of salt
4 tablespoons hoisin sauce
4 tablespoons water

Heat the oil in a wok or large frying pan and stir-fry the turkey strips for 3 to 4 minutes until lightly brown.

Meanwhile trim the spring onions and cut into 5 cm (2 inch) lengths, peel and slice the onion across the grain into 5 mm (¼ inch) slices, and cut the bamboo shoots into 5 mm (¼ inch) strips. Add all the vegetables to the turkey and stir-fry together for 2 to 3 minutes until the vegetables are hot right through. Crush the garlic and ginger with the point of a knife and a pinch of salt. Add this to the mixture with the hoisin sauce and water. Stir and toss together for 1 to 2 minutes until thoroughly coated with the sauce, then serve immediately.

7. Minced turkey

Minced turkey is an excellent product and can be used as a low-fat alternative to conventional mince. It makes excellent dishes in its own right, too, as in this recipe.

Turkey polpette in soured cream

Serve this dish with long, flat noodles like tagliatelle.

Serves 4

1 large slice wholemeal bread, broken into chunks
1 small onion, peeled and quartered
450 g (1 lb) minced turkey
½ teaspoon freeze-dried chives
½ teaspoon freeze-dried marjoram
1 egg
Salt and freshly ground black pepper
1 tablespoon oil
150 ml (5 fl oz) soured cream
1 tablespoon chopped fresh parsley

Purée the bread and onion in a food processor. Add the turkey, herbs and egg and process briefly for 5 to 10 seconds until thoroughly mixed. Bring a large pan of water to the boil. Divide the meat mixture into 16 portions and roll into balls – you'll find that wetting your hands stops it sticking – and slide them carefully into the gently boiling water. Cook for 4 to 5 minutes until they have risen to the surface, then drain them carefully, reserving the liquid. In a frying pan into which they will all fit, heat a smear of oil and fry the meatballs until lightly browned. Add 120 ml (4 fl oz) of the poaching liquid, season generously and stir in the soured cream. Bring the sauce to the boil and simmer for a further 5 minutes. Sprinkle with the chopped parsley and serve.

89

This simply flavoured dish could match well with English Seyval Blanc or one of the spicy Hungarian Rieslings. Appley cider or sparkling apple juice would also be good.

Goose

Goose is a bird slowly coming back into fashion, though it will remain an adult taste, being rich and strongly flavoured. It's also not an economical bird as there is a surprisingly large amount of bone to meat. It is, however, worth doing on high days and holidays, and some of the old methods of cooking, when it was the first-choice celebration bird, still make for good eating. Buy geese weighing between 3.2 kg (7 lb) and 5.4 kg (12 lb) – any smaller and the amount of meat is not worth having, any larger and they tend to be very strongly flavoured and slightly tough.

THREE STEPS TO GREAT ROAST GOOSE

- **Blanching** Like duck, goose has a reputation for being greasy. This can be avoided by pouring a large pan of boiling water over the goose in a colander or on a rack before you cook it. Treat all sides of the goose like this. It loosens the skin from the fat and ensures that the cooked bird is not at all greasy.

- **Stuffing** Goose has to be very thoroughly cooked and is very succulent so it can be stuffed with some quite astringent tastes and flavours. A herb that used to be popular was sage, but that's out of fashion these days. A delicious stuffing can be made using dried fruit – principally apricots and dried pears – 225 g (8 oz) of each, cut up and soaked for 2 to 3 hours, then mixed with fresh white breadcrumbs, a finely chopped onion, generous seasoning and an egg to bind the mixture. It needs no butter or fat because the goose will provide plenty.

- **Cooking** A medium oven, gas mark 4, 180°C (350°F) is best for roasting goose. It needs about 15 to 18 minutes per 450 g (1 lb), stuffed weight. The bigger the bird, the less time per 450 g (1 lb), but make sure it's cooked well through. It's also best roasted on a rack so that the abundant fat runs out and pours away into the pan and the goose doesn't sit in it while it's cooking. When it's cooked, allow the goose to stand for 10 to 15 minutes before carving. A sharp knife is essential for this and it's best to separate the legs from the body and to carve those individually to get the meat off. The fat used to be highly prized for frying potatoes and adding flavour to other fried foods or casseroles. It may be worth storing a little of it in a jar in the fridge for occasions of self-indulgence, but most of it, I'm afraid, is probably best discarded. Serve the goose with apple sauce – made from English cooking apples with a little sugar and a generous seasoning of cloves or cinnamon – potatoes, mashed or roasted and red cabbage cooked as on page 115 to make up the perfect balance.

 WINE *tip* This rich, fatty bird needs rich, fruity French red Rhônes like the pricey Hermitage or the cheaper Crozes-Hermitage, or Châteauneuf-du-Pape.

THREE INTERESTING IDEAS FOR SPARE BITS OF
GOOSE

- **Giblets** Geese usually come complete with their giblets, which are quite substantial. The French have a tradition for cutting the neck and gizzard up with the heart and making a small casserole using a little of the goose fat, onions and carrots, plenty of herbs and slow cooking it at the same time as the goose (or after it if your oven isn't big enough). It improves well with keeping for a few days before re-heating and eating.

- **Liver pâté** The liver of the goose is usually quite hefty, making an excellent basis for goose liver pâté. Sauté the liver with 225 g (8 oz) of chicken livers, a clove of garlic and a good pinch of mixed herbs in 1 or 2 tablespoons of the goose fat (instead of butter). When they're cooked but still pink inside, purée with a wine glass of apple juice, and chill in a soufflé dish for 6 hours.

- **Confit of goose** This is the French recipe used to make a preserve with goose that will keep for months, even out of the fridge. In France it's used to enrich slow-cooked country dishes like Cassoulet, the wonderful bean dish of south-west France. Unless you happen to have a lot of surplus goose as the *foie gras* farmers do, I think it's an indulgence. But if you've got some spare bits or you haven't eaten all the roast goose, cut it into moderate-sized pieces, on the bone if that's appropriate, place in preserving jars, cover with goose fat and a teaspoon of coarse salt per jar. Bake for 30 minutes at gas mark 4, 180°C (350°F). Make sure all the meat is under fat before the jars cool and you seal them. They will keep for 6 months, at least, in a cool place. To use, the technique is to stand the jar in a pan of boiling water until the fat melts. Retrieve the pieces of goose and add to soups, stews or Cassoulets or even grill and eat in their own right. Store the rest by allowing the fat to harden again.

WINE tip For the giblet casserole – a big old-fashioned Spanish red, such as Toro. For the liver pâté – a sweet wine like French Monbazillac or the fortified Pineau des Charentes from the Cognac region. And for the *confit* – a simple, solid red with body – French Cahors, Madiran or Côtes du Ventoux.

Guinea fowl

Guinea fowl are occasionally available and are a happy half-way house between poultry and game. They can be roasted in the French style like a chicken (see page 68) or make an excellent casserole, particularly when cooked with fruit. Dried apricots and a mild spicing of garam masala is one interesting option, or cooked like Pheasant vallée d'Auge with apples and cream (see page 99) is another.

91

CHAPTER SEVEN

• •

'Game' traditionally meant a source of meat that is hunted rather than raised. Although that division is a bit blurred these days as pheasants are hand-reared and deer are raised on land not suitable for other kinds of farming.

game

The great divide: fur versus feathers

Meat from game is either furred – like venison, hare and rabbit – or feathered – like pheasant, grouse and wild duck. Whichever it is, it has a number of common characteristics. It tends to be:

• High in flavour.
• Lower in saturated fat than domestic animals.
• Dense in texture.
• Usually dark in colour.

Many supermarkets now stock game or will order it. But butchers with a game-dealing licence are the experts.

Furred game

Venison: three cuts and three ways to cook them

1. HAUNCH

This is the most expensive cut, the Robin Hood cut, and is essentially a rear leg. It is similar to a leg of lamb. Haunch of venison is traditionally marinated before cooking.

*Above: **Jugged hare** (page 96). Below: **Country rabbit casserole** (page 98)*

Marinated roast haunch of venison

A wide variety of marinades is used for venison, often with red wine or beer as the base, but any acidic juice will do equally well – cranberry or even cloudy apple juice. With the addition of vegetables and herbs, crushed peppercorns and juniper berries the marinade will, over a period of 24 hours, tenderize the meat and add flavour.

Serves 8

2.25 kg (5 lb) haunch of venison
600 ml (1 pint) red wine or acidic juice
225 g (8 oz) carrots, sliced
225 g (8 oz) onions, peeled and sliced
6 juniper berries, crushed
Salt and freshly ground black pepper

Place the meat in a deep bowl. Mix together the marinade ingredients, pour over the meat, cover and leave in a cool place for 24 hours, turning occasionally.

Pre-heat the oven to gas mark 5, 190°C (375°F). Drain the meat off the marinade (which you can then strain and boil as a basis for gravy or sauce). Cover the meat loosely with butter papers or buttered foil and roast in a gas mark 5, 190°C (375°F) oven, 170°C (340°F) fan oven, or the bottom of the roasting oven in an Aga for 20 minutes per 450 g (1 lb) plus another 20 minutes. Allow the meat to stand in a warm place for 10 to 15 minutes. Make the sauce from the pan drippings and 150 ml (5 fl oz) of the marinade thickened with 2 teaspoons of cornflour. Check the sauce for seasoning and balance then slice the venison as for leg of lamb. A purée of potato and celeriac, and either sprouts or red cabbage go very well with this dish.

2. LOIN

This is the cut that in beef would be sirloin, or in lamb, half a saddle. Get your butcher to remove it from the bones (these can be used for a game soup or stock). You should now have a sausage-shaped piece of meat weighing about 900 g (2 lb) ready for the next recipe.

Braised venison with quince jelly

Serves 4

1 tablespoon plain flour
½ teaspoon ground bay leaves
¼ teaspoon salt
1 loin of venison
1 tablespoon oil
4 tablespoons quince jelly or redcurrant jelly
150 ml (5 fl oz) water

Pre-heat the oven to gas mark 7, 220°C (425°F).

Mix the flour, bay and salt together and use this to dredge the meat. Heat the oil in a heavy frying pan and brown the meat quickly on all sides. Cook in the oven for 15 minutes per 450 g (1 lb) plus another 5 minutes. Remove from the oven and keep in a warm place for at least 10 minutes. Add the water to the drippings in the pan and scrape up. Add the quince jelly to the liquid, stir and bring to the boil until the jelly melts and a thin sauce is made. This can be thickened, if you choose, with arrowroot but is nicest used as a gravy on meat which has been sliced across the grain into rounds.

WINE *tip*   **Venison is a strongly flavoured meat, so it needs heavier, more robust red wines with mature flavours. The fruit jellies and juices in the recipes give bags of sweet fruit so match them with a wine from the sunny southern hemisphere such as Cabernet Sauvignon, or Shiraz. Big-flavoured wines, such as Fitou, or Rioja Reserva will match the loin, and a well chilled full-bodied rosé such as Spanish Navarra rosé makes a different but delightful alternative for stews.**

3. STEWING VENISON

Stewing venison is much cheaper than a whole joint and makes a delicious, warming, winter stew. This can be made into a much fancier presentation by adding a pastry lid, traditional in Scotland.

Daube of venison

Serves 4

900 g (2 lb) stewing venison
225 g (8 oz) button mushrooms
225 g (8 oz) button onions, peeled
4 stalks of celery
2 carrots
1 tablespoon butter
1 tablespoon oil
25 g (1 oz) plain flour
2 bay leaves
Salt and freshly ground black pepper
2 allspice berries, crushed
2 juniper berries, crushed
1 tablespoon chopped fresh parsley
300 ml (10 fl oz) liquid (cranberry juice, red grape juice or red wine)
225 g (8 oz) puff pastry (optional)
1 egg, beaten (optional)

Cut the venison into 2.5 cm (1 inch) cubes. Cut the mushrooms, onions and celery into 5 mm (¼ inch) slices and the carrots into 1 cm (½ inch) dice. Melt the butter and the oil in a flameproof casserole and fry the venison until golden. Dredge with flour and continue to fry until the whole mixture has a dark brown colour, but do not allow it to burn. Add the carrots, onions, celery, bay leaves, parsley, allspice and juniper, and season generously. Pour in the liquid, which you should stir well into the meat and vegetables, cover and cook gently over a very low heat for 45 minutes. Season generously and cook for another 15 to 30 minutes until the meat is tender.

You may either serve this directly from the casserole or cover it with home-made, or one of the very acceptable shop-bought, puff pastry. If you are using a casserole, roll out the pastry to make a lid and lay it on top. If using a pie dish, make a pastry rim first and then add a lid to that. Decorate the lid with offcuts of pastry, brush with a beaten egg and bake for 20 minutes in a maximum heat oven until the pastry is risen and brown. This is known in Scotland as a Venison pasty.

Braised venison with quince jelly

- **Don't catch it** We're not talking about whether you chase it across the field. Catching a hare means removing the iridescent skin that is under the fur coat; any good game dealer or butcher should have done this already.

- **Don't save the blood to thicken the sauce** Despite tradition, it's an unpleasant process and produces a very strong and often unacceptable flavour.

- **Don't overcook it** Hare will cook in 45 minutes to 1 hour, despite the recipes that recommend 3 hours stewing.

- **Don't worry** It's easy to cook, rich in flavour and, if you follow the above instructions, highly acceptable for most people to eat.

96

TWO DELICIOUS HARE DISHES

Jugged hare

Boiled potatoes, carrots and crisp cooked cabbage – red or green – are a wonderful accompaniment to this traditional dish.

Serves 4 to 6

1 hare, cut into sections
Salt and freshly ground black pepper
1 blade of mace, crushed, or 1 teaspoon ground mace
1 bundle of herbs: parsley, thyme, celery and bay leaf
600 ml (1 pint) beef stock
2 anchovy fillets
2 onions, peeled and stuck with 4 cloves
A pinch of cayenne pepper
1 tablespoon redcurrant jelly
1 tablespoon made mustard
2 teaspoons cornflour

Pre-heat the oven to gas mark 3, 160°C (325°F).

Put the hare in a bowl and season it generously with salt, pepper and the crushed or ground mace. Put it into a tall, thin casserole or an ovenproof jug. Add the bundle of herbs and the beef stock, the anchovies and clove-studded onions. Pour in enough water to come just below the surface of the hare. Cover the jug or casserole tightly, put it in a baking dish or ovenproof bowl with 5 cm (2 inches) of boiling water and place the whole thing into the oven for 1½ to 2 hours until the hare is tender. The water jacket slows the cooking so much the length of time is okay. Remove the pieces of hare and pour the liquid through a sieve into a saucepan. Add the cayenne pepper, the redcurrant jelly and mustard, and the cornflour mixed in a little water. Stir together over a gentle heat, bring to the boil and allow to thicken. Place the hare in a serving dish and pour the sauce over it.

Lepre in agrodolce

This is an Italian recipe for hare, the Italians being great game-eaters. It has an unusual combination of flavours and some totally unexpected ingredients but is worth trying as it is so delicious. It is often served with polenta in Italy and mashed potato is probably the best alternative.

Serves 4 to 6

2 tablespoons olive oil
1 hare, jointed
2 tablespoons balsamic or red wine vinegar
Salt and freshly ground black pepper
300 ml (10 fl oz) chicken stock
25 g (1 oz) bitter chocolate
1 teaspoon soft brown sugar
25 g (1 oz) butter
175 g (6 oz) button onions or 3 small English onions
Chopped fresh parsley to garnish

Heat the oil and fry the hare pieces until well browned. Pour in the vinegar and allow to bubble for a minute or two. Season generously and add the chicken stock, the chocolate and the brown sugar. Bring to the boil, cover and cook over a very gentle heat for about 45 to 50 minutes until the hare is tender. In a separate pan, melt the butter and add the remaining sugar. Turn the onions in this mixture until browned and then tip the whole mixture, onions and butter, into the hare casserole and stir well. The sauce should be much reduced and almost syrupy with a sweet and sour flavour. Check it for balance. Place the hare on a serving dish, spoon the sauce over and sprinkle with finely chopped parsley.

 WINE *tip* **Hare is rich, solid grub which demands wine of similar character. What about aged Barolo, which is a thunderbolt in its own right, or alternatively Portuguese Periquita or Dão.**

THREE REASONS TO BUY RABBIT

- **Flavour** A mild but distinctive flavour which, where the influence of Beatrix Potter does not extend, is as well liked as chicken.

- **Value** A cheap meat with a high proportion of flesh to bone.

- **Health** Low in fat and high in nutritive values.

THREE WAYS TO BUY RABBIT

- **Wild** Often available, particularly towards the beginning of autumn in country areas. They're smaller than domestically reared rabbits but have a better flavour.

- **Rabbit portions** Domestic rabbits reared for the table are usually in portions when they arrive, very much like jointed chicken.

- **Cubed** Frozen rabbit from, of all places, China. An acceptable cheap meat but not ideal for the rabbit dishes in this book.

97

THREE RABBIT RECIPES

Rabbit with two mustards

A French dish best served with green cabbage and boiled potatoes.

Serves 4

2 tablespoons olive oil
1 rabbit, jointed
1 tablespoon white wine vinegar
1 large onion, finely chopped
250 ml (8 fl oz) chicken stock or water
1 tablespoon Bordeaux mustard
1 tablespoon Meaux grain mustard

In a deep frying pan, heat the oil and fry the rabbit pieces until brown. Add the vinegar and allow to bubble almost dry. Add the onion and stock and sauté over a medium to low heat for 35 to 40 minutes until the rabbit is cooked through, turning at least once half-way through. There should be a small amount of sauce left in the pan. Stir the mustards into the sauce, adding a little more stock or water if the sauce is too thick. Coat the rabbit with the sauce and serve.

Country rabbit casserole

A basic rabbit casserole with a lot of vegetables flavouring and enriching the dish. New potatoes in their skins are the perfect accompaniment.

Serves 4

1 tablespoon oil
1 tablespoon butter
1 rabbit, jointed
225 g (8 oz) carrots
225 g (8 oz) onions
225 g (8 oz) leeks
1 teaspoon freeze-dried marjoram
1 teaspoon freeze-dried thyme
1 bouquet garni or a stick of celery, some parsley stalks
*   and a bay leaf tied together*
Salt and freshly ground black pepper
2 teaspoons cornflour

Heat the oil and butter and fry the jointed rabbit until golden brown. Clean and trim the vegetables and cut into 1 cm (½ in) dice. Stir into the juices, add the herbs and bouquet garni, season generously and just cover with water. Simmer on top of the oven, or cook in a pre-heated oven at gas mark 4, 180°C (350°F) for 40 to 45 minutes until the rabbit is tender. Remove the bouquet garni. Slake the cornflour with a little water, stir it into the sauce and allow to thicken over a very gentle heat.

Rabbit with prunes and grape juice

Another French favourite from the south-west of France whence the best prunes also come. I like this served with broad, flat noodles like tagliatelle, though in Aquitaine they often serve rice.

Serves 4

175 g (6 oz) prunes
300 ml (10 fl oz) white grape juice
1 tablespoon oil
1 rabbit, jointed
1 clove garlic, peeled and finely chopped
2 teaspoons cornflour
150 ml (5 fl oz) double cream
Juice of ½ lemon
Salt and freshly ground black pepper

Put the prunes to soak in the grape juice for at least 30 minutes before you begin to cook; up to 2 hours is okay.

Heat the oil and sauté the rabbit and garlic until golden, about 5 minutes a side. Add the prunes and the grape juice and simmer gently, uncovered, for about 30 minutes until the rabbit is tender and the prunes are plump. Make sure that the liquid doesn't boil or the prunes will disintegrate. Stir the cornflour into the cream, add the lemon juice. The mixture will thicken almost immediately. Stir it spoonful by spoonful into the rabbit and sauce, season generously and test for balance in the flavours. The lemon juice should balance the sweetness of the prunes and grape juice. The sauce should be thick and creamy.

WINE *tip* Simple country wines match rustic dishes such as rabbit. Try Spain's rosados (rosés), France's Vins de Pays from the Syrah grape, and Cahors, Portugal's Dão, and Sicily's chunkier reds. Or, for a complete contrast – vintage cider! Its refreshing dryness makes a pleasing change from wine.

Feathered game

Our choice of the five best game birds

- **Pheasant** Very much like a rich-flavoured chicken and the palest and lightest of game birds, it's widely available in season. The cock will serve four people and the hen three.

- **Partridge** Comes in grey- and red-leg varieties but it's very difficult for anyone but an expert to tell them apart. When very young they make a good sauté but are usually best braised or casseroled.

- **Pigeon** Widely available and the cheapest of all game birds, only the breast is really worth the bother and is often sold separately from the rest of the carcass.

- **Mallard** A kind of wild duck with two superb *magrets* (duck breast steaks) to each bird. Once again, the legs and wings are scarcely worth the bother.

- **Quail** Now reared for the table, quail are tiny. You need two for a decent main course per person. Very delicately flavoured.

Four outrageous opinions about game

- **Don't hang it for long** A couple to three days is fine for the larger of the game birds. Any bird that smells or looks significantly 'off' is worth avoiding.

- **Don't roast it** Traditional game birds were roasted for landowners by their own cooks after being shot and hung on the estate. We're much better sautéeing, baking or casseroling.

- **Game chips are just soggy crisps** The vaunted accompaniments to roast game, including bread sauce and game chips, are like the method of cooking itself – over-rated and a relic of another era.

- **Grouse isn't worth the bother** Although an enormous fuss is made about grouse, and 'the glorious twelfth' when it can first be shot on the Scottish and northern English moors, it's one of the less appetizing birds to eat, with a slightly piney flavour about it. Rarely worth the money.

TWO PERFECT PHEASANT RECIPES

Pheasant vallée d'Auge

This recipe comes from the great valley in northern Normandy famous for its apples and cream and, in season, for its pheasants cooked in them.

Serves 4

2½ tablespoons butter
1 cock pheasant, jointed (like a chicken, see page 67)
300 ml (10 fl oz) apple juice
1 bouquet garni made of a stick of celery, a bay leaf, a sprig of thyme and 4 sprigs of parsley
Salt and freshly ground black pepper
1 tablespoon cornflour
150 ml (5 fl oz) double cream
2 eating apples
Chopped fresh parsley to garnish

Melt 2 tablespoons of butter in a deep-sided frying pan and fry the pheasant pieces until golden brown. Add the apple juice and the bouquet garni, season generously and simmer on top of the stove for 25 minutes. Stir the cornflour into the cream then stir the mixture into the sauce. Blend thoroughly and heat gently until thickened. Core the apples but don't peel them, and cut them into 12 segments each (an apple corer is an ideal tool for this). Melt the remaining butter in a separate pan and turn the apples for a minute or so until they are very pale gold. Arrange them neatly on serving plates, add the pheasant and spoon the sauce around. A sprinkling of parsley adds a touch of colour to the event.

WINE tip Pheasant is a classy bird and if your pocket can run to a French St-Estèphe or a Beaujolais Cru (that's a Beaujolais named after a village, see page 270) then go for it. But French Syrah de l'Ardèche or South African Pinotage will slide down very happily with either of these pheasant recipes.

99

Pheasant with walnuts and pomegranates

This is known as Fasainjan in northern Turkey and Iran, from where it originally comes. The combination may seem strange but is delicious and complements the rich flavour of the pheasant excellently.

Serves 4

2 tablespoons olive oil
1 pheasant, jointed (like a chicken, see page 67)
100 g (4 oz) shelled halved walnuts
2 pomegranates or the juice of 1½ lemons
1 small onion, finely chopped
250 ml (8 fl oz) water
Salt and freshly ground black pepper

Heat the oil and fry the pheasant gently until well browned. Crush or process the nuts until they are the texture of fine breadcrumbs. Cut the pomegranates in half and squeeze them on a citrus squeezer, or if you prefer, scoop them into a blender and strain the remaining juice. Add the onion to the pheasant and stir for 2 to 3 minutes until the onion is transparent. Add the pomegranate juice and an equal amount of water (you can top up with a lemon juice and water mixture if you prefer). Season generously and simmer for 20 to 25 minutes until the pheasant is cooked through. Transfer the pheasant to a warming plate. Stir the crushed walnuts into the sauce; they will thicken the sauce as well as adding flavour and texture. Pour this over the pheasant and check for seasoning.

Partridge

Partridges are plump birds but, with the best will in the world, one will only feed two people. Very young partridges are traditionally roasted but they are hard to come by and it's difficult to be sure so I always braise them with two cabbages.

Braised partridge with two cabbages

Serves 2

1 tablespoon oil
1 tablespoon butter
1 partridge, quartered
1 large onion, peeled and sliced
225 g (8 oz) Dutch coleslaw-style cabbage, sliced
2 juniper berries
½ teaspoon caraway seeds
1 teaspoon cider vinegar
Salt and freshly ground black pepper
250 ml (8 fl oz) water
225 g (8 fl oz) Savoy cabbage

Heat the oil and butter and fry the quartered partridge lightly until golden on all sides. Remove the partridge. Mix together the onion and Dutch cabbage and add to the pan. Fry in the partridge fat for 3 to 4 minutes until well coated and the onion is starting to turn translucent. Add the juniper and caraway and cider vinegar and season generously. Put in the partridge pieces. Add water, just to the level of the bird, cover and simmer on top of the stove, or in a pre-heated oven at gas mark 4, 180°C (350°F), for 45 minutes to 1 hour depending on the size and age of the partridge.

Meanwhile, wash and cut the Savoy cabbage into 2.5 cm (1 inch) squares, discarding any coarse stalks. When the partridge is cooked, remove the casserole from the heat, put the green cabbage on top and return to the simmer or the oven for 10 to 15 minutes until the green cabbage is cooked through but still emerald-coloured. Serve, making sure each person gets a portion of both cabbages as well as of partridge.

WINE tip — **From France – young red Burgundy from the Côtes Chalonnaise, such as Mercurey or Givry, or try Romanian or Californian Pinot Noir.**

Pigeon

TWO KEY FACTS ABOUT PIGEON

- Pigeon is widely available.

- It's rich, strong-tasting with a dense texture. The breast of one pigeon can flavour a beef casserole with enough for six people.

Otherwise, eat the breast as a main course and use any remaining flesh for a pâté. 100 g (4 oz) of a meat to 225 g (8 oz) of chicken livers, an egg, herbs and seasoning minced and baked in a mould in a bain marie for 45 minutes make a terrific pâté.

Spatchcock pigeon

Serve this dish with a green salad and French bread. If you cool it and slice the breasts very thinly, they make an exciting salad served with frisée or endive lettuce (see page 105).

Serves 1

2 juniper berries
2 allspice berries
4 black peppercorns
Juice of ½ lemon
2 tablespoons olive oil
½ teaspoon salt
1 pigeon breast

Crush the spices in a mortar or use a spice mill. Mix the lemon juice and oil together and add the spices and salt. Originally the whole bird was used, but in this case, flatten the pigeon breast with a large frying pan, a meat mallet or the flat of a cleaver so that it is as flat as possible. Push a skewer through it to keep it in position and coat with the flavoured oil and lemon. Allow to marinate for at least 2 hours; 8 to 12 hours is ideal. Pre-heat the grill to maximum and line the grill pan with foil. Grill the pigeon breasts about 7.5 cm (3 inches) from the heat for 5 to 7 minutes a side. Baste with a little of the marinade.

WINE tip   **Needs a biggish wine – Bulgarian Gamza, Chianti Classico or Châteauneuf-du-Pape.**

Above: *Pheasant vallée d'Auge (page 99).*
Below: *Braised partridge with two cabbages*

CHAPTER EIGHT

Firstly, an introduction to the wide range of ingredients that have come to replace the limp lettuce and vinegared beetroot of the past.

salads

Eleven variations on four super salad greens

1. Lettuces

- **Conventional cos** Long, green, crunchy leaves usually of a good flavour, best in the summer.

- **Baby cos** Also known as Little Gem. Quite sweet, tightly curled, yellow and green leaves, slightly bitter aftertaste. Available all year round.

- **Iceberg/Webbs Wonder** Dense lettuces with crisp, crunchy leaves, solid hearts and comparatively little flavour.

- **Lollorosso** A curly-leaved lettuce with red-tipped leaves, no heart, but interesting flavour.

- **Oak leaf or salad bowl** Loose-leaved lettuce with bronze or green leaves, good flavour, very decorative.

2. Chicory

- **Belgian chicory** Bullet-shaped chicons, pale white to gold with green tips to the leaf. Very crisp and quite bitter to the taste.

- **Sugar loaf chicory** Similar in shape to Cos lettuce, pale green, curly leaves, often tightly packed. Mild, bitterish flavour.

- **Radicchio** Orange-sized, dark red balls of chicory with densely packed hearts. A mild, rich flavour and a vivid colour to add excitement to salads.

3. Watercress

Try to buy this fresh and with big crisp stalks as they add greatly to the peppery flavour and texture of watercress.

4. Batavia

- **Frisće** The English for this is frizzy! Long thin leaves with frilly ends, pale gold to pale green, quite bitter and with a terrific texture. Winter time only.

- **Batavia proper** A thick, oak-leaf lettuce lookalike, with succulent texture and a slightly bitter flavour. Another winter special.

 SALAD WASHING
All salad stuffs should be thoroughly washed in cold water and then dried before using – a salad spinner, tea towels or kitchen paper help. Always tear, never cut greens – they go limp. Putting them in the fridge for 15 minutes after washing crisps most greens up remarkably well.
It is advisable to wash pre-packaged salad greens, too, even though they often claim they have been washed.

105

From top: *California salad* (page 108); *Winter salad* (page 108); *French salad* (page 107) *with croûtons garnish* (page 110)

Tomatoes – a four-point buyers' guide

1. Flavour

Many tomatoes are bred for shape and size but not for flavour, but this is changing. A number of tomatoes, usually the more expensive, have been grown especially for flavour, often based on old varieties. Supermarkets have led the way in this and it's worth looking on their labelling to see those varieties designated as high in flavour.

2. Size

The choice of different-sized tomatoes has also improved dramatically. Tiny cherry tomatoes are readily available, as are the large beefsteak-sized ones. The latter should only be bought in the summer. They may come from France or northern Spain and – at best – have the flavour for which the French Marmande tomatoes are justly famous.

3. Colour

106

Always look for dark red tomatoes. In Britain pale or slightly green ones are simply not ripe and will not have the richness of flavour that you hope for. There are now some yellow tomatoes on sale, once again depth of colour is an indication of ripeness.

4. Shape

Most tomatoes are still round, though the big beefsteak, Marmande kind are often slightly misshapen. It's also possible to buy Italian plum tomatoes which are long and thin. In Italy they are primarily used for their superb cooking quality.

A cucumber for all seasons

Most cucumbers on sale in Britain are hothouse-grown throughout the year. It's very rare to find open-ground cucumbers these days, not least because even fine cross-breeding hasn't prevented them generating what used in polite circles to be known as wind. Look for long, straight cucumbers with a uniform dark green colour, and a crisp texture.

Spring onions

Spring onions eaten raw are for the brave. But they should be used frequently in cooking, both oriental and the modern lighter European style. Look for onions without any yellowed or greying leaves and buy them (if you can) comparatively untrimmed as they will stay fresher longer.

Beetroot

Lovely – hot with butter or soured cream – okay pickled. Never in salads unless it is part of a mixture like Russian salad.

WINE tip Don't! Salads dressed with vinaigrette do not take kindly to wine – the vinegar murders it.

Nine crucial salad combinations

Each of these is a really successful combination from somewhere around the capitals of the salad world. These tend to be the USA and the shores of the Mediterranean. You can adopt or adapt these as you choose but do try the basic combinations first as they are tested by time and palate.

1. Three greens

Put together a mixture of three different lettuces, one crisp-textured, one slightly bitter and possibly frilly-edged and one loose-leaved or soft. The last might have a tinge of red in it if it's oak leaf or lollorosso. Tear the leaves into equal half postcard-sized pieces. Dress with the French Dressing on page 111. Serves 4.

2. Lettuce and herbs

We rarely use herbs in British salads and certainly not in the profusion our ancestors did. Try using a basic lettuce, a cos or Webbs Wonder lettuce. Wash it thoroughly and drain it, break it into postcard-sized pieces, sprinkle with either half a cup of chives cut into 5 mm (¼ inch) strips, or 2 tablespoons of mint leaves torn up finely, or 2 tablespoons of basil leaves torn up finely, and dress with the Lemonette Dressing on page 24. You can add marigold petals (no, really!); nasturtium leaves and/or flowers; some fresh thyme rubbed between your fingers, particularly the lemon-scented ones; or the leaves of lemon balm, or salad burnet which has a cucumber flavour. Don't use more than one, or at most two, complementary herbs at a time. Serves 4.

3. New York style salad

In New York they slice iceberg lettuce in steak-thick pieces and cover it with a layer of the Blue Cheese Dressing you'll find on page 111. It's eaten as a separate course either before or after the main course. Serves 4.

4. French salad

French salads have a high reputation but a small range. The reputation is based on high quality green stuffs with a much wider catchment than we normally use. They would include dandelion leaves, rocket and a range of other plants we haven't eaten since the seventeenth century. But most crucial of all is the dressing. Pick one or two green salad ingredients, use the French Dressing on page 111 and add a judicious amount of blue or Gruyère cheese, some crushed walnuts or some herb croûtons (see page 110). Serve it after the main course as a separate dish.

5. Greek salad

Greek salads use local ingredients almost exclusively and often have no green in them at all, being a combination of tomatoes, onions, cheese and olives. Some prefer a little green as a base if it's available. Start with ribbon-sliced, crisp lettuce with layers of thickly sliced ripe tomatoes. Sprinkle over them feta cheese in small cubes. (This is properly made with sheep's milk but is also available with northern European substitutes. It often comes in a jar or container with brine.) Add black olives to taste and a chopped spring onion. Dress with the Lemonette Dressing on page 24.

6. Italian salad

Italian salads are similar to French but with the addition of more flavourings in the dressings. See the dressing on page 111. They also tend not to have cheese in them, which is as well because so many other Italian dishes do. They also, however, make use of a very wide range of non-salad vegetables and cook some of them.

Take a red, green and yellow sweet pepper, de-seed them, slice them very thinly, sauté them in a little olive oil in a heavy-based frying pan until they are wilted but not totally soggy. You can add a finely chopped clove of garlic to the oil while you're doing this. Allow to cool for a couple of minutes then add the fresh juice of a lemon and a good pinch of salt. Cool and, if possible, chill for up to 2 hours. Check the dressing for balance before serving. Serves 4.

7. Winter salad

Though we don't think in these terms very much, winter vegetables make very good salads, as do rice and pasta.

Try pasta with the Italian Dressing on page 111 and a good sprinkling of fresh oregano or basil, or . . .

Try 350 g (12 oz) cooked rice with a handful of toasted pine nuts (see page 110), the same of good raisins, a couple of finely chopped spring onions and the Garlic Dressing on page 111. Then the winter vegetables themselves:

Grated carrot and celeriac with French Dressing (see page 111) and a Mustard Mayonnaise (see page 24) respectively. They are nice cooked too. Try a mixture of 175 g (6 oz) each of lightly simmered carrot batons, young turnip slices and 1 cm (½ inch) leek chunks in a herb-flavoured Lemonette Dressing (see page 25).

Here are the final two crucial salads

Caesar salad

108

One of the great American substantial salads, this was invented, so they say, in Miami in the 1920s for an eponymous gang leader down from the frozen North.

Serves 4

1 cos lettuce
1 clove garlic
1 egg
2 tablespoons white wine vinegar
Pinch of salt
½ teaspoon sugar
4 tablespoons oil
4 tablespoons croûtons (see page 110)
2 tablespoons grated Parmesan cheese

Wash and break up the lettuce into half postcard-sized pieces and dry thoroughly. Cut the garlic in half and rub a salad bowl with the cut side so that it's smeared all over. Allow to dry. Bring a small saucepan of water to the boil and boil the egg for 1 minute. Break and scoop into a bowl. Add the white wine vinegar, salt, sugar and oil and whisk thoroughly. Put the croûtons on the lettuce, pour the dressing over, toss thoroughly then sprinkle with Parmesan cheese.

California salad

This is a salad so named because of the commitment in California to healthy eating, sometimes of a slightly unexpected kind.

Serves 2 as a main course, 4 as starter

1 ripe avocado
½ iceberg-type lettuce, shredded
1 ripe peach or pear, peeled and cored
4 tablespoons cottage cheese
100g (4 oz) sprouted seeds (not bean sprouts but alfalfa, sunflower or even, at a pinch, mustard and cress)
1 quantity Lemonette Dressing (see page 24)

Halve the avocado, remove the stone and peel. Cut each half vertically into 5 mm (¼ inch) slices. Place the lettuce, on a large salad plate or platter and fan the avocado slices over the top of it. Slice and fan the peach or pear, on top. Pile the cottage cheese into the middle of the salad and surround with the sprouted seeds. Pour the dressing over the top and chill for 10 minutes before serving.

From top: *Thousand island dressing* (page 111); *Yoghurt dressing* (page 111); *Blue cheese dressing* (page 111)

vegetables

We have a marvellous variety of vegetables to choose from. Here we've pinpointed the best cooking methods to maintain their wonderful flavours – with several unexpected recipes, too.

Six great greens

1. Spinach

Spinach now comes pre-packed and tender, requiring little picking over of stems. It can be delicious eaten raw as a salad. To cook, wash it thoroughly and plunge it into boiling water for 2 minutes. It will shrink in volume dramatically. Drain it carefully and then:

- **Spinach with garlic** For 450 g (1 lb) of cooked spinach, chop 1 clove of garlic and heat gently in 2 tablespoons of olive oil until golden. Add the spinach and turn thoroughly until the flavours are mixed. Season with salt and freshly ground black pepper.

- **Orange spinach** Put a tablespoon of butter and 4 tablespoons of fresh orange juice into a frying pan. Bring to the boil, add 450 g (1 lb) of cooked spinach and turn until the spinach has absorbed all the orange and butter mixture.

2. Sprouts

Sprouts are much underrated, and if bought and eaten small (which also means young) are a delicious delicately flavoured vegetable. Trim them but never put a cross in the bottom (they cook too quickly).

- **Buttered sprouts** Cook in boiling water for 6 to 8 minutes until cooked through but still bright emerald green. Then butter them and serve.

- **Sprouts polonaise** Toss 450 g (1 lb) of cooked sprouts in a frying pan with 2 tablespoons of fresh breadcrumbs, 25 g (1 oz) of butter and the chopped white and yolk of a hard-boiled egg. Good enough to eat as a course on its own.

- **Sprout purée** Boil 450 g (1 lb) of sprouts in 5 cm (2 inches) of salted water for 9 minutes. Put them into a food processor with 4 tablespoons of fromage frais, a teaspoon of salt and a generous flavouring of black pepper and process until finely chopped. Serve as a purée.

113

Above: *Sauté spring greens* (page 115). Below left: *Broccoli with almonds* (page 115). Below right: *Red cabbage with apples* (page 115)

3. Cabbage

Cabbage comes green or white and loose-leafed or firm. Raw, it makes great coleslaw salad. Or try these two ace ways of cooking it.

Quick tossed cabbage

This is for green, English-style cabbage. It's very rapidly cooked indeed – please trust the timings even though they don't seem generous.

Serves 4

450 g (1 lb) green leafy cabbage (any variety except Savoy)
25 g (1 oz) butter
100 g (4 oz) water
Salt and freshly ground black pepper

Cut the hard stalk out of the cabbage, wash and slice across into 1 cm (½ inch) ribbons. Put the butter and water into a large saucepan with a well fitting lid, bring to the boil, add the cabbage ribbons, season generously, put the lid on and shake vigorously. Put over maximum heat for 45 seconds, shake vigorously once more, 45 seconds more heat, and serve the cabbage, draining it of the surplus water and butter as you do so. The cabbage will be bright green and steamed hot right through but still crisp.

Creamed Savoy cabbage

A simple winter cabbage dish which transforms the crinkly-cut Savoy into something of a luxury. It's finished off flashed under the grill like a gratin but shouldn't be cooked too long (or it becomes khaki coloured).

Serves 4

1 Savoy cabbage
Salt
2 teaspoons cornflour
2 teaspoons butter
175 ml (6 fl oz) milk
Pinch of freshly grated nutmeg
4 tablespoons double cream or fromage frais
1 teaspoon caraway seeds

Pre-heat the grill.
   Cut the cabbage into 2.5 cm (1 inch) chunks and plunge these into boiling salted water for just 4 minutes. Remove and drain. Make a white sauce by whisking the cornflour and butter into the milk, heating through and adding the nutmeg, cream or fromage frais and caraway seeds. Mix with the blanched cabbage. Place in a gratin or baking dish that it fills just to the brim and flash under the hot grill for a couple of minutes until the top is bubbling and golden.

Red cabbage with apples

A delicious cabbage idea based on Central European recipes.

Serves 4

1 tablespoon vegetable oil
1 onion, peeled and thinly sliced
1 cooking apple, peeled, cored and thinly sliced
675 g (1½ lb) red cabbage, stalks removed, cut into
  1 cm (½ inch) slices
Salt and freshly ground black pepper
2 tablespoons cider vinegar
1 tablespoon soft brown sugar
1–2 tablespoons water
Pinch of ground cloves
Pinch of ground allspice

Pre-heat the oven to gas mark 3, 160°C (325°F).

Heat the oil in a flameproof casserole and fry the onion for 5 minutes until soft but not browned. Add the apple and cabbage and toss to coat. Season generously, stir in the cider vinegar, sugar and water. Cover the casserole and bake in the oven for 25 minutes. Remove from the oven, add the spices and mix well – add more water if the cabbage is drying out. Return to the oven for another 25 minutes, then serve at once.

4. Broccoli

Broccoli provokes strong feelings – it was even banned from the US White House at one time. What we now buy as broccoli is strictly calabrese but it's available all year round. It has wonderful texture and flavour and is a terrific source of vitamins. It should be served after boiling or steaming for not more than 6 to 8 minutes, while it is still bright emerald green and has some crispness left. It can be simply buttered or you can try the following ideas.

● **Broccoli with almonds** Toss 50 g (2 oz) of slivered almonds in 25 g (1 oz) of butter, add the juice of half a lemon and turn 450 g (1 lb) of freshly cooked broccoli in the mixture before serving.

● **Chinese broccoli** An alternative with a Chinese flavour is to use 2 tablespoons of oyster sauce, a readily purchased thick soy sauce variety. Steam 450 g (1 lb) of broccoli, pour 4 tablespoons of the sauce in a thin stream decoratively over the hot vegetable and serve immediately.

5. Spring greens

A very loose-leafed young cabbage variety that makes an excellent vegetable cooked as in the Quick Tossed Cabbage on page 114 or:

● **Sauté spring greens** Slice 450 g (1 lb) of spring greens across very thinly into 1 cm (½ inch) ribbons. In a large saucepan or covered frying pan, put 2 tablespoons of oil and a finely chopped clove of garlic. Add the spring greens and stir-fry for 1 minute over a high heat. Add 4 tablespoons of water, put the lid on tight, return to the heat and toss for another 45 seconds. This will produce a bright green, garlic-flavoured and still crunchy vegetable.

115

VITAMIN E
Leafy vegetables are a good source of vitamin E (along with vegetable oils and wholemeal cereals). It is an essential vitamin for the body and more recent research indicates that it may help prevent heart disease and some cancers.

6. Cauliflower

As well as white cauliflower there are also the purple and green kinds. While these taste the same as a conventional white cauliflower, they are extremely attractive, especially presented whole.

- **Cauliflower cheese** The secret is to blanch the cauliflower first for just 2 to 3 minutes in boiling water. Then place the florets in a gratin or baking dish and pour a measure of Mornay Sauce over it (see page 20). Season generously with nutmeg and add a further 50 g (2 oz) of grated cheese (Cheddar, Gruyère or Parmesan), before putting in a pre-heated oven at gas mark 6, 200°C (400°F) for 15 to 20 minutes. When the top is golden and bubbling and the cauliflower cooked through . . . enjoy it immediately.

- **Cauliflower vinaigrette** Boil the cauliflower in salted water for 6 to 8 minutes until the stem is just tender. Drain thoroughly and, while still warm, divide into 4 sections for 4 servings. Dress each section with 2 tablespoons of Lemonette Dressing (see page 24). Sprinkle generously with snipped fresh chives and/or chopped fresh parsley and allow to chill thoroughly before serving as an hors d'oeuvre.

WINE tip Cauliflower cheese needs a dry French white such as Côtes de Gascogne to cut through the rich cheese or a red southern French Merlot to complement it.

STEAMING VEGETABLES
Many of our vegetable recipes suggest cooking vegetables in shallow water rather than immersing them completely. This helps keep them *al dente*, preserving both flavour and vitamins. Soggy veg are not only bland-tasting but also nutritionally poor. The best way to preserve both flavour and vitamins is to steam:

- Either in a microwave.
- Or in a purpose-built double saucepan steamer.
- Or in a colander inside a saucepan of shallow water.

Microwaving – in which the water molecules in vegetables are agitated – is essentially a steaming technique. It can preserve 80 per cent of the vitamin C in broccoli; a steamer will preserve 70 per cent while conventional boiling will only leave 35 per cent.

You can ignore all questions of vitamin retention if you want, but steamed vegetables are a complete revelation of flavour.

Above: *Stuffed peppers* (page 121). **Below:** *Leeks provençal* (page 119)

Six rustic roots

Root vegetables are no soft option and properly cooked can be just as much of a treat as their more exotic or delicate above-ground relatives. Like green vegetables they need careful cooking or the result is a dismal mush.

1. Turnips

The smaller the turnip the better the flavour (large ones can be too strong).

- **Glazed turnips** Select 450 g (1 lb) of turnips not more than 5 to 7.5 cm (2 to 3 inches) across. Peel them and cut them into quarters. Place in cold water and bring to the boil, simmering for approximately 6 minutes until just tender. Drain them thoroughly and toss them in a tablespoon of butter, a teaspoon of sugar and a teaspoon of white wine vinegar over heat. When the turnips are glazed and the vinegar has evaporated, serve at once.

- **Turnip purée** Put 450 g (1 lb) cooked turnip into a food processor with a generous 25 g (1 oz) of butter, salt and pepper, and purée to a delicate white mousse – delicious with grilled meats and sausages.

2. Parsnips

This English vegetable, scarcely known in other countries, has a wonderful hint of sweetness to set off its generous texture.

- **Roast parsnips** Place the parsnips in cold water, bring to the boil, then poach for about 6 minutes. Drain thoroughly and roast like roasted potatoes in hot fat in a hot oven.

- **Buttered parsnips** Cook for 10 to 12 minutes and when just tender but not soggy, drain thoroughly. Add 25 g (1 oz) of butter to 450 g (1 lb) of parsnips and toss gently to allow the butter to soak into the golden flesh.

3. Celeriac

This looks like an extremely knobbly, large turnip. When peeled it has a white flesh with a crisp texture and a mild flavour of celery.

- **Celeriac rémoulade** It can be cut into matchstick-sized strips and served with mayonnaise which has a teaspoon of Dijon mustard added to it – a great French winter salad.

- **Potato and celeriac mousse** Boil 225 g (8 oz) of peeled and diced celeriac with 675 g (1½ lb) of potatoes and mash them thoroughly together with plenty of black pepper, a pinch of salt, some butter and a little milk to produce a delicately flavoured alternative to mash.

4. Leeks

The great trick with leeks is to clean them thoroughly. Trim them and then split them lengthways before washing in plenty of cold water.

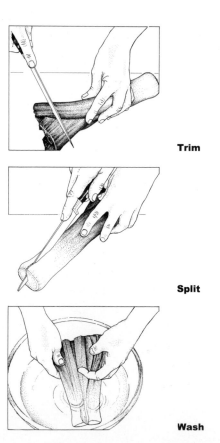

Trim

Split

Wash

- **Leeks au gratin** Slice 450 g (1 lb) of leeks into 2.5 cm (1 inch) lengths, drop into boiling water for 3 minutes, drain and pour a white sauce over them (see page 19). Brown quickly under the grill before serving either as a course on its own or with roast meat.

- **Leeks provençal** Cut 450 g (1 lb) of leeks into 15 cm (6 inch) lengths. Fry them in a tablespoon of olive oil. Add 200 g (7 oz) of tinned chopped Italian tomatoes, a teaspoon of chopped fresh basil, and season generously. Simmer for 10 minutes until the liquid has almost all gone and the tomatoes form a thick sauce for the leeks. Check for seasoning and either serve hot, or cold as an hors d'oeuvre with a squeeze of lemon juice over them.

5. Carrots

Baby carrots need nothing more than a good scrub, a quick boil from cold, and butter, salt and pepper to season them. For older, bigger carrots:

- **Vichy-style carrots** Peel 450 g (1 lb) of carrots and cut them into rounds. Place them in a saucepan almost covered by water. Add a tablespoon of butter, half a teaspoon of salt, a teaspoon of white sugar, and bring to the boil. Cook till all the water has evaporated. The carrots will be just tender and glazed – half a teaspoon of dried mint is a good addition.

- **Punchnep carrots** Carrots also go very well in a puréed mixture of root vegetables, mixed 50/50 with peeled and diced swede. Cook from cold in salted water for 12 to 15 minutes until both vegetables are soft. Drain thoroughly and either process or mash with a potato masher to a coarse purée. Season generously with butter or fromage frais, salt and pepper, and serve hot.

Above: *Ratatouille* (page 122). Below: *Vichy-style carrots*

6. Onions

Onions are very rarely eaten in their own right, this is a pity because they make marvellous dishes.

- **Baked onions** Try baking an onion per person alongside the potato the next time you bake potatoes. Trim them first but don't take all the peel off and allow about 15 to 20 minutes less for the onion than you would allow for an equivalent-sized potato in a medium to hot oven. Serve with salt, soured cream and/or butter. If you're eating them on their own, a little brown bread and butter goes well with them.

- **Marmalade of onions** Peel and slice 900 g (2 lb) of onions. Put 3 tablespoons of oil, preferably olive, in a heavy-based saucepan that has a good lid. Cook the onions in the oil very gently for about 35 minutes, until softened and well blended without allowing them to brown. Add a tablespoon of Ribena or equivalent blackcurrant drink. This adds sweetness, colour and depth of flavour. Bring to a rapid boil until the liquid is all evaporated and the onions have taken on a little colour. Serve well seasoned as a vegetable dish with simply cooked meats or sausages.

7. Swede

A golden vegetable without much flavour of its own. Great in soup or purées, particularly with carrots (see page 119).

8. Beetroot

Particularly good baked like a potato. Wash but don't peel the beetroot, bake till tender (about 1½ hours in a medium oven) and then peel. Eat with butter, salt and pepper.

Also try baby beetroot – boiled, skinned and then heated in a little butter with a dollop of sour cream. These are known as *Harvard Beets* in the United States.

Five Mediterranean vegetables: facts and flavours

1. Aubergines

Although aubergines range in size from a pea to a small pumpkin and in colour from black to white, we are most familiar with purple ones. They have a white, slightly spongy flesh and can be used to make a wide variety of dishes from creamy dips to batter fritters. Here are two of the best ideas.

- **Crisp fried aubergines** Slice the aubergine across into 5 mm (¼ inch) slices and pat the inside dry with kitchen paper. Dip in a little flour and fry in shallow oil for 2 to 3 minutes a side until lightly gold. Drain and serve as a first course or vegetable.

Moussaka

Aubergines also make the wonderful layered dish, Moussaka.

Serves 4

450 g (1 lb) aubergines, sliced
2 tablespoons plain flour
2 tablespoons oil
450 g (1 lb) minced lamb
1 onion, peeled and finely chopped
1 clove garlic, peeled and crushed
1 × 400 g (14 oz) tin chopped tomatoes
Salt and freshly ground black pepper
¼ teaspoon freshly grated nutmeg
300 ml (10 fl oz) Béchamel Sauce (see page 19)
50 g (1 oz) hard cheese, grated

Pre-heat the oven to gas mark 4, 180°C (350°F).
Pat the aubergines dry on kitchen paper then dip in flour. Heat the oil and lightly fry the aubergines until golden; drain well. Add the lamb, onion and garlic to the pan and fry until soft. Add the tomatoes, salt, pepper and nutmeg and simmer for 30 minutes. Make the Béchamel Sauce. Layer the aubergines in an ovenproof dish with the lamb mixture, finishing with a layer of aubergine. Stir the cheese into the sauce and pour over the top. Bake for 40 minutes. Serve with a green salad.

WINE *tip* Go for Greek! Château Carras or the typical piney Retsina.

2. Courgettes

Once thought of as baby marrows, courgettes are now a normal, in fact almost basic, part of our vegetable diet. Excellent eaten raw in salads when sliced thinly or grated. Cut into 2.5 cm (1 inch) batons they make an excellent ingredient in a stir-fry, or cooked with a clove of garlic in a little olive oil for 4 to 5 minutes make an excellent vegetable in their own right. They are also delicious steamed. Cut them into 2.5 cm (1 inch) lengths and steam in a colander or steamer basket over boiling water for 7 to 10 minutes.

They can then be salted and buttered and served or, best of all, covered in a light Béchamel Sauce (see page 19), seasoned and served either as a dish on their own or as an accompaniment to simply cooked meat or fish.

3. Peppers

Sweet peppers now come in a variety of colours – green, yellow, orange and red. The red are the sweetest and the orange the spiciest (although all are mild in flavour). They all need to be split and have their seeds removed as those are not edible.

- **Pepper salad** For a perfect pepper salad, the waxy skins should be removed as well. To do this place the pepper halves in a very hot oven until the skins are literally charred. Take them out of the oven very carefully, place them in a plastic bag holding it closed for 30 seconds, then the skins will rub off easily in cold water. Slice the peppers thinly and dress with the Lemonette Dressing (see page 24). Allow to chill in the dressing for an hour before serving.

- **Stir-fries** Peppers make a splendid ingredient for stir-frying, particularly with strong-tasting meats like beef or lamb. Cut the meat and peppers into equal-sized strips with onion and fry together before seasoning with soy sauce.

- **Stuffed peppers** Peppers are also excellent stuffed. To do this, remove the seeds by cutting a ring round the stalk and pull out, leaving a large empty case. Check for stray seeds inside the pepper and remove.

Cut a ring round the stalk

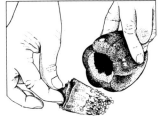

Pull out and check for stray seeds inside the pepper

Use a stuffing of your choice. Try mixing cooked rice with chopped onion, green parsley and pine nuts flavoured with a little lemon juice and rind. Put the peppers into a baking dish, bake in an oven at gas mark 4, 180°C (350°C) for 35 to 40 minutes. Delicious served with Tomato Sauce (page 21).

4. Tomatoes

Tomatoes come in all shapes and sizes from the tiny cherry to the large beefsteak. Make sure you've got really ripe ones whatever you're going to do with them (see page 106).

- **Provençal tomato salad** To make an excellent summer salad, thickly slice 450 g (1 lb) of tomatoes. Mix a sliced salad onion with them and dress them with the French Dressing on page 111 and sprinkle them with chopped fresh basil. Marinate for an hour before serving.

- **Provençal grilled tomatoes** This is an excellent way of using the giant Marmande or beefsteak tomatoes. Cut them in half across, score the surface lightly with a knife and sprinkle with a little salt. For each tomato (half is a serving with other foods), a chopped clove of garlic, 2 tablespoons of fresh breadcrumbs and 2 tablespoons of chopped fresh parsley. Mix the ingredients together, pat into the cut surface of the tomatoes and sprinkle a teaspoon or so of olive oil over the top. Grill 5 cm (2 inches) away from a hot grill for 6 to 7 minutes until the edges of the tomato start to char.

121

5. Garlic

The essential Mediterranean ingredient – look for the purple tinged kind in spring and summer as that is the best-flavoured of all and tends not to taint the breath! The easy way to peel garlic is to put a clove down on a firm surface and either with the heel of your hand or the flat of a large knife (sharp edge pointing away from you) press down until the garlic crushes slightly. The papery skin will then peel off. Trim the ends and you can make Crispini:

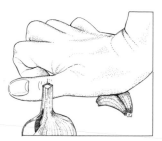

Place the clove down on a firm surface and press down until the garlic crushes slightly

Peel off the papery skin and trim the ends

- **Crispini** Split the clove of garlic. Take 6 slices of good white bread from a large French or similar loaf, put these into an oven at gas mark 4, 180°C (350°F) to toast for 6 or 7 minutes until crisp on the outside. Remove from the oven and rub with the cut side of the clove of garlic. Allow the garlic juice to dry and cover 3 of the Crispini with sun-dried tomatoes preserved in oil (available in all supermarkets or speciality grocers), the other 3 with slices of Mozzarella cheese sprinkled with chopped fresh basil; or sliced hard-boiled egg with anchovy; a wafer thin slice of pastrami or smoked turkey, or any other topping you fancy.
  Garlic is also the centrepiece of the famous Spanish cold soup called Gazpacho.

- **Gazpacho** Crush 2 cloves of garlic thoroughly with a teaspoon of salt until they make a fine purée. Stir this in to 600 ml (1 pint) of tomato juice and add the finely chopped flesh of a red and green pepper, a chopped bunch of spring onions and 175 g (6 oz) of skinned, chopped tomatoes. To serve, add a handful of ice cubes to the soup to chill it thoroughly and stir in a tablespoon each of olive oil and wine vinegar. Pour the soup over wholemeal croûtons in individual bowls.

FACT FILE

GARLIC
Many things are claimed for garlic and a few are probably true. We cannot vouch for its properties as a vampire repellent, but some medical researchers believe:
- **that garlic can help disperse blood clots (but only if you eat ten cloves a day!);**
- **that it may lower blood cholesterol;**
- **that it can alleviate cold symptoms;**
- **that it can cause skin irritation if the hands are exposed to it for long periods.**

- **Ratatouille** All the Mediterranean vegetables added together make one of the great dishes of the world – ratatouille. In addition to 225 g (8 oz) each of aubergines, peppers, courgettes, tomatoes and onions, you need 2 cloves of garlic and 4 tablespoons of olive oil. Prepare all the vegetables and cut them in neat 5 mm (¼ inch) slices. Crush the garlic and add it to the olive oil in a large pan. Bring this up to a high temperature until the garlic is golden. Add the onions, peppers, aubergines and courgettes and sauté over a medium heat for 5 minutes. Add the tomatoes, season generously and turn the heat down and allow to cook, partly covered, for another 25 to 30 minutes until all the vegetables are cooked through but not disintegrated. This can be eaten hot or cold and is best seasoned with a generous amount of chopped fresh parsley.

WINE *tip*   **A strongly-flavoured red would suit these garlic-laced dishes – try a Portuguese Dão or Douro.**

Exotic vegetables from near and far and some key cooking tips

1. Asparagus

Reputed to have been brought to Britain by the Romans, asparagus is now imported from all over the world all year round, though our season in May and June still produces the best-flavoured asparagus. Cook asparagus in boiling water for 20 minutes, if possible standing up so that the tips are steamed rather than boiled. If the stalks are very tough (test with a thumbnail) you can peel them with a potato peeler before cooking them. Nicest with melted butter and lemon juice or Hollandaise Sauce (see page 20).

2. Artichokes

Not to be confused with the root vegetables called Jerusalem artichokes, these look like a giant thistle and, in fact, that's what they are. Trim the stalks off parallel with the base and cook in plenty of boiling water with a tablespoon of wine vinegar for 25 to 30 minutes. To eat, peel off each leaf, dip it in melted butter or Hollandaise Sauce (see page 20) or, if the artichoke is eaten cold, in Vinaigrette Dressing, (see page 24), and bite off the fleshy base with your teeth. When you get to the hairy bit in the middle scoop it out and discard. What is left, the whole of the base (the heart) of the artichoke, is edible.

3. Chinese leaves

Looking like a pale, thick cos lettuce, these are now commonplace all over Britain. They are excellent thinly sliced for a winter salad, particularly with an even more thinly sliced red pepper and an olive oil-based vinaigrette. They are also delicious cooked quickly as a stir-fry, sliced once lengthways and then across into 2.5 cm (1 inch) ribbons, tossed in hot oil flavoured with a clove of garlic and 5 mm (½ inch) of crushed root ginger. The Chinese often add a little chilli sauce to the stir-fry at the end but very rarely soy sauce with this light, clean-tasting vegetable.

PREPARING AND EATING ARTICHOKES

123

Trim the stalks off parallel with the base

After boiling, to eat, peel off each leaf; dip in melted butter or Hollandaise sauce and bite off the fleshy base with your teeth

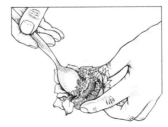

When you get to the hairy bit in the middle scoop it out and discard

4. Okra

These are also known as lady's fingers and are the small, green, bean-shaped vegetable often sold in Indian and other speciality grocers. They have a glutinous texture which thickens stews and dishes made with them. They are also used extensively in Cajun cooking in New Orleans, mixed with chicken or shrimp to make a Gumbo. They are best used in small quantities in curries or Southern American dishes.

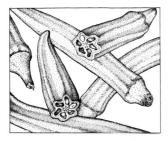

Okra

5. Sweet potatoes

These are much larger than British conventional potatoes and usually have a red or ochre skin. When well scrubbed they can be baked like an ordinary potato and are absolutely delicious eaten with butter and plenty of salt and pepper. When boiled and then sliced into 2.5 cm (1 inch) thick rounds, sprinkled with a little brown sugar, cinnamon and butter and glazed under a grill for candied sweet potatoes, they are the traditional accompaniment in America for roast turkey. Don't fry them or even *think* of making chips with them!

6. Chocho

This is a vegetable that looks like a large, green, slightly furry pear. Inside it has a flesh very like a marrow. It's very popular in the Caribbean and best eaten like a marrow, either stir-fried or steamed, with a white or cheese sauce.

Five luminous legumes

All the legumes are high in protein as well as being delicious vegetables in their own right, and are therefore an important part of any diet which is vegetarian in inclination.

1. Green peas

Very rarely seen now in their fresh state unless you grow them yourself, almost all the British domestic production is destined for the commercial freezer.

Petits pois à la française

This is the way the French have cooked peas since they were first introduced from Italy in the sixteenth century.

Serves 4

4 spring onions
4 lettuce leaves
1 tablespoon butter
350 g (12 oz) shelled peas, fresh or frozen
Salt and freshly ground black pepper
3 tablespoons double cream or 8 per cent fromage frais

Shred the spring onions and the lettuce finely. Melt the butter and cook the spring onions and lettuce gently for 10 minutes until thoroughly wilted and reduced but not browned. Add the peas (if frozen, straight from the freezer) and cook 3 minutes for frozen or 12 minutes for fresh with 120 ml (4 fl oz) of water, until the water has all evaporated. Season well. Add the cream or fromage frais and stir gently, heating through before serving without allowing the mixture to boil.

125

Above: *Petits pois à la française.* **Below:** *Asparagus* **(page 123)** *with Hollandaise sauce* **(page 20)**

2. Mangetout

These are edible pea pods and come in two forms – the flat, true mangetout ('eat all' in French), and sugar snap peas which have the bumps of immature peas inside them and are American in origin. They are both cooked in the same way – topped and tailed, popped into boiling water for 3 to 4 minutes and lightly buttered and seasoned. A sprig of fresh mint is an interesting addition. They also stir-fry very well, being added to a mixture of vegetables and tossed for 3 to 4 minutes in the hot oil.

3. String beans

These come in all sizes from genuine shoelace thinness up to bobby beans which can be nearly 1 cm (½ inch) across. They all share the virtue of having no string in them, despite their name, and should be topped and tailed. They are also occasionally known as French beans.

Beans amandine

126 Serves 4

350 g (12 oz) beans, topped and tailed
50 g (2 oz) slivered almonds
25 g (1 oz) butter
Salt and freshly ground black pepper

Put the beans into boiling water and cook for 6 to 8 minutes, depending on thickness, until they are bright green but cooked through. Drain well. Add the butter to the hot pan and when it has melted, add the almonds and fry till they are light golden. Add the beans and turn briskly for 1 minute then serve. A squeeze of lemon is an alternative finish to this dish.

Chinese-style beans with garlic

Serves 4

1 tablespoon cooking oil
2 cloves garlic, peeled and chopped
350 g (12 oz) beans
120 ml (4 fl oz) water
Salt and freshly ground black pepper

Put the oil into a flat frying pan or sauté pan, into which all the beans will go in virtually one layer, and heat it gently. Add the garlic and fry until light golden. Add the beans and toss in the oil for 2 to 3 minutes. Add the water and cook over a high heat until the water has all evaporated and the beans are sautéeing again gently. They should be cooked through, bright green, but still crisp. Season to taste.

4. Runner beans

The traditional English bean, this can also now be grown (if not always bought) virtually stringless. If they need it, string both sides of the bean when topping and tailing, then shred them across the grain on the diagonal into 5 mm (¼ inch) slices or cut into 2.5 cm (1 inch) chunks.

● **Grandma's beans** Put 450 g (1 lb) of shredded beans into 250 ml (8 fl oz) of well salted boiling water, allow to cook for 6 to 8 minutes then drain thoroughly. Place in a basin, add 40 g (1½ oz) of butter and 3 or 4 leaves of fresh or 1 teaspoon of dried savory. Stir thoroughly and eat from bowls as a course on their own with brown bread and butter.

Beans with tomato and onion

Serves 4

450 g (1 lb) runner beans, trimmed
1 tablespoon oil
1 onion, peeled and finely chopped
200 g (7 oz) tinned chopped Italian tomatoes
Salt and freshly ground black pepper
½ teaspoon chopped fresh basil
½ teaspoon chopped fresh oregano

Blanch the beans in boiling water for 5 minutes then drain thoroughly. Heat the oil and fry the onion for about 3 minutes until translucent. Add the tomatoes and cook for another 3 to 4 minutes. Add the blanched beans and mix thoroughly. Simmer for 4 to 5 minutes until the beans are cooked through. Season generously, add the herbs and serve.

5. Broad beans

Broad beans have a wide following in countries like Greece or Turkey where they regard them as a salad vegetable. In Britain, we almost inevitably eat them cooked. They make a splendid soup and interesting vegetable dishes in their own right. *Never* peel the individual beans – if they're really old and tough they can go into the soup pot. They also freeze well and are available all the year round in that form.

Broad beans in white sauce

This is a simple, classic recipe that never fails to taste good. It's particularly nice with things like salt beef or grilled chops that benefit from the saucing as well as the flavour of the beans.

Serves 4

300 ml (10 fl oz) water
Salt
350 g (12 oz) broad beans, shelled
1 quantity of Béchamel Sauce (see page 19)
Pinch of freshly grated nutmeg

Pre-heat the grill.
    Bring the well salted water to the boil, add the beans and cook them for 6 to 8 minutes. Drain them thoroughly. Season the Béchamel Sauce with the extra grating of nutmeg. Mix with the beans and pour into a flameproof gratin dish. Put under the grill for 3 to 4 minutes for the flavours to blend.

Broad bean purée

If the beans are a bit tough or you're looking for an alternative vegetable, try this recipe.

Serves 4

350 g (12 oz) shelled broad beans
2 tablespoons fromage frais
Salt and freshly ground black pepper
½ teaspoon dried sage or savory

Cook the beans for 12 minutes in boiling well salted water until soft and then drain. Put in a food processor with all the other ingredients, making sure there's plenty of black pepper, and process until a smooth pale green purée. This can be put into a basin or serving dish and kept warm for up to 15 to 20 minutes without suffering any damage.

Dried beans

Dried beans come in many shapes and sizes all over the world, from the tiny aduki beans of Japan, less than 5 mm (¼ inch) across and dark red, to the giant white beans of South America, up to 5 cm (2 inches) long. All dried beans are a marvellous source of protein and an extremely economical basis for a wide variety of dishes.
    They all need the same basic treatment. Soaking them for at least 6 hours in plenty of fresh water without salt or any additions. Bring to the boil in fresh water and cook rapidly for 20 minutes. Then reduce the heat and cook the beans for the length of time it requires to make them tender. This varies according to the age and size of the beans but is normally between one and two hours. There's no virtue in undercooked beans (see below) and they come to little harm if cooked for slightly longer than necessary, so always err on the side of overcooking. Chick peas need the same sort of soaking and cooking.

127

 POISONOUS BEANS
Despite their healthy image, beans contain several toxins. Cooking them at high temperatures (i.e. boiling point) for at least 20 minutes destroys the toxins and makes them entirely safe. Red kidney beans are the best known example but all dried beans should be treated this way. Tinned beans have already been cooked and are ready for consumption.

Cassoulet

This is a vegetarian version of the famous southern French bean dish. In its traditional form, it could contain sausages, a roast and cut up shoulder of lamb, preserved goose (see page 91) or duck prepared in the same way, or a combination of these.

Serves 6

450 g (1 lb) dried haricot or cannellini beans, soaked
   and cooked as on page 127
2 onions, peeled
1 head celery
1 × 400 g (14 oz) tin chopped Italian tomatoes
4 tablespoons oil
3 tablespoons tomato purée
2 cloves garlic, peeled and chopped
½ teaspoon dried oregano
½ teaspoon dried thyme
2 bay leaves
225 g (8 oz) chestnut mushrooms
2 teaspoons salt
2 teaspoons soft brown sugar
Freshly ground black pepper
2 slices wholemeal bread, processed or grated to
   breadcrumbs

Pre-heat the oven to gas mark 4, 180°C (350°F).

   Put the cooked beans into an ovenproof casserole dish. Trim the onions and celery, chop both into 1 cm (½ inch) chunks and add them to the dish with the tomatoes and all the remaining ingredients except the breadcrumbs. Mix thoroughly but gently and season with black pepper. Cover and cook in the oven for 1 to 1½ hours. Remove, stir gently, check for seasoning, sprinkle the top with the breadcrumbs, return to the oven and bake for a further 30 minutes before serving.

WINE *tip* A full, warming rustic dish needs a full, warming wine to complement it – Madiran from the south of France or Californian Zinfandel.

Crafty Boston baked beans

This is the North American version of Cassoulet which has, over the years, turned into British tinned baked beans. It's very easy to make and very appealing to children. Once again we give a vegetarian version though the original could contain various sausages and salted meats. It also contained rum and a very considerable amount of brown sugar and molasses. Although some modern tinned baked beans still contain high amounts of sugar, this version reduces it.

Serves 4

450 g (1 lb) dried haricot or navy beans, soaked and
   cooked as on page 127
2 tablespoons tomato purée
1 onion, peeled and finely chopped
2 teaspoons soft brown sugar
2 teaspoons treacle (molasses)
½ teaspoon paprika
½ teaspoon ground bay leaves
1½ teaspoons salt
1 tablespoon butter

Pre-heat the oven to gas mark 3, 160°C (325°F).

   Mix all the ingredients into the beans in an ovenproof pot and bake in the oven for 1 hour (or, if you prefer, cook very gently on top of the stove or on an asbestos mat). It can be cooked, if you have an Aga or similar cooker, in the plate warming oven overnight once it's been brought to the boil. It's traditionally eaten with a very dark and slightly sweetened, steamed bread. The nearest thing to it, though I don't recommend it with the beans, is one of our currant malted loaves.

Sweetcorn

Sweetcorn comes in large and baby sizes.
   Large – nothing beats boiling large sweetcorn in unsalted water for 15 minutes and eating with butter, salt and freshly ground pepper. It can also be roasted in its husk on a barbecue for 35 minutes.
   Baby – now widely available in supermarkets. Eat whole as part of a stir-fry (see page 121) or steam with green beans and serve buttered.

128

Above: *Broad bean purée (page 127)*. Below: *Chinese-style beans with garlic (page 126)*

Gratins

Pommes dauphinoise

Potatoes make the most marvellous gratins, or baked dishes. The classic gratin of all time is Pommes Dauphinoise, which comes from the eastern part of France. There are lots of different opinions on whether it should or shouldn't contain cheese, and whether you should wash the potatoes before cooking them or not. This version is one that's been developed over many years of happy trial and error. It's certainly good enough to eat on its own but absolutely scrumptious with some grilled liver and well seasoned spinach.

Serves 4

675 g (1½ lb) potatoes that keep their shape well when
* boiled*
1 clove garlic
1 tablespoon butter
Salt and freshly ground black pepper
150 ml (5 fl oz) milk
150 ml (5 fl oz) double cream

Pre-heat the oven to gas mark 4, 180°C (350°F).

Peel the potatoes and slice them across into 5 mm (¼ inch) slices. If you like a light gratin, at this stage wash them in a colander to remove some starch and leave them to drain. (A refinement for the purists.) Take a gratin or baking dish, cut the clove of garlic in half and rub the cut side round the baking dish until the whole area is smeared. Allow this to dry. Take half the butter and spread that round the baking dish with a piece of kitchen paper or butter paper. Put in half the potato slices in layers, season generously, add the remaining butter and the second half of the potato slices, finishing with an attractive arrangement on the top. Season again. Mix the milk and cream together and pour over the potatoes. Bake in the oven for 45 to 50 minutes until the top is golden and bubbling. You will find the centre still creamy and smooth and the flavour of garlic will have permeated very gently through the whole dish.

Mushroom gratin

This is a variation on Pommes Dauphinoise, making use of the marvellous marriage that mushrooms, particularly wild mushrooms, and potatoes make. It's a course, or indeed a meal, in its own right. Take the ingredients for the Pommes Dauphinoise as above plus 175 g (6 oz) of wild or chestnut mushrooms or 100 g (4 oz) of ordinary cultivated mushrooms and 25 g (1 oz) of dried cèpes. If you're using the dried cèpes, soak them in a cup of boiling water for 15 minutes before cooking. You can substitute some of the water for the milk in the recipe as the water will be flavoured by the mushrooms. Wash and thinly slice the mushrooms. Garlic-rub and butter the dish as before, add half the potatoes and then the mushrooms in a complete layer across the potatoes. Season generously, add the remaining potatoes and then pour on the cream and milk or mushroom water mixture and bake as above for 50 minutes. This is particularly good as a vegetarian meal served with coarse grained wholemeal bread and butter with a green salad to follow.

132

*Above: **Cassoulet** (page 128). Below: **Thick-cut jacket chips** (page 131)*

A key guide to culinary herbs – their affinities and uses

In Britain we use very few herbs in our cooking, but British recipes from the seventeenth and eighteenth centuries often list a wide variety of herbs and flavourings that we now only meet in imported cuisines. Here are some favourites. Happily they're now available in a variety of forms in most supermarkets and many greengrocers.

1. Fresh

Both growing in pots and picked, in special wrappings, six or seven fresh herbs are commonplace in most supermarket vegetable sections these days. Buy them individually, not as mixed herb bunches.

2. Freeze-dried

New techniques developed originally for luxury coffees have been applied to herbs with the result that freeze-dried, green herbs now have both the flavour and colour and, even occasionally, some of the texture of fresh herbs after they've been cooked.

All they need to be added to liquid in some form or another in order to re-hydrate them and for you to get the full benefit of the flavour.

3. Traditionally-dried

Despite their not being so fashionable, the intensity of flavour that can be obtained from traditionally-dried herbs is remarkable and many expert chefs use them when that quality of flavour is particularly required.

All the herbs listed here (with the foods that they best accompany) are available in the three forms above.

BASIL

The 'holy' herb, mentioned in many of the world's religious books, basil has a superb, slightly orangey and spicy flavour, particularly when fresh. Terrific with tomatoes, excellent in cream sauces, and the basis for that wonderful northern Italian/southern French conglomeration known as Pesto or Pistou.

BAY

The glossy (when fresh), aromatic leaves of the 'noble' laurel, bay is an essential part of bouquet garni with celery, parsley and thyme. In whole leaf form, it is almost always welcome in stocks and casseroles. It is useful in its ground form as a seasoning on grilled meats and chicken before roasting.

CHIVES

Not just an addition to cream cheese but excellent anytime you want a mild flavour of onion. Chives are particularly good with salads and as an addition to sauces for delicate flesh like chicken or fish.

CORIANDER

Coriander seed has a warm, spicy, almost orangey flavour and is widely used in Indian and Middle Eastern dishes. Coriander leaves look like flat-leaved parsley but have a much more astringent flavour. The leaves are much favoured as a herb flavouring in India and South-East Asia, particularly in Thailand and especially in their hot soups.

DILL

The green fronds are widely used in Scandinavia for potato dishes (try dill with new potatoes instead of mint) and for flavouring fish – particularly gravadlax (salmon) and pickled herring. Dill seed is mostly used to flavour 'digestive' spirits and in speciality bread making.

FENNEL

Fennel comes as green, feathery fronds or seeds. The seeds are much used in Italian cooking to provide a light, sweet-and-sour flavour, particularly with bread or in veal dishes. The green fronds are a perfect foil for fish dishes.

MARJORAM

A very old English herb with a warm, homely smell and flavour, this is excellent in casseroles and meat dishes, nice added to things like Shepherd's Pie, and an excellent flavouring for dumplings.

134

MINT

There are many varieties of mint with flavours as varied as pineapple and pepper. The culinary varieties, though, tend to be spearmint – long, thin, green leaves – or apple mint – round, pale green, and slightly furry. Apart from lamb and new potatoes, mint makes an interesting addition to a variety of vegetable dishes and salads. It's good finely chopped and added to carrots before they're puréed, or mixed with fresh chives in small quantities into a dressing for a summer green salad. It's also increasingly used as a garnish for fruit desserts, particularly with strawberries and other soft fruits.

OREGANO

The Italian version of marjoram, much stronger in intensity and more aromatic, oregano is a key ingredient in pizza and pasta sauce flavourings and most Italian cooking that involves tomatoes.

PARSLEY

Perhaps the most common of all herbs, it comes in curly and flat-leaved varieties. The flat leaves are far stronger in flavour but in both kinds the stalks have the edge if it's intensity you're after. Use the leaves for dressing and garnishing and use the stalks for flavouring soups, casseroles and stews – they can be removed after cooking. Parsley is high in vitamin C and helps neutralize garlicky and oniony flavours (if such things worry your family or guests).

ROSEMARY

Spiky-leaved rosemary is a Mediterranean herb. It has particular affinities for lamb, chicken and rabbit. It needs to be used in judiciously small quantities as it's very pungent. Often used on barbecues directly on to the coals, it gives an aromatic flavour to the grilling meat.

SAGE

Whatever the colours of sage leaves – and they vary from pale gold to dark purple – the flavours tend to be very similar. It's a strong-tasting herb traditionally used with pork and as a flavouring for stuffings and dumplings. In European cooking it's often teamed with veal and in Britain makes an interesting flavour variant for turkey, a meat with a similar texture which, when portioned, is used in similar recipes.

TARRAGON

Tarragon has a slightly aniseed flavour – the ultimate herb for chicken dishes, roasts and casseroles. Also excellent in creamy sauces for fish. 'French' tarragon has by far the best flavour so beware of the blander 'Russian' tarragon which is easier to grow.

THYME

Another old English herb which again has a wide variety of flavours. As well as traditional thyme, it comes in lemon and wild forms. It's a pot herb by tradition, used in soups and casseroles, but also an indispensable ingredient in small quantities in most Mediterranean, and particularly Italian, cooking. A background rather than a foreground flavour.

135
....

CHAPTER TEN

Pasta comes in all shapes and sizes, and also, these days, a variety of colours. Its versatility makes it an extremely popular basis for a whole range of dishes.

pasta

Key colours and contents

Here is an outline guide to these colours, the eight most crucial shapes and what to do with them.

- **White** This is the basic pasta made with just flour and water. It's fine as a basis for other foods but makes little flavour contribution itself.

- **Brown** Brown pasta is wholemeal pasta, high in fibre with a more substantial texture and a slightly earthy flavour. It requires cooking for almost twice as long as other forms of pasta.

- **Gold** This is egg pasta. The dough includes egg as well as water and it has a lighter texture and creamier flavour.

- **Red** Red pasta has been coloured with tomato paste. There is barely any tomato flavour but the colour is attractive.

- **Green** Green pasta is flavoured and coloured with puréed spinach. It's often available as tagliatelle or lasagne, the sheets of which have sufficient size for the flavour of the spinach to be just perceptible when you're eating it. Green pasta tends to be slightly heavier than its equivalent in gold or white, though it cooks in the same time.

- **Other colours** Recently, exotic-coloured pastas – dark red (beetroot), black (squid ink), and other variations – have appeared in some speciality shops. The best advice is to avoid them like the plague as they are hugely expensive and the colouring mostly washes out in the cooking. When it doesn't, you might be left wishing it had.

Fresh and dried pasta

If you make pasta at home yourself you will have to follow the instructions on the machine or system you have. These vary so much it's impossible to give generalized instructions. However, soft, fresh pasta is available now throughout Britain in speciality shops and supermarkets. Some of the most exciting are those with the addition of garlic and herbs. Fresh pasta cooks in 3 to 4 minutes when plain, and in 8 to 10 minutes when stuffed. The stuffings vary from varieties of cheeses and mushrooms through to meat and, occasionally, fish combinations as well.

Dried pasta comes in even more shapes than fresh (in Italy designers are even employed to dream up new shapes!). The trick is to use pasta shapes that are suitable for what you're going to eat them with. Thus a chunky sauce is best suited to chunky styles of pasta and a more liquid creamy sauce to longer, thinner tagliatelli or spaghetti-type pasta. Some pastas (such as penne) have grooves on the inside which have been specifically designed to hold a sauce.

139

Above: *Tagliatelle with cream and mushroom sauce* (page 141). Below: *Linguine with seafood sauce* (page 143)

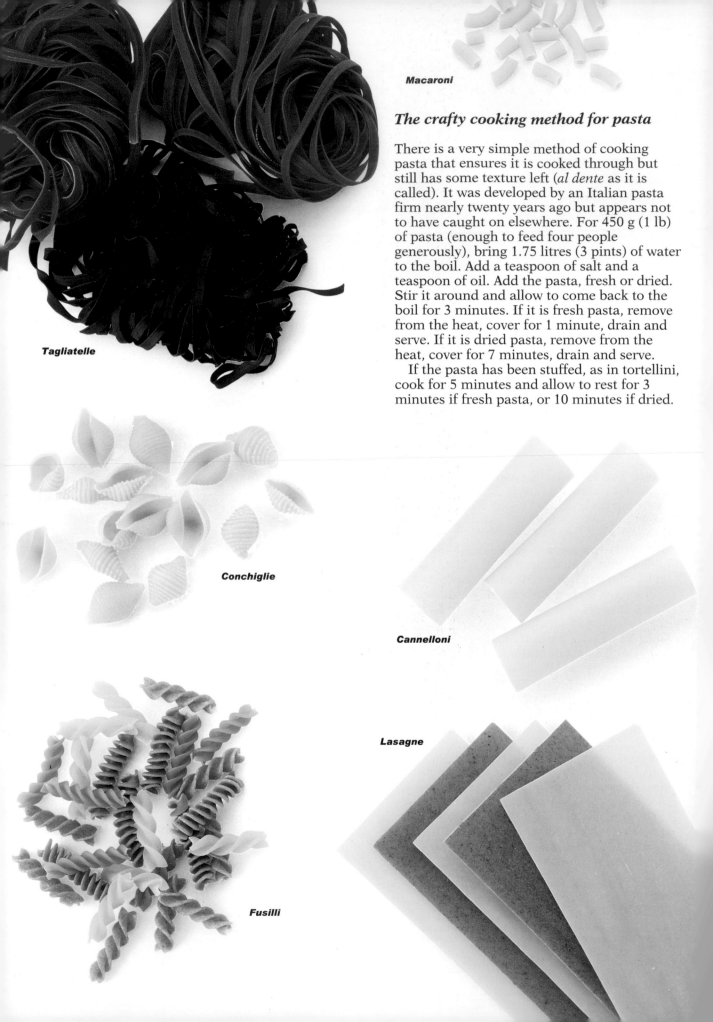

Macaroni

Tagliatelle

Conchiglie

Cannelloni

Lasagne

Fusilli

The crafty cooking method for pasta

There is a very simple method of cooking pasta that ensures it is cooked through but still has some texture left (*al dente* as it is called). It was developed by an Italian pasta firm nearly twenty years ago but appears not to have caught on elsewhere. For 450 g (1 lb) of pasta (enough to feed four people generously), bring 1.75 litres (3 pints) of water to the boil. Add a teaspoon of salt and a teaspoon of oil. Add the pasta, fresh or dried. Stir it around and allow to come back to the boil for 3 minutes. If it is fresh pasta, remove from the heat, cover for 1 minute, drain and serve. If it is dried pasta, remove from the heat, cover for 7 minutes, drain and serve.

If the pasta has been stuffed, as in tortellini, cook for 5 minutes and allow to rest for 3 minutes if fresh pasta, or 10 minutes if dried.

Nine key shapes

1. Spaghetti

Long, round and thin, still the most popular pasta though not always the easiest to eat. Cook it as above and serve it with a proper ragù, the original of our 'spag bol' sauce.

Ragù

Use a teaspoon of each of the herbs if you are using fresh. Serve with spaghetti.

Serves 4

2 tablespoons olive oil
450 g (1 lb) minced beef
1 large onion, peeled and finely chopped
1 clove garlic, peeled and finely chopped
1 carrot, grated
1 × 400 g (14 oz) tin chopped Italian tomatoes
1 tablespoon tomato purée
Salt and freshly ground black pepper
100 g (4 oz) chicken livers, chopped
½ teaspoon freeze-dried oregano
½ teaspoon freeze-dried thyme
½ teaspoon freeze-dried basil
150 ml (5 fl oz) beef stock or water (optional)

To serve:

2–3 tablespoons double cream (optional)
Grated Parmesan cheese

Heat the oil and fry the meat until lightly browned. Add the onion, garlic and grated carrot and continue to fry for 3 to 4 minutes. Add the tomatoes and tomato purée, season generously and cook for a further 15 to 20 minutes. Add the chicken livers and herbs, plus a little beef stock or water if you want a thinner sauce. Cook for a further 15 to 20 minutes until the sauce is well blended. In Bologna they add 2 to 3 tablespoons of thick cream before serving the sauce with the spaghetti and freshly grated Parmesan cheese.

WINE tip Italian red Lambrusco, if you can find it, is the traditional glug (dry not sweet in its native country). Or of all other Italian reds perhaps the best partner is Teroldego Rotaliano.

2. Tagliatelle

Tagliatelle is like spaghetti but flat and 5 mm (¼ inch) wide. It comes fresh or dried.

Tagliatelle with cream and mushroom sauce

In the Veneta, the area around Venice, they might add 225 g (8 oz) cooked green peas to this dish, in which case they might not sprinkle it with the parsley.

Serves 4

2 teaspoons cornflour
2 teaspoons butter
250 ml (8 fl oz) double cream
Salt and freshly ground black pepper
½ teaspoon freshly grated nutmeg
225 g (8 oz) button or chestnut mushrooms, thinly sliced
50 g (2 oz) Pecorino or Gruyère cheese, grated
450 g (1 lb) tagliatelle, cooked as on page 140
1 tablespoon chopped fresh parsley

Whisk the cornflour and butter into the cream and bring gently to the boil, stirring until it is thick and smooth. Season generously and add the nutmeg. Add the mushrooms and cook for 2 to 3 minutes. Stir in the grated cheese, pour over the drained tagliatelle, and serve sprinkled with parsley.

141
....

PARMESAN CHEESE
Fresh Parmesan is expensive but well worth the effort. Buy it in chunks and grate it yourself. Most ready-grated Parmesan comes from Holland and tastes of soap. There is ready-grated from Italy now available but the flavour does not compare with the real thing. The real thing is so good you should also try it with bread or biscuits as a Cheddar substitute.

7. Lasagne

Lasagne is the name for the flat sheets of pasta about 15 to 20 cm (6 to 8 inches) long and 5 to 10 cm (2 to 4 inches) wide. Traditionally they were boiled before using, but the crafty method with lasagne is to dip the sheets into warm water before using, and to lay them directly into the dish with the appropriate sauce. The Ragù on page 141 is an excellent meat sauce, the fish sauce for the linguine (see page 143) also is extremely satisfactory, or try the following tasty vegetarian sauce.

Whatever the sauce, the method of baking the lasagne is the same. You need 450 g (1 lb) of lasagne, 600 ml (1 pint) of white sauce (see page 19) and an equivalent quantity of your chosen vegetable, fish or meat sauce. You also need a large square or rectangular dish at least 4 to 5 cm (1½ to 2 inches) deep.

Vegetarian lasagne with ricotta and aubergines

A delicious southern, Italian-style lasagne with a surprise layer of Ricotta cheese.

144

Serves 6

For the sauce:
1 large onion, peeled and chopped
3 cloves garlic, peeled and chopped
2 large courgettes, diced
450 g (1 lb) aubergines, unpeeled and diced
100 g (4 oz) mushrooms, sliced
2 × 400 g (14 oz) tins chopped Italian tomatoes
1 glass water
Sprig fresh thyme or 2 teaspoons freeze-dried
Sprig fresh rosemary or 1 teaspoon freeze-dried
Salt and freshly ground black pepper
350 g (12 oz) green lasagne (the sort that needs no pre-cooking)
100 g (4 oz) Mozzarella cheese, finely sliced
25 g (1 oz) Parmesan cheese, grated

For the Ricotta filling:
225 g (8 oz) fresh Ricotta cheese
50 g (2 oz) Parmesan cheese, grated
25 g (1 oz) chopped fresh parsley
2 eggs
½ teaspoon freshly grated nutmeg
Freshly ground black pepper

For the Béchamel Sauce:
40 g (1½ oz) butter
40 g (1½ oz) plain flour
450 ml (15 fl oz) skimmed milk
Pinch of freshly grated nutmeg
Salt and freshly ground black pepper

Pre-heat the oven to gas mark 6, 200°C (400°F).

Put the onion, garlic, courgette, aubergines and mushrooms in a large saucepan. Stir in the tomatoes, wine or water, herbs and season with salt and pepper. Cover and cook over a low heat for 15 minutes. The juices will have come out of the vegetables making the sauce quite watery. Uncover and cook over a higher heat for another 15 minutes, stirring frequently to avoid burning. The sauce will reduce until there is almost no excess liquid.

Make the Ricotta filling by mixing all the filling ingredients into a smooth paste. Put to one side. Then prepare a Béchamel sauce (see page 19).

Assemble the lasagne in a large ovenproof dish. Brush the bottom and sides with a little oil and cover the bottom of the dish with pasta. Spoon on half the vegetable sauce, avoiding getting too much juice in the baking dish. Put the slices of Mozzarella on the vegetable sauce. Cover with another layer of lasagne. Spread on the Ricotta filling, making sure all the lasagne is covered. Cover with another layer of lasagne. Spoon on the rest of the vegetable sauce. Cover with another layer of lasagne. Finally pour on the Béchamel Sauce, again making sure all the lasagne is covered. Sprinkle with grated Parmesan and bake in the oven for 30 to 35 minutes. Serve with a green salad.

Above: *Vegetable lasagne (page 146).* **Below:** *Ricotta and spinach cannelloni with tomato sauce (page 147)*

Chicken pilau

This is the Indian version of the ubiquitous rice dish. It uses chicken, undoubtedly the favourite meat to eat with rice across the world. It's very simple to make and provides a touch of the exotic without putting off people who don't like their food 'too foreign'. Serve it with a cucumber and tomato salad and some mango chutney.

Serves 4

2 tablespoons butter
1 tablespoon oil
2 chicken breasts
1 teaspoon ground ginger
1 teaspoon turmeric
3 cardamom pods or ½ teaspoon cardamom powder
1 large Spanish onion, peeled and finely chopped
1 clove garlic, peeled and crushed
275 g (10 oz) basmati or patna rice
1 teaspoon salt
225 g (8 oz) frozen unminted peas

Melt the butter in the oil in a saucepan with a well-fitting lid. Cut the chicken into small pieces about the size of half a walnut and add to the butter and oil with the ginger, turmeric and cardamom. Fry gently for 3 to 4 minutes until the chicken is opaque and the spices are giving off a warm aroma. Add the onion and garlic. Measure the rice in a cup or jug and add it to the pan. Turn the whole lot over until the rice is coated with the flavoured and spiced oils. Add the salt and twice the volume of water as you had of rice. Stir the whole lot together, bring to the boil, reduce the heat to minimum, cover and simmer for 15 minutes. Uncover and add the frozen peas, stirring them in gently with a fork. Cover again and leave for 5 minutes then turn onto a warm oval plate to serve.

152

The curry flavour of this Pilau, even though mild, would be best with beer, lager for choice: Bavaria offers good uncluttered flavours, or from Britain try Samuel Smith's. But if you feel like wine, match the slight sweetness with an Italian Orvieto Abboccato.

Stir-fried rice

Should you have any rice left over, this is the most wonderful dish for using it up. It's also incredibly quick and easy for putting a meal together at very little notice. You can use things you've got left in the fridge – bits of cold meat or cooked vegetables – but don't put in everything otherwise the result can be a hotchpotch. It's nicest served with a bowl of soup.

Serves 4

2 tablespoons cooking oil (not olive)
1 clove garlic, peeled and chopped
2.5 cm (1 inch) piece fresh ginger root, peeled and chopped
1 onion, peeled and finely chopped
175 g (6 oz) cooked chicken, meat or prawns (or other appropriate ingredients), cubed
1 tablespoon soy sauce
175 g (6 oz) frozen mixed vegetables (or frozen peas, or cold cooked vegetables, cubed)
2 eggs, beaten
Salt
275 g (10 oz) cooked long-grain rice
1 teaspoon roasted sesame oil (optional)

Heat the oil in a large frying pan or, if you've got one, a Chinese-style wok. Add the garlic and ginger and fry for about 30 seconds. Add the onion, then the meat and/or prawns and cook over a high heat, stirring or tossing, for about 1 minute. Add the soy sauce and vegetables (if they're frozen they don't need to be de-frosted), and stir over a high heat for another 1 to 2 minutes. Beat the eggs and salt, stir them into the pan and allow them to set, then scramble them and the meat and vegetable mixture together. Add the rice and use a spatula or big metal spoon to stir and toss the rice and vegetable and meat mixture together gently until the rice is thoroughly hot and the other ingredients are dotted through it like jewels. Transfer to a warm serving bowl and sprinkle with the sesame oil, if using. This adds a special and delicate fragrance.

Above: *Brown rice cooked using method one* (page 150). Below: *Stir-fried rice*

Coarse cracked wheat recipes

Poussin with cracked wheat and apricot stuffing

Poussin, little spring chicken, is an ideal vehicle for exotic stuffings – not too much, though. The cracked wheat also gives a nutty and substantial texture to the dish. They are delicious served with a couple of vegetables other than potatoes or other grains as the stuffing is quite substantial.

Serves 4

100 g (4 oz) medium to coarse cracked wheat, bulgar or pod ghouri
250 ml (8 fl oz) water
1 small onion, peeled and finely chopped
100 g (4 oz) dried apricots, coarsely chopped
1 tablespoon chopped fresh or freeze-dried parsley
1 tablespoon honey
Juice of 1 lemon
2 oven-ready poussin

Pre-heat the oven to gas mark 5, 190°C (375°F).

156

Mix the cracked wheat with the water until it's thoroughly moistened. Add the onion, apricots, parsley, honey and lemon juice and stir well. Use this to fill the cavities of the poussin. Any you have left over can be baked in a small dish alongside the chicken. Put the poussin on a rack in a baking dish and pour 300 ml (½ pint) of water beneath it. Cover them with a piece of foil or butter paper and roast for 30 minutes. Turn the heat down to gas mark 3, 160°C (325°F) and cook for another 20 minutes. Remove the foil or butter paper and cook for a further 15 minutes to allow the chicken to brown.

The neatest way to serve the dish is to split the chickens with poultry shears or a very sharp knife and serve half each, roasted side up, on the bed of stuffing. The liquid in the pan under the chickens makes an ideal sauce.

Frumenty

A kind of savoury or sweet porridge made with wheat which was eaten for centuries. It only really went out of fashion at the beginning of the Second World War. It was particularly eaten in savoury form with game and roast meats, while its sweetened form is held to have been one of the origins of the British Christmas pudding.

Sweet frumenty

This can be served warm or poured into little cups and served cold as a pudding.

Serves 4

225 g (8 fl oz) medium or very coarsely cracked wheat
300 ml (½ pint) milk
300 ml (½ pint) water
3 tablespoons honey
50 g (2 oz) sultanas
50 g (2 oz) flaked almonds

Soak the wheat in the milk and water overnight in a non-stick saucepan. Bring to the boil then simmer very gently for 15 to 20 minutes until the wheat turns into a soft and quite stiff porridge. It may need a little more liquid – wheat varies in how much liquid it will absorb – but it should never be thicker than clotted cream. Stir in the honey and sultanas and sprinkle with the almond slivers before serving.

Above: Couscous (page 155). Below: Polenta with leek and sausage sauce (page 159)

CHAPTER TWELVE

Recipes and advice for beef, lamb, pork, offal and good ideas for barbecues.

meat

Beef

Beef, the traditional meat of Britain, is now eaten much less than it used to be. This is partly for health and partly for cost reasons. But it's also because of the challenge involved in cooking some of the dishes that show beef at its best. Here are the crafty solutions to that part of the dilemma.

Three categories of beef

1. Tender

In Britain only about half the beef carcase can be classed as tender. That is, meat which can be grilled, fried or roasted. These are the more expensive cuts of beef but they often suit the simplest and quickest recipes.

2. Tough

Often the tastiest joints, but the cuts require gentle, prolonged and moist cooking. They make excellent casseroles, stews and, of course, minced meat dishes.

3. Untouchable

The 'untouchables' are offal. For many people the inedible part of the animal, for others these offer the greatest treats of all. They are also extremely good value because of the lack of demand for them. Offal, of course, comes from other animals, too, so we have given it a section of its own later in this chapter.

Quality and quality marks

The quality of the meat depends on the way the animal was raised, how well it was butchered, and whether it has been properly hung – that is, allowed to mature after slaughter. There are a number of ways of buying premium quality beef. The Scots have developed a quality mark that ensures that the meat was raised properly, fed (by and large) on grass, and hung and aged for at least three weeks before selling. The Irish are about to introduce a similar quality mark indicating particularly tender beef. Some specialist butchers, particularly those displaying the 'Q' Guild mark, are committed to providing meat that's been properly reared, carefully butchered, and matured for the correct length of time. Mature beef, by the way, has a dark red colour to it and pale gold fat rather than the white fat and bright red of immature meat.

1. Tender

FILLET

The most expensive cut of all, fillet comprises a single boneless joint about 1.65 kg (3½ lb) in weight, tapering to a thin tail. Cut across the grain it makes tournedos or fillet steaks but can, with the tail folded round to equalize the shape of the meat and its thickness, be roasted whole.

Filet rôti (page 162) with Pommes dauphinoise (page 132) and green vegetables (see chapter nine, page 113)

Steak Diane

Serves 4

50 g (2 oz) butter
4 × 100–175 g (4–6 oz) fillet steaks
100 g (4 oz) onion, peeled and very finely chopped
Juice of ½ lemon
2 tablespoons Worcestershire sauce

In a heavy frying pan, melt the butter and fry the steaks for about 2 to 3 minutes until brown on one side. Turn over, allow to brown for 1 minute on the other side, add the onion and cook with the steaks for 2 to 3 minutes for rare or 3 to 4 minutes for medium. Squeeze the lemon juice over the steaks, add the Worcestershire sauce and bring rapidly to the boil.

Serve the steaks, stir the sauce mixture together and pour carefully over the steaks.

Filet rôti

Get your butcher to tie the fillet for roasting. It should be about 46 cm (18 inches) long and an equal thickness all the way along. Serve the beef with Pommes Dauphinoise (see page 132) and a green vegetable for the most luxurious roast beef ever.

162

Serves 4 to 6

3 tablespoons oil
1 × 1.5 kg (3 ¼ lb) beef fillet
50 g (2 oz) butter
Salt and freshly ground black pepper
250 ml (8 fl oz) beef stock, cranberry juice or red wine

Pre-heat the oven, to gas mark 8, 230°C (450°F).

Heat a frying pan, into which the fillet can be placed, until very hot. Add the oil and immediately roll the fillet in it for about 2 to 3 minutes, ensuring that all sides are brown. Remove from the pan and place on a rack in a roasting tin. Spread with the butter, season generously with salt and pepper and roast in the oven for 10 minutes per 450 g (1 lb).

Remove from the oven and allow to stand for 5 minutes while you deglaze the juices in the bottom of the roasting pan with your chosen liquid. Bring the mixture quickly to the boil then reduce to 120 ml (4 fl oz) of juice to use as a gravy. Slice the fillet across the grain in 1 cm (½ inch) slices; they should be still pink in the middle.

RUMP

Traditionally a large roasting joint, rump is now more frequently cut into steaks, often quite thick and with a cushiony appearance. It cooks a little more slowly than sirloin and fillet but has a good flavour and, if well marbled, a good texture as well.

Barbecue-flavour rump steaks

Serves 4

2 tablespoons hoisin sauce
1 tablespoon Worcestershire sauce
Juice of ½ lemon
1 clove garlic, peeled and crushed
½ teaspoon salt
½ teaspoon freshly ground black pepper
4 × 225 g (8 oz) rump steaks, cut at least 25 cm (1 inch) thick

Mix the seasoning ingredients together, spread over the steaks and leave to marinate for at least 1 and up to 8 hours. Pre-heat a grill and grill the steaks 5–7.5 cm (2–3 inches) away from the heat for 3 minutes each side for rare, 4½ minutes each side for medium. You can baste the steaks with the marinade as you cook them to produce a lovely shiny finish.

WINE tip **Something robust to stand up to the marinade such as wines from the Syrah grape – from the Rhône and southern France, or Australia, where it is called Shiraz.**

SKIRT

This is not a cut of beef easily obtainable in supermarkets but most butchers can still provide it. It has a ribbed, almost knitted, appearance but is surprisingly tender. It makes extremely good stir-frys or an excellent dish of stroganoff, a great favourite in Paris and the Russian court at the turn of the century.

Beef stroganoff

Serve this delicious dish with tagliatelle or wild rice. Vegetables or salad can form a second course to follow.

Serves 4

25 g (1 oz) butter
2 tablespoons cooking oil
450 g (1 lb) Spanish onions, peeled and sliced into 1 cm (½ inch) ribbons
675 g (1 ½ lb) beef skirt, sliced into 1 cm (½ inch) ribbons
225 g (8 oz) button or chestnut mushrooms, cut into 1 cm (½ inch) slices
300 ml (10 fl oz) soured cream
Salt and freshly ground black pepper

Heat the butter in the oil in a large, heavy-based frying pan. Add the onions and fry them rapidly for about 1½ minutes until translucent. Remove the onions and fry the skirt strips at maximum heat for 1 to 1½ minutes until brown. Return the onions to the pan with the mushroom slices and turn together for another minute before adding the soured cream. Bring to the boil and season well with salt and pepper. Serve immediately.

WINE tip French red Burgundy is the first choice – but look out for Alsace Pinot Noir as an alternative.

SIRLOIN

Sirloin is the piece of beef that on a lamb chop would make up the eye of the chop. It can be eaten as steaks or as roast, on or off the bone. If off the bone as a roast, it can be cooked in a very similar way to the Filet Rôti (see page 162) except that it docsn't need buttering – it already has a layer of fat on it. Cook for 12 minutes per 450 g (1 lb) plus 10 minutes resting time for sirloin, which should be sliced more thinly than the fillet. On the bone it should be roasted without pre-browning for 12 minutes per 450 g (1 lb) at gas mark 6, 200°C (400°F). Allow it to stand for 15 minutes before carving. You may wish to remove it from the bone and carve it.

SIRLOIN STEAK

Often held to bc the best steak as it combines tenderness with good flavour, it's important to cut through or remove the fat line down one side of the steak which would otherwise cause it to curl up as it cooks. If you don't want to remove all the fat, cut through the fat at right angles, making sure you sever the membrane underneath the fat next to the flesh itself in two or three places.

163

Remove the fat line down one side of the steak to prevent it curling as it cooks

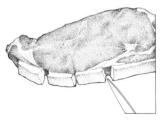

If you prefer not to remove all the fat, cut through it at right angles and sever the membrane underneath the fat next to the flesh in two or three places

Sirloin steaks à la crème

Serves 4

1 tablespoon olive oil
25 g (1 oz) butter
4 × 175–225 g (6–8 oz) sirloin steaks
Salt and freshly ground black pepper
150 ml (5 fl oz) double cream
2 teaspoons grainy French mustard
2 tablespoons chopped fresh parsley

In a large, heavy-based frying pan, heat the oil
and the butter until the butter stops sizzling.
Put in the steaks and brown for about 1 to 2
minutes on one side. Turn them over, brown
for another 1 to 2 minutes then season
generously. Pour in the cream, stir and allow
to bubble. Add the mustard and stir
thoroughly until mixed. Turn the steaks once
in this mixture. Transfer the steaks to a warm
serving plate, stir the parsley into the cream
sauce and pour over the steaks. They should
be served on hot plates and not kept waiting.

164

WINE
tip

**An astringent red to offset the
creamy sauce – try Bergerac or
young Côtes-du-Rhône.**

Rib of beef

**Also known as fore ribs, these used to be
regarded as the 'butcher's cut' – customers
rarely ordered them but they were held to be the
best roasting joint there is. They can be sold on
or off the bone. It's not worth buying less than
1.4–1.8 kg (3–4 lb) of beef as the shrinkage and
weight loss makes it uneconomic. The other
advantage to a large joint is that it makes
delicious cold roast beef. This method works
perfectly whether your rib is on or off the bone.**

Serves 4 to 6

½ tablespoon plain flour
½ teaspoon garlic salt
½ teaspoon ground bay leaves
½ teaspoon paprika
1 × 1.8 kg (4 lb) rib roasting joint (or larger)

Pre-heat the oven to gas mark 7, 220°C
(425°F). Mix the flour and spices together and
dredge the beef with them, patting it well into
all surfaces. Place the beef on a rack in a
roasting pan and put into the oven. With every
oven but an Aga, turn the heat down to gas
mark 4, 180°C (350°F) and roast for 12
minutes per 450 g (1 lb) rare, or 15 minutes
per 450 g (1 lb) for medium. If in an Aga, half-
way through the time remove the beef to the
next oven down in temperature and cook for
the remaining time. Take out of the oven,
remove the beef to a warm place and cover
loosely with foil. Allow to stand for 15
minutes before carving. This will make the
beef much more tender and juicy. Use the
drippings in the pan to make gravy if you
haven't been making Yorkshire Pudding in it.

Yorkshire pudding

Makes 4 individual puddings

50 g (2 oz) plain flour
1 egg
A pinch of salt
150 ml (5 fl oz) milk
4 teaspoons oil

Whisk the flour, egg, salt and milk together
until smooth. Leave to stand for 5 to 10
minutes. Heat 1 teaspoon of oil in each
individual Yorkshire tin. Pour in the
Yorkshire pudding mixture and bake in the
same oven as the rib of beef for 15 minutes
until well risen and golden. You can bake the
pudding in the pan below the beef so long as
the beef is a good six inches above on a rack.

Hereford-style braised beef

Serves 4 to 6

So-called because Herefordshire, one of the great British beef counties, is also a great centre for apples. Beef cooked this way produces succulent and delicious results. Serve it with plenty of mashed potatoes. The Quick Tossed Cabbage on page 114 is an ideal accompaniment.

1 tablespoon cooking oil
1 × 1.4 kg (3 lb) topside
450 g (1 lb) onions
450 g (1 lb) cooking apples
A pinch of ground cloves
1 teaspoon freeze-dried thyme
1 teaspoon freeze-dried marjoram
2 teaspoons made English mustard
250 ml (8 fl oz) apple juice
Salt and freshly ground black pepper

Pre-heat the oven to gas mark 4, 180°C (350°F).

Heat the oil in a large frying pan or casserole and brown the beef for 2 to 3 minutes. Peel the onions and apples, core the apple and cut both into walnut-sized pieces. Use these to line the bottom of a casserole into which the beef will just fit. Sprinkle with the cloves and herbs. Spread the browned beef with the mustard, then put the beef on top of the apples and onions. Pour in enough apple juice to come a quarter of the way up the beef. Season generously with salt and pepper. Cover and cook in the oven for about 1½ hours until just tender. Take out the beef and keep it warm while you make the sauce. Blend the apples and onions together in a liquidizer or food processor to produce a smooth sauce. Slice the meat across the grain and serve.

This needs a red wine with a cutting edge to match the acidity of the apple – a red from the Loire such as Saumur or Anjou Rouge would be good – or why not try dry cider?

Christmas spiced beef

To make this you need to start at least twelve days before Christmas with a piece of topside at least 2.25–2.7 kg (5 lb–6 lb) in weight. This produces one of the perfect cold meats for the 'groaning sideboard' with a wonderful old-fashioned flavour to it.

Serves 12

50 g (2 oz) soft brown sugar
1 × 2.7 kg (6 lb) topside
100 g (4 oz) sea salt
25 g (1 oz) black peppercorns
25 g (1 oz) allspice berries
1 teaspoon cardamom seeds
1 teaspoon cloves
2 star anise

Rub the sugar into the beef then place it in a large glass or earthenware bowl (not in a metal container) in which it can lie flat. Cover with a cloth or lid and leave for a day. Mix the salt and all the spices together in a pestle and mortar, a spice grinder or strong liquidizer until well ground. Rub into the beef, put back into the container and leave for 3 days. Turn, rubbing the beef thoroughly with the liquid which will have emerged. Repeat this process twice over the next 6 days. It can be kept in the fridge but a cool larder is probably even better.

When you're ready to cook it, pre-heat the oven to gas mark ½, 120°C (250°F). An Aga is perfect for this. Scrape but don't wash off any surplus spices and put it in a baking or oven dish – a self-basting roaster is ideal. Add a cup of water and bake in the oven for 5 hours. A fan oven is not ideal for this particular kind of cooking as it dries the meat very rapidly. When cooked, allow to cool, wrap in greaseproof paper and then in foil and leave to set for at least a day in the fridge. To carve, slice thinly across the grain.

165
·············

2. Tough – slow cooking beef

BRISKET

Brisket is the beef cut that equates to breast of lamb. In beef it can be quite fat and comes in two forms: boned and rolled like a roasting joint, or cut into ribs of beef rather like giant spare ribs. Either way it needs slow cooking but has one of the best flavours of any beef joint.

Chinese red ribs

This is a method of cooking brisket as the Chinese do, with quite vivid flavours to produce meat that can be eaten hot or cold. It can be sliced across the grain and eaten with its juices, rice and Stir-fried Vegetables or allowed to cool and sliced thinly across the grain as part of a Chinese-style hors d'oeuvre.

Serves 4

900 g (2 lb) brisket ribs, meat on
4 tablespoons soy sauce
2 cloves garlic, peeled and crushed
2.5 cm (1 inch) piece fresh ginger root, peeled and crushed
1 tablespoon brown sugar
1 teaspoon salt

Pre-heat the oven to gas mark 2, 150°C (300°F).

Trim off any substantial bits of fat from the ribs of beef. Put them into a shallow casserole with a lid. Mix the remaining ingredients together and marinate the ribs in the mixture for at least 1 hour. Add a cup of water to the casserole and cook it in the oven for 3 to 4 hours until the meat is completely cooked through, turning at least twice during the cooking.

Something cold and fizzy: lager, or if you must have wine, Blush Frizzante, chilled Asti Spumante or Moscato Spumante.

CHUCK STEAK

An excellent cut for casseroling and for *daubes* – low-liquid casseroles.

Traditional beef stew

A very English casserole with optional dumplings.

Serves 4

675 g (1 ½ lb) chuck steak, trimmed
1 large onion, peeled
225 g (8 oz) carrots, peeled
225 g (8 oz) turnips, peeled
2 tablespoons oil or beef dripping
1 tablespoon plain flour
½ teaspoon freeze-dried thyme
½ teaspoon freeze-dried marjoram
2 bay leaves
1 tablespoon chopped fresh parsley
Salt and freshly ground black pepper

For the dumplings:
50 g (2 oz) shredded suet
50 g (2 oz) self-raising flour
50 g (2 oz) fresh white breadcrumbs
1 egg, lightly beaten
1 tablespoon chopped fresh parsley

Pre-heat the oven to gas mark 4, 180°C (350°F).

Cut the beef, onion, carrots and turnips into 2.5 cm (1 inch) cubes. Heat the oil or dripping in a flameproof casserole and fry the beef until brown. Sprinkle over the flour and continue to turn and brown until the flour is the colour of milk chocolate. Do not allow it to burn! Immediately add the prepared vegetables and all the herbs except the chopped parsley. Season generously and add enough water just to cover the ingredients; the quantity will depend on the shape and size of your casserole. Cover and cook in the oven for 1 to 1½ hours until the meat is thoroughly cooked. Add the parsley and serve or . . .

If you're making dumplings, mix together all the dumpling ingredients except the parsley to make a cohesive paste. Add the parsley, season generously and add to the stew in tablespoon-sized dollops 25 minutes before you're ready to eat. You can, if the mixture is quite stiff, roll these into balls in your hand or add them directly from the spoon. Cover again and cook with the stew.

WINE tip

Robust dish, robust wine – French Corbières or Portuguese Dão.

French-style daube

Serves 4

900 g (2 lb) chuck steak
2 tablespoons oil or beef dripping
2 cloves garlic, peeled and chopped
1 onion, peeled and chopped
3 tablespoons red wine vinegar
250 ml (8 fl oz) water
1 bouquet garni of 1 stalk celery, 2 stalks parsley, a bay
*   leaf and a sprig of thyme*
1 tablespoon plain flour
1 tablespoon butter

Pre-heat the oven to gas mark 2, 150°C
(300°F).

Cut the meat into 2.5 cm (1 inch) cubes.
Heat the oil or dripping and gently brown the
meat. Add the garlic and onion and fry until
they start to brown. Pour in the wine vinegar
and deglaze (raise the heat to high and use the
liquid to scrape up the brown bits on the
bottom of the casserole or pan). When the
liquid has almost evaporated, add the water
and the bouquet garni – the liquid should
come about half-way up the meat. Cover and
cook in the oven for 1½ to 2 hours. You can
stir this casserole once during cooking to
make sure all the meat remains moist.

When the meat is cooked, mash the flour
and butter together until they make a smooth
paste. Add this, teaspoon by teaspoon, to the
casserole, preferably on a gentle heat,
allowing each teaspoon to dissolve and mix in
before adding the next. The sauce will go
glossy and thick and will just coat the meat.
Remove the bouquet garni and serve.

WINE
tip
**A traditional southern French
casserole – try it with a southern red
to match, such as red Coteaux du
Languedoc.**

Variations

If you add some capers and black olives at the
end it makes it a *Daube Provençal*. And 225 g
(8 oz) of button mushrooms instead of the
capers and olives makes it a *Daube À La Mode
Parisienne*. Use light beer instead of red wine
vinegar and water makes this a French or
Flemish-style dish called a *Carbonade*.

Leg of beef and shin of beef

The toughest meat which needs the slowest
cooking, these two cuts can be used in dishes
instead of chuck steak but require almost
double the length of cooking time. They're
very gelatinous and when cooked properly
produce a sauce of unexpected silkiness and
richness. The Mediterranean version of the
daube used to be cooked slowly in bakers'
ovens after the bread was removed.

Stifado

**This is the Greek version of an almost universal
Mediterranean stew. Serve it with rice or lots of
mashed potatoes and save any vegetables for a
separate course.**

Serves 4

900 g (2 lb) shin or leg of beef
1 tablespoon olive oil
225 g (8 oz) onions
2 cloves garlic
225 g (8 oz) tinned chopped tomatoes
2 tablespoons tomato purée
Juice of 1 lemon
1 teaspoon freeze-dried oregano
1 pinch freeze-dried thyme
1 teaspoon sugar
Salt and freshly ground black pepper

167
....

Pre-heat the oven to gas mark 2, 150°C
(300°F). Perfect for an Aga simmering oven.

In a casserole, heat the olive oil. Cut the
beef into 2.5 cm (1 inch) cubes and fry until
lightly browned. Add the onions and garlic
and fry until golden. Add the tomatoes, the
tomato purée, the lemon juice, herbs and
sugar, a little salt and pepper (save the final
seasoning until it's cooked) and enough water
to come half-way up the beef. Turn
thoroughly to mix all the ingredients together,
cover and cook in the oven for about 3 hours.
Stir it at least once during cooking. The sauce
will reduce to an almost jam-like consistency
by the end of this time and the meat will be
completely tender.

WINE
tip
**Amazing thunderous flavours need a
mighty wine – Greece's Château
Carras is a good (though rather
expensive) idea. Otherwise try a
mature Haut Medoc from Bordeaux or a cheaper
generic claret.**

Pot roasted silverside

Pot roasting is a technique worth reviving. Not only does it create moist joints of meat, it also cooks with the minimum of fat and makes its own sauce. Although we suggest silverside for this dish, you can use a number of braising joints, like aitch bone or short ribs, with equal success.

Serves 4 to 6

1 × 1.4 kg (3 lb) silverside
2 onions, peeled and halved
4 cloves
1 bay leaf
2 parsley stalks
1 celery leaf
450 g (1 lb) carrots
4 tablespoons cider (not malt) vinegar
120 ml (4 fl oz) water

Heat a flameproof casserole until very hot. Cook the joint on all sides for 2 to 3 minutes until 'sealed'. This will cause some spluttering, but don't worry: just open a window! Remove the joint from the dish. Stick the onions with the cloves and add them to the pan. Tie the bay leaf, parsley stalks and celery leaf together and put into the pan with the carrots. Splash in the cider vinegar, let it sizzle, add the water and put the meat on top. Cover and cook on a very low heat for 2½ hours. Remove the meat and leave to stand for 5 minutes before carving. Discard the herbs and cloves. Serve the carrots with the meat and purée the onions with the juices to make the sauce.

To match the acidity of the cider vinegar, try an Italian Merlot – or why not try dry cider?

Salted silverside

Silverside looks like a roasting joint but won't roast at all satisfactorily. It does however make marvellous salt beef and the basis of a Bollito Misto. You can buy it salted or salt it yourself. Saltpetre is difficult to buy, though your chemist might order it for you. You can follow the recipe omitting the saltpetre but the result will not be the lovely pink colour that's associated with traditional salt beef. Salt beef can be eaten hot or cold with gherkins, mustard and coleslaw (see page 114).

Serves 6 to 8

1.4–1.8 kg (3–4 lb) piece of silverside in a roll
1.75 litres (3 pints) water
100 g (4 oz) salt
1 teaspoon saltpetre (optional)
2 bay leaves
6 peppercorns

Bring the water to the boil and add the salt, saltpetre, bay leaves and peppercorns. Stir until the salt and saltpetre are dissolved, allow to cool then put in the beef. You must use a non-metallic container. Cover and keep it in a cool place, a larder or fridge will do, for 4 to 6 days, turning it occasionally.

169

To cook the salt beef; drain it from the brine, put into a large saucepan with fresh water and simmer gently for 3 hours or place in a pressure cooker according to instructions with about an 2.5 cm (1 inch) of water and the spices from the brine and cook for approximately 1 hour.

Alternatively you can cook silverside fresh.

WINE *tip* **Something from near the sea is a romantic idea, such as Colares from Portugal. As a contrast, try 'white' Zinfandel, the softly medium rosé from California.**

Boiled beef and carrots

Follow the cooking instructions and time for Salt Beef. Add a leek and carrot at the beginning of the cooking time, and add 900 g (2 lb) of carrots, peeled and split lengthways 15 minutes before serving. Discard the original leek and carrot, cut the beef across the grain and serve with the carrots, newly boiled potatoes and English mustard.

Or, try it the Italian way as:

Christmas spiced beef (page 165)

Bollito misto

You can serve some pre-cooked tagliatelle or boiled, whole potatoes to go with this if you please. Italian bread is also traditional.

Serves 8

1 salted tongue
900 g (2 lb) silverside
4 leeks
450 g (1 lb) carrots
1 medium-sized head fennel
1 medium-sized chicken
2 bay leaves

For the green sauce:
2 large gherkins
1 teaspoon capers
25 g (1 oz) fresh parsley
50 g (2 oz) fresh white breadcrumbs
Juice of ½ lemon
2 tablespoons olive oil
1 tablespoon red wine vinegar
3 tablespoons chopped fresh parsley
50 g (2 oz) Parmesan cheese, grated

Tie the meats with string so that they can be removed individually, or have some large meat forks ready. Take a large saucepan and half fill it with water. Put in the tongue and the silverside and, without any further seasoning, bring to the boil, cover and simmer gently for 1 to 1½ hours.

Meanwhile, clean the leeks, leaving them as whole as possible, and tie them in a bundle. Peel the carrots but don't cut them up. Trim the fennel and tie that together as well. After the meat has been cooking for 1½ hours, add the chicken and bay leaves. Continue to poach for 45 minutes. Add the leeks, carrots and fennel, topping up with water, if necessary, to make sure everything is covered, and continue to simmer for 15 minutes.

Meanwhile, put all the sauce ingredients into a food processor or blender (if it's a blender you may need to add a little water), and process until a coarse green purée. After the chicken has been cooking an hour and the vegetables about 15 minutes, remove the meats which should be tender. Skin the tongue (this will come off very easily with a sharp knife and a moment's patience). Put the tongue and drained chicken and silverside on to a large carving board and keep them warm. Transfer the vegetables to a serving dish. Split the fennel, untie the leeks and pile the carrots together. Serve the broth as a first course if

you choose with a teaspoon of parsley and some Parmesan cheese over each serving. Slice the meats and carve the chicken and serve with the vegetables and the green sauce.

WINE tip

Time-honoured Italian fare – try Barbera for a lighter, jumpier style of red or Barolo for a heavier, meatier mouth-filler.

Mince

Minced beef is not only a great convenience it also forms the basis of a very substantial cuisine in its own right. In places where tender beef was not available, mincing meat was the only way to make use of the tough carcase of work animals. But it's also economic on fuel and preparation time. You can buy various grades of mince – look for lean as there are no ratios for the amount of fat to lean in basic butchers' mince. You can also buy it as minced steak, the most expensive of all, and in coarse and fine ground form. The coarse is best for stews and casserole dishes, the fine for hamburger-type patties and meatballs.

MEAT AND FAT
● **First things first – fat is essential for flavour and 'mouth-feel'. Over-lean meat can taste awful (unless helped along with strong flavours such as smoke, herbs or spices).**

● **Modern butchers are adopting continental methods of meat preparation, cutting away most of the excess fat and then adding a little back to add flavour and moistness. But beware – this can turn into a racket, selling fat at meat prices. Added fat should not amount to more than 10 per cent of the overall weight. If it comes in higher than that, you are being ripped off.**
● **If you feel that you are eating too much animal fat (whether for specific health reasons or through concern at its high calorific value) you may like to know the following:**
1 Meat and meat products account for one-fifth to one quarter of the fats and oils we eat.
2 Bacon, ham, beef and lamb are the fattiest meats but . . .
3 . . . meat products such as pies, pasties and sausages make up one-fifth of the meat fat we consume. They are the fattiest (adding fat is a cheap way of bulking them out).

Chilli con carne

This much-maligned beef dish comes from the Texas/Mexico border. Made well, it's really delicious and far superior to the microwaved pub versions that have taken over from spaghetti bolognese as our most prevalent and worst-cooked dish. Serve it with rice and an avocado or green salad.

Serves 4

2 tablespoons oil
675 g (1½ lb) coarse ground minced beef
1 large onion, peeled and finely chopped
1 clove garlic, peeled and finely chopped
225 g (8 oz) tin chopped Italian tomatoes
1 tablespoon tomato purée
½ teaspoon chilli powder or chilli sauce
½ teaspoon cumin seed
½ teaspoon ground cinnamon
300 ml (10 fl oz) water
450 g (1 lb) cooked red kidney beans (either tinned or
  cooked as on page 127), drained and rinsed
Salt and freshly ground black pepper

Heat the oil in a large saucepan or deep frying pan. Add the beef and brown it thoroughly, breaking it up with a spoon. Add the onion and the garlic, the tomatoes, tomato purée, and spices and stir well. Stir in the water. If using freshly cooked red kidney beans, you can add these now. If using tinned ones, add them 5 minutes before the end of the cooking time. Simmer the chilli con carne for 45 minutes on a low heat, making sure it doesn't catch or dry out too much. Add the beans if tinned. Make sure the mixture has enough liquid in it to avoid a look of greasiness on the surface; another half cup of water will cure this if it appears. Season to taste with salt, pepper and chilli.

Minced meat loaf

It may be not so popular in Britain, but in the US this dish is regarded as a national treasure. It's often eaten there as a main course for Sunday lunch and comes in many forms. This is the simple version that can be eaten very much as we would eat a joint with vegetables, gravy and potatoes. You can change the spicing, add cheese or various chopped vegetables such as mushrooms or courgettes, use different varieties of meat, or ring the changes in almost any other way you like. There is a veal version on page 182.

Serves 6

900 g (2 lb) finely ground lean minced beef
2 eggs
4 tablespoons soft white breadcrumbs
2 tablespoons tomato ketchup
2 teaspoons made mustard
1 tablespoon chopped fresh parsley
1 teaspoon freeze-dried thyme
1 teaspoon freeze-dried oregano

Pre-heat the oven to gas mark 4, 180°C (350°F)

Mix all the ingredients thoroughly in a basin with your hands. If it's a bit dry you can add a few tablespoons of water until the mixture is soft but not runny. Pack the mixture into a 900 g (2 lb) loaf tin. Invert a roasting tin on to the loaf tin and turn the whole lot upside down so that the meat slides out of the tin on to the roasting tin but with its loaf shape intact. Cook it in the oven for 45 to 60 minutes. It should be brown on the outside and cooked through on the inside. You may want to cover the top of it with a butter paper after half-time to make sure it doesn't burn on the outside, especially in a fan oven. Make gravy from the pan drips and serve with potatoes and vegetables like a roast.

171

WINE *tip* The well-herbed meat loaf needs a good punchy red such as Californian red Zinfandel.

Crafty hamburgers

Purists will tell you that the best hamburgers are made from minced beef alone. But the following recipe produces more coherent patties that stay together better when they're cooked. And they taste delicious. Serve them in a bun, with mashed potatoes, with onions, or any way you please.

Makes 4 large hamburgers

450 g (1 lb) finely ground lean minced beef
1 egg
50 g (2 oz) onion, finely chopped
50 g (2 oz) fine white breadcrumbs
1 tablespoon tomato purée
½ teaspoon freeze-dried thyme
½ teaspoon salt
½ teaspoon freshly ground black pepper

In a bowl or, if you prefer, in a food processor, mix all the ingredients together until thoroughly cohesive. Divide into 4 and form into hamburger-shaped patties, making sure the centre is no thicker than the perimeter. Either heat a large heavy frying pan till very hot and smear with oil before dry frying, or grill under a hot grill for 2 to 3 minutes a side.

Accompaniments for beef

Horseradish

This is one of the two traditional accompaniments to roast beef and braised beef in Britain. It's also sometimes used for smoked fish. It's very difficult to obtain fresh these days – it looks rather like a grimy, shrivelled parsnip. If you do buy it fresh, peel about 2.5 cm (1 inch) of it and grate it very carefully, making sure none of it gets in your eyes or into cuts or scratches on your hands – it's fiercely powerful! You can store the rest in the fridge for up to 2 or 3 weeks. Mix a grated tablespoonful with a teaspoonful of cider or wine vinegar, a pinch of sugar and salt, and 2 tablespoons of double cream or fromage frais. Leave the flavours to blend for 1 or 2 hours before using. You can also buy it in a ready-grated form and, of course, ready-made. Many of these, however, are too sweet and sickly.

Mustard

English mustard is the strongest and is bright yellow. Normally mixed with just a little water and allowed to develop its flavour for up to 10 minutes. It can also be bought ready-made.

Grain mustard is often bought ready-made as Moutarde de Meaux, but is also available as a coarse powder to be mixed with wine vinegar and a pinch of sugar or, for a milder version, with fruit juice and a little honey.

Dijon and Bordeaux mustard are French mustards made from special blends of mustard seed which are available dried but are much better bought ready-made.

American mustard is mild and pale gold. It is flavoured and coloured with turmeric; ideal for eating in generous quantities on hot dogs, etc.

Flavoured mustards are available in more than 30 or 40 varieties, from garlic through green peppercorn to various herbs. The best of all in a tasting test conducted with over 76 varieties was the Maille's Provençal-style mustard.

Gherkins

Eaten with cold roast beef and pâtés, the smaller sizes are better as the large ones are really dill pickles. Those are good for hamburgers and American-style hot salt beef.

Pickles

A wide variety of pickles and chutneys are traditionally eaten with meat. The old English tradition is for pickles – onions, cauliflower, piccalilli, etc, with a strong and often highly spiced flavour. There's an increasing taste for chutneys with their sweet and sour flavour and softer texture – mango, peach, apricot, apple, etc. Some recipes for these can be found on page 243.

Lamb and mutton

Seven cuts and twelve dishes

Lamb is naturally grown on grass and killed young so the meat is tender. In Britain our produce comes in a variety of choices, and there's also New Zealand chilled and frozen lamb. Welsh and Scottish quality marks aim to guarantee premium meat butchered and hung to high standards. They are worth seeking out in specialist butchers. New Zealand lamb, although often sold frozen, is in fact outstanding value both in terms of price and quality. Increasingly it is available chilled. The long journey in this state gives it the maturity that hanging would otherwise provide.

1. Best end of neck

This is also known as a rack of lamb and is a row of eight chops sold as a mini-joint or sometimes separated. Either way it needs chining, which is removing the line of bone along the bottom end which prevents the chops being separated before or after they're cooked.

Lamb chops milanese

An Italian dish which makes the quite small chops from a rack of lamb go much further. They're often eaten in Italy with pasta served with a tomato vegetable sauce but they're nice, too, with new potatoes and green beans.

Serves 4

100 g (4 oz) fresh white breadcrumbs
Grated rind of 1 lemon
8 rack of lamb chops, separated
1 egg, beaten
2 tablespoon oil
2 tablespoons butter
1 lemon, quartered

Mix the breadcrumbs and lemon rind together. Dip the chops in the beaten egg, keeping a bit of the bone end free for handling purposes, and then roll in the breadcrumbs and lemon rind mixture. Repeat with all the chops. Heat the oil and butter in a large frying pan into which all the chops will fit in one layer. Over a medium heat, fry the chops for 3 to 4 minutes a side until golden and pale brown but not burnt. Remove and serve with a quarter of lemon on each plate.

Roast rack of lamb

This is served three chops to a portion in French restaurants and makes the neatest, quickest individual roast available. If you're cooking it for a group of people it's probably best to roast it as a complete rack and separate it at the table into appropriate numbers. Two to three chops are a minimum for an adult serving.

Serves 6

2 racks of lamb
Grated rind of 1 lemon
1 tablespoon chopped fresh parsley
2 cloves garlic, peeled and puréed
1 egg yolk
1 teaspoon freeze-dried rosemary
Salt and freshly ground black pepper

Pre-heat the oven to gas mark 6, 200°C (400°F).

Get your butcher or supermarket to prepare the lamb by trimming the meat off the ends of all the bones so that they have 2.5 cm (1 inch) of clean bone sticking out. Also have the outer skin removed from the meat so that the fat is clean and white. You may want to trim off some of the fat if the lamb is oversupplied with it. Mix all the other ingredients together with a good pinch of salt and some black pepper and spread it on the fat side of the lamb. Put the lamb, fat side up, on a roasting rack in a roasting tin. Cook in the oven for 10 minutes. Turn off the heat if possible (in an Aga take down to the simmering oven), cook for another 10 minutes for pink and 15 to 20 minutes for medium to well done. Slice into individual chops or, if you prefer, into two to three chop portions.

173

WINE tip Lamb is a lovely juicy meat and slightly on the sweet side. So no matter what you do to it, juicy, fullsome wines will whack your tastebuds into action – Californian Petite Syrah, Italian Valpolicella, French Côtes de Duras, heavier rosés or Spanish Rioja.

2. Breast of lamb

Breast of lamb is a very cheap joint and often very fatty. It's available with or without the bone in. Sometimes when it's boned it has also been rolled.

Rolled breast of lamb

Whether the meat's been rolled or not, this quantity of stuffing will fill one boned breast. It's particularly nice served with a Pilau-style rice (see page 152).

Serves 2

50 g (2 oz) dried apricots, finely chopped
2 spring onions, finely chopped
½ teaspoon freeze-dried rosemary
50 g (2 oz) fresh white breadcrumbs
2 tablespoons milk
Salt and freshly ground black pepper
1 breast of lamb, boned

Pre-heat the oven to gas mark 4, 180°C (350°F).

174   Mix all the ingredients together until they form a cohesive mixture. Cut any excess fat you can from the breast of lamb. Spread the stuffing on the inside and roll up gently. Tie with string in 3 places and roast in the oven for 45 to 50 minutes. You can make gravy with the dripping. Slice the lamb in thick chunks across the grain.

WINE *tip*   **To complement the apricots – try a French red Burgundy.**

Lamb spare ribs

This is a simple way of using the very economical breast of lamb to make a dish that's quickly cooked and finger-licking good.

Serves 4

2 unboned breasts of lamb
2 tablespoons hoisin sauce
2 tablespoons soy sauce
1 tablespoon Worcestershire sauce
2 tablespoons tomato purée
1 teaspoon garlic salt
½ teaspoon ground ginger
A pinch of five-spice powder (optional)
2 tablespoons lemon juice

Cut the lamb vertically between the bones into 1 cm (½ inch) mini chops or spare ribs. Mix all the sauce ingredients together in a china or glass dish and use to coat the lamb. Leave to marinate from 1 hour up to 12 hours before cooking. Either pre-heat the grill, or pre-heat the oven to gas mark 8, 230°C (450°F), and line a roasting tin with kitchen foil.

Put the lamb on a rack in the roasting tin and grill or hot bake for 20 to 25 minutes, turning as necessary. You can use the remaining marinade as a basting sauce while this takes place. When the lamb is thoroughly cooked, remove and serve while hot and bubbling.

Roast rack of lamb (page 173)

3. Shoulder

One of the popular cuts of lamb, this is nevertheless inclined to be quite fatty and difficult to carve. The French often bone it completely and use it as a braising joint, but there is a way of preparing it for roasting which makes it very easy to handle.

Easy to carve roast shoulder of lamb

Serves 4

1 shoulder of lamb
1 sprig fresh rosemary
Salt and freshly ground black pepper

Using a very sharp, thin knife, cut around the edge of the shoulder blade bone (the flat end) of the shoulder of lamb. On the underside this is easy as it's flat. On the upper side there's a ridge which you need to cut round and over, preferably without breaking the skin. Cut as far back into the joint as possible but don't try to remove the bone at this stage.

176

Cut around the edge of the shoulder blade bone (the flat end)

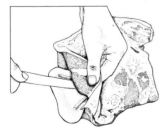

On the upper side of the shoulder cut round and over the ridge without breaking the skin

Pre-heat the oven to gas mark 4, 180°C (350°F).

Place the lamb in a roasting tin, tuck the rosemary alongside and season well with salt and pepper. Roast for 15 minutes per 450 g (1 lb) for pink, 18 for medium and 22 for ruined. Allow the lamb to stand for 10 minutes while you make gravy with the pan drippings, discarding the rosemary.

To carve, hold the shank end of the lamb down firmly with a carving fork and, with a towel or cloth wrapped round your hand, seize the shoulder blade *bone* and twist it resolutely. When you get it round to 360° you will find that it will come undone from the joint and slide out without too much trouble if you've freed it properly with a knife before roasting. You can then cut across the joint almost like slicing bread until you get to the shank which should be cut rather like a miniature leg of lamb.

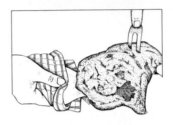

Hold the shank end down with a carving fork and, with the other hand, seize the shoulder blade bone and twist it resolutely

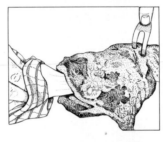

Once you have twisted it 360° you will find that it will come away from the joint and slide out

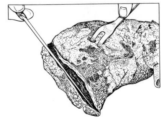

You should now be able to cut across the joint in slices

Braised shoulder of lamb

This can be done with a completely boned shoulder. Ask your butcher or your supermarket to supply one (they will need 24 hours notice). Or you can use one of the half shoulders, preferably the shank end, that are also widely available. You can cook the lamb in the oven or on top of the stove. Serve it with rice, noodles or freshly boiled new potatoes.

Serves 4

1 large onion, peeled and finely chopped
1 clove garlic, peeled and finely chopped
225 g (8 oz) ripe tomatoes, coarsely chopped
1 boned shoulder tied in a parcel or shank end of lamb
  shoulder
1 teaspoon freeze-dried or chopped fresh basil
1 teaspoon freeze-dried or chopped fresh oregano

If cooking in the oven, pre-heat it to gas mark 4, 180°C (350°F).

Mix together the onion, garlic and tomatoes. In a heavy casserole or pan, brown the lamb gently in its own fat. Remove from the pan and add the tomato and onion mixture, turning it in the fat until hot. Return the lamb to the pan and add the herbs and enough water to come 1 cm (½ inch) up the pan; the quantity will depend on the size of the pan and the volume of meat. Cover and simmer on top of the stove or in the oven for 20 minutes per 450 g (1 lb) plus 20 minutes. To serve, remove and slice the lamb. Purée the sauce in a liquidizer or food processor.

4 and 5. Loin and chops

What a pleasure lamb chops can be when well cooked. Loin of lamb is a row of chops not separated which can be used as a small roasting joint similar to the carré or rack of lamb (see page 173). It can be treated in exactly the same way and will take about half as long again to cook (30 minutes for pink, about 40 minutes for medium, and just under 50 for ruined!).

Grilled lamb chops

For loin or chump chops there's no question that they are best cooked under a grill. Chops like this are best served simply with new potatoes or a Pommes Dauphinoise (see page 132) and a green vegetable.

Serves 4

4 lamb chops
Either:
4 teaspoons redcurrant jelly
4 teaspoons Dijon mustard
Or:
4 teaspoons olive oil
4 teaspoons lemon juice
A pinch of freeze-dried rosemary

Pre-heat the grill for at least 10 minutes before you start to cook and line your grill pan with foil to reflect heat, catch splashes and reduce washing up.

Choose your flavouring and either mix together the redcurrant jelly and mustard; or the oil, lemon juice and rosemary.

If you're using the jelly and mustard, grill the chops on one side for 3 to 4 minutes until sizzling. Spread with a little of the mixture, turn over, spread with the rest of the mixture and grill for another 3 to 4 minutes before serving.

If using the lemon and herbs, spread with half the mixture before the first side is grilled, turn over, spread the remaining mixture on the other side of the chops and continue to grill for the 3 to 4 minutes.

177

WINE *tip* | **For delicate chops, a delicate wine – Italian Pinot Noir (called Pinot Nero) or a Cabernet from Grave del Friuli.**

6. Leg of lamb

Leg is a prime cut. It is almost always roasted and with good reason because it makes an extremely succulent and easy to carve joint, particularly if you get your butcher to remove the little saddle bone at the fat end of the leg. If he doesn't know how, or you're buying from a supermarket, take a sharp knife and remove the bone with a hole in it you'll find running across the flat end of the thick part of the joint, separating it from the knuckle. This will make the whole thing much easier to carve.

Garlic and herb roast lamb

Serves 6

1 leg of lamb
3 cloves garlic, peeled and crushed
4 tablespoons olive oil
2 teaspoons freeze-dried rosemary
300 ml (10 fl oz) warm water

Pre-heat the oven to gas mark 6, 200°C (400°F).

178

Mix the garlic with the olive oil and rosemary. Spread the mixture over the lamb, scoring it in places if you wish the flavour to penetrate deep into the meat. Place it on a rack on a roasting pan and add the water to the pan. This will facilitate making gravy and prevent the drippings burning. Roast in the oven for 15 minutes per 450 g (1 lb) for pink or 18 minutes per 450 g (1 lb) for medium. Take out of the oven and allow to stand in a warm place, covered with a loose tent of foil, for at least 15 minutes. The meat will continue to cook and will be much more tender to carve.

Make the gravy with the remaining drippings, thickening it if you feel inclined with some cornflour, and carve to serve (see page 176).

WINE tip Good old-fashioned English-style roast lamb, and traditional French garlic and rosemary roast – both would go well with Merlot. Look out for some of the southern French examples named after the grape.

Welsh honey-roast lamb

This is a way of cooking lamb that is traditional in Wales and produces a delicious sweet and sour mahogany-coloured crust. It is excellent served with creamed potatoes and a strong-tasting green vegetable like leeks or broccoli.

Serves 6

2 sprigs fresh thyme
2 bay leaves
1 large leg of lamb
Salt and freshly ground black pepper
4 tablespoons runny honey

Pre-heat the oven to gas mark 6, 200°C (400°F) and line your roasting pan with some foil – it will make washing up much easier.

Put the thyme and bay leaves on the foil, a rack over it, place the lamb on the rack and season generously with salt and pepper. Roast in the oven for 10 minutes per 450 g (1 lb). Remove and spoon half the honey over the lamb. Put back into the oven and allow to roast for a further 15 minutes. Remove again and add the rest of the honey, turning the lamb to make sure it is all coated. Put back into the oven for 20 minutes.

Remove from the oven and allow to stand in a warm place for 15 minutes before carving. It is possible to make a sauce from the pan dripping but for many this is too sweet.

WINE tip Roast leg of lamb with honey would go well with a Portuguese Dão or Bairrada

7. Minced lamb

Traditionally Shepherd's Pie was made with the remains of a cooked joint, minced up. In fact it's much nicer made with fresh minced lamb which you can either mince yourself or, very often these days, buy ready minced. It's also the ideal ingredient for a number of dishes from southern Europe and indeed even further afield than that. As well as the Shepherd's Pie that follows do try Moussaka – a dish eaten all over the Middle East (see page 120 of Vegetable chapter).

Super shepherd's pie

Serves 4

450 g (1 lb) minced lamb
225 g (8 oz) onions, peeled and finely chopped
1 tablespoon tomato purée
1 tablespoon soy sauce
1 tablespoon Worcestershire sauce
½ teaspoon freeze-dried or chopped fresh thyme
½ teaspoon freeze-dried or chopped fresh marjoram
Salt and freshly ground black pepper
120 ml (4 fl oz) water
225 g (8 oz) carrots, finely grated
900 g (2 lb) potatoes, peeled
120 ml (4 fl oz) milk
25 g (1 oz) butter
½ teaspoon freshly grated nutmeg
25 g (1 oz) cheese, grated

Fry the lamb in its own fat in a heavy-based saucepan or frying pan until well browned. Add the onions, tomato purée, sauces and herbs. Season generously with salt and pepper and add the water. Put the mixture into an oven or baking dish at least 4 cm (1½ inches) deep. Place the grated carrots on top of the lamb. Put the potatoes in a saucepan of water, bring to the boil then simmer until tender.

Pre-heat the the oven to gas mark 4, 180°C (350°F).

Mash the potatoes with the milk, butter, nutmeg and salt and pepper. Spoon on to the carrot and lamb mixture and level with a fork. Sprinkle over the grated cheese. Bake in the oven for 35 to 40 minutes until the potato and cheese are well browned on top and the whole mixture is bubbling.

Bobotie

A dish brought to South Africa by the Cape Malay people who became the best cooks in that subcontinent, it's a very simple dish with a surprisingly sophisticated appeal. It's normally eaten with yellow rice; that is, long-grain rice cooked by Method Two (see page 150) but with a dessertspoon of turmeric mixed into the water to give it a bright orange colour. A handful of raisins is added at the same time. Also eaten with it are a variety of chutneys – mango, apricot, etc. – and a salad made from finely chopped tomatoes, spring onions and parsley.

Serves 6

2 slices white bread
300 ml (10 fl oz) milk
2 onions, peeled and chopped
1 clove garlic, peeled and chopped
450 g (1 lb) minced lamb
4 tablespoons apricot jam or chutney
2 teaspoons mild curry powder
1 teaspoon salt
2 eggs
2 bananas
2 bay leaves

Pre-heat the oven to gas mark 4, 180°C (350°F).

Place the bread in a bowl, pour over half the milk and allow it to soak in. Fry the onions, garlic and minced lamb gently until the onions and garlic are translucent and the lamb lightly browned. Remove from the heat and add the soaked bread, mixing it together thoroughly with a fork or, after it's cooled, with your hands. Add the jam or chutney, curry powder and salt. Pack this into a baking or gratin dish about 4 cm (1½ inches) deep. Beat the eggs with the remaining milk. Peel the bananas and slice them lengthways. Place the bananas in an attractive pattern on top of the meat, garnish with the bay leaves and pour the milk and egg mixture over the top. Bake in the oven for about 45 to 50 minutes until the meat is cooked through and the custard on the top has set and turned golden. Serve it in hot slices like a pie.

8. Mutton

Mature tasting, hard to find (try ethnic butchers), but great for stews.

Irish stew

Serves 4

450 g (1 lb) floury or old potatoes, peeled and sliced
450 g (1 lb) onions, peeled and sliced
900 g (2 lb) mutton chops (lamb chops will do)
450 g (1 lb) waxy or new potatoes, scrubbed
Salt and freshly ground black pepper
1 tablespoon chopped fresh parsley

Pre-heat the oven to gas mark 3, 160°C (325°F).

Use the floury potatoes to line the base and sides of a casserole into which the rest of the ingredients will fit comfortably. Add half the onions in a layer then add the chops, and top with the rest of the onions. Trim the new potatoes to a uniform size and add them to the casserole. Season generously with salt and pepper, add the parsley and put in enough water to come up to the top of the new potatoes. Cover and bake in the oven for 1 to 1½ hours depending on the age of the mutton. The floury potatoes should have dissolved to thicken the sauce and the chops and new potatoes should be cooked to perfection. Make sure everyone gets a portion of everything.

Veal

Veal is a meat which raises hackles, to say the least. Many gave up eating it in protest against cruel rearing of veal calves in crates. This is now outlawed in Britain but persists in Holland. So if you like veal escalopes – and they are delicious – you should look for a label in the butcher's or supermarket that confirms the veal was raised in Britain. But there's a price to pay for animal welfare – veal escalopes are very expensive.

This is a favourite recipe for *the* classic veal escalope dish. If you make your own fresh white breadcrumbs in a food processor then they are wonderfully light and fluffy. The lemon lends a sharpness to what is, after all, fried food.

Wiener schnitzel

Serves 4

4 × 175–225 g (6–8 oz) veal escalopes
Juice of 1 lemon
40 g (1½ oz) flour seasoned with salt and freshly
*   ground black pepper*
1 egg
120 ml (4 fl oz) milk
175 g (6 oz) fresh white breadcrumbs
2 tablespoons vegetable oil
50 g (2 oz) butter
Lemon wedges to serve

Place the escalopes between sheets of damp greaseproof paper and use a heavy frying pan to flatten them to a 5 mm (¼ inch) thickness. Peel off the paper. Dip the escalopes in the lemon juice, then in the flour and leave for a few minutes. Beat together the egg and milk, dip the escalopes in the mixture, then coat in breadcrumbs. Heat the oil in a large frying pan and add the butter when the oil is hot. Fry the escalopes for 2 minutes each side until golden and just cooked through. Serve at once with the lemon wedges.

Above: *Irish stew.* **Below:** *Wiener schnitzel*

Hungarian goulash

Although it's usually made with beef in Britain, Hungarian Goulash was traditionally made with what we would think of as quite mature veal. The modern, acceptable methods of rearing (no force feeding in crates) produce a similar, darker meat. It's a heart-warming, extremely generous casserole to be eaten on cold winter nights when comfort and flavour are the order of the day. Serve it in bowls with flat noodles like tagliatelle.

Serves 4

675 g (1½ lb) boneless stewing veal
2 tablespoons cooking oil
1 large onion, peeled and finely chopped
1 teaspoon caraway seeds
Salt and freshly ground black pepper
2 tablespoons tomato purée
2 tablespoons paprika
675 g (1½ lb) new potatoes, scrubbed
2 teaspoons cornflour
150 ml (5 fl oz) soured cream

Cut the veal into pieces the size of half a walnut. Put the oil in a large heavy-based saucepan and heat it gently. Add the veal and brown it lightly all over. Add the onion and the caraway seed and turn together for about 3 to 4 minutes until the onion is translucent. Season generously with salt and pepper, stir in the tomato purée, the paprika and enough water just to cover the veal. Cover and simmer gently for 30 minutes. Trim the new potatoes to even sizes, add them to the pan and cook for a further 15 minutes or so until cooked through. Stir the cornflour into a little water then stir that into the stew to thicken it. Bring it gently to the boil then turn off the heat immediately and serve with a tablespoon or two of soured cream on the top of each bowl.

Italian meat loaf

Another variation of the much-loved American meat loaf, this is a light version with a strong Italian flavour. Once again it uses stewing veal or minced veal, both of which are surprisingly widely available these days. It is possible to make this with the minced turkey that's also recently come on the market. Ricotta is an Italian cottage cheese – British cottage cheese will do at a pinch. This is nicest eaten with mashed potatoes or pasta with a creamy mushroom sauce. A Béchamel Sauce (see page 19) with 225 g (8 oz) of button mushrooms sliced into it and simmered for 5 minutes is ideal.

Serves 4

675 g (1½ lb) minced veal or stewing veal minced at
  home
100 g (4 oz) fresh white breadcrumbs
100 g (4 oz) Ricotta cheese
1 small onion, peeled and very finely chopped
2 cloves garlic, peeled and very finely chopped
1 heaped teaspoon freeze-dried or 1 tablespoon
  chopped fresh basil
1 heaped teaspoon freeze-dried or 1 tablespoon
  chopped fresh oregano
2 eggs
100 g (4 oz) Parmesan cheese, grated

Pre-heat the oven to gas mark 5, 190°C (375°F).

Mix together all the ingredients except the Parmesan cheese. Mix in half the Parmesan and press into a 900 g (2 lb) loaf tin. Invert a roasting dish over the loaf tin and turn the whole lot upside down again so that the meat slides out of the bread tin on to the roasting tin in a loaf shape. Sprinkle the remaining Parmesan along the top to form a crust and bake in the oven for 45 to 50 minutes until the meat is cooked through but not dried out. You may need to put a butter paper or two over the top for the last 10 to 15 minutes of cooking to make sure that it doesn't, but do that before the loaf is cooked through.

Pork and bacon

Michael Barry doesn't eat pork, Jilly Goolden can take it or leave it but Peter Bazalgette loves it. Here are some favourite recipes.

Roast pork with amazing gravy

Good crackling is essential. Make sure your butcher scores the skin of the joint. The gravy recipe has a few unexpected ingredients. If you like an oriental flavour, use sesame oil and smear the flesh with soy sauce. Roast potatoes are obligatory (see page 130).

Serves 4 to 6

For the pork:
A loin or leg of pork 350 g (12 oz) per person with bone, 225 g (8 oz) per person without Vegetable oil
Salt and freshly ground black pepper
For the gravy:
Pork fat and roasting juices
About 1 tablespoon plain flour
250 ml (8 fl oz) strong tea
1 onion stock cube
1 teaspoon chilli paste
250 ml (8 fl oz) red wine
4 teaspoons redcurrant jelly

Pre-heat the oven to gas mark 9, 240°C (475°F).
  Rub the scored pork skin with vegetable oil. Sprinkle the skin well with salt. Put the joint into a very, very hot oven for 20 minutes. Then reduce the heat to gas mark 4, 180°C (350°F) and cook the joint for 25 minutes per 350 g (1 lb) until tender. Drain off the fat and juices into a separation jug and leave the joint in a warm place. When the fat and meat juices have separated, pour a little of the fat into a large frying pan. Fry enough flour in it to thicken it (but ensure it remains a liquid and does not become a paste). Fry the flour until dark brown. Add the tea and stir it in with an onion stock cube and a teaspoon of chilli paste. Then add the red wine and enough of the meat juices to achieve a thick, liquid consistency. Add redcurrant jelly and season.

WINE tip The sweet, strawberry flavours of the Pinot Noir grape go succulently well with roast pork. Look out for affordable ones – try Romania and southern California.

Above: *Roast pork with amazing gravy.* **Below:** *Hot boiled gammon* (page 184) and *Pease pudding* (page 184)

Hot boiled gammon

Serves 4 hot or more when cold

1 × 1.8 kg (4 lb) piece of centre-cut smoked gammon
5 medium onions, peeled but whole stuck with cloves
1 fat clove of garlic, peeled and halved
1 small parsnip, peeled and halved
450 g (1 lb) carrots, sliced
1 tablespoon brown sugar
1 tablespoon red wine vinegar
1 tablespoon black peppercorns
2 bay leaves with edges torn
1 stalk celery, cut into 4
Crushed parsley stalks

Place the gammon in a very large saucepan. Cover with water and leave for 1 hour. Drain. Re-cover with fresh water and add all the peeled vegetables and other ingredients. Cover the saucepan and bring to the boil slowly then cover the pan and turn down the heat to simmer gently. The cooking time from boiling point is 20 minutes per 450 g (1 lb), plus another 20 minutes.

To serve hot:
When the meat is ready, lift it on to a warm plate and remove the string and rind. Carve. Add the vegetables from the saucepan, which you can remove with a slotted spoon.

To serve cold:
After the meal, replace the gammon in the stock until cool. Lift out, wrap in tin foil and refrigerate. (The stock is excellent for soups, particularly lentil.)

If you want to eat the gammon cold in the first instance, use only 2 carrots and just 1 onion stuck with cloves. The other ingredients remain the same.

WINE tip For such a salty meat you need a pungent, powerfully flavoured white such as Muscat – made as a dry wine, as it increasingly is in Hungary and Portugal, for instance. Look out for the Portuguese João Pires.

Pease pudding

The traditional complement to boiled gammon, 'hot' or 'cold' in the words of the rhyme.

Serves 6

225 g (8 oz) split peas
Salt and freshly ground black pepper
50 g (2 oz) butter
2 eggs
Chopped fresh parsley (optional)

Soak the split peas in water overnight. Ensure that the water is about 2.5 cm (1 inch) above the level of the peas – they will soak up a lot of water. Then tip the split peas and the remaining liquid into a saucepan and add enough extra water to cover the peas. Add a pinch of salt and bring to the boil. Then turn down the heat and simmer very slowly for 45 to 60 minutes until tender. Beware – the peas can boil over very easily, spreading a messy foam across your hob. After cooking, strain nearly all the water off but retain a little liquid in the saucepan, about 1 cm (½ inch). Put the peas and the retained water into a food processor or blender with the butter, eggs and freshly ground black pepper. Process until smooth. Grease a 1.2 litre (2 pint) pudding basin and pour in the mixture (you can stir in a handful of chopped parsley at this stage if you like). Butter a piece of greaseproof paper and tie the paper over the top of the pudding basin, grease side down. Stand the basin in a pan of water, bring to the boil, cover and steam for 1 hour, topping up with boiling water as necessary. Serve hot or cold.

Bacon pudding

Fresh butcher's suet is best for this recipe but you can use shredded suet if necessary. This is a Victorian favourite well worth serving.

Serves 4 to 6

225 g (8 oz) rashers, streaky bacon, rinded
50 g (2 oz) frozen peas
1 sprig fresh mint
1 teaspoon sugar
Salt and freshly ground black pepper
100 g (4 oz) butcher's suet, grated
225 g (8 oz) self-raising flour
1 onion, peeled and chopped
2 tablespoons chopped fresh parsley (imperative!)
1 tablespoon mixed chopped fresh sage and thyme
or 1 teaspoon dried mixed herbs

Cut out any small 'dots' of bone from the bacon then cut the rashers into roughly 2.5 cm (1 inch) square pieces. Cook the frozen peas in water with mint and sugar and salt until tender, then drain. Put all the ingredients into a mixing bowl. Add very little salt (remember the bacon) and plenty of freshly ground black pepper. Mix with water to a stiff consistency like bread dough.

Grease a pudding basin and a piece of greaseproof paper with butter. Put the mixture in a basin large enough to leave about 2.5 cm (1 inch) of the basin above the surface of the mixture. Pleat the greaseproof paper, and tie butter side down over the basin. Place in a steamer above boiling water, or in a large saucepan with water half-way up basin (in which case keep an eye open for replenishing) for 2 hours. Turn out on to a warm plate. Serve with Mrs Beeton's Tomato Sauce (below).

Mrs Beeton's tomato sauce

This classic recipe for tomato sauce has one or two crafty additions and a little technological help. Spinach makes a good accompaniment.

Serves 4

4 rashers streaky bacon, rinded and chopped
2 tablespoons cooking oil
1 clove garlic, peeled and chopped
1 small onion, peeled and chopped
1 tablespoon plain flour
1 × 400 g (14 oz) Italian tomatoes
Brown sugar to taste
A shake of Worcestershire sauce
Salt and freshly ground black pepper
1 bay leaf
1 tablespoon red wine vinegar

Cut out any 'dots' of bone from the bacon then chop it. Heat the oil and fry the garlic and onion until soft. Add the bacon and cook until firm. Remove from the heat and mix in the flour. Return to the heat, add the tomatoes and stir until bubbling. Turn the heat down, add all other ingredients, cover and cook for 25 minutes, stirring occasionally. Take out the bay leaf. Pour into a blender and whizz until smooth. To re-heat, melt a knob of butter in a saucepan and add the sauce. Stir over a low heat until hot. Pour over the bacon pudding.

185
·············

BRINGING HOME THE BACON
The most common, cheapest bacon is cured by injection with brine. This leads to watery meat and bacon which shrinks, leaving white scum in the frying pan (instead of good, honest fat). There *are* better hams and bacons and here's how to find them:
● **Bacon rashers: Look for 'Dry' or 'Traditional Cure' on the label – a superior curing process that does not rely on injected brine. It yields firmer, drier meat – bacon like it used to be (except, more expensive, unfortunately).**
● **Bacon joints: Gammon, collar, shoulder or hock. Hock is the cheapest but more gristly. If you are buying the joint in a butcher then ask about the curing method (see above). The method used dictates how long the joint needs soaking (the more traditional methods produce saltier meat that needs longer soaking).**
● **Ham: Ham prices have risen quite a lot but for a good reason – we have rebelled against plastic, watery ham. Look for 'no added water' and you will pay more but get a satisfying, meaty ham. Cured, uncooked hams (such as Bayonne from France and Parma from Italy) are increasingly available. Delicious.**

Country pie

This pie started life in 1949 as egg and bacon flan when food was still rationed. The following quantities are for a 21 cm (8½ inch) diameter spring clip tin.

Serves 8 to 10

*Shortcrust pastry, using about 450 g (1 lb) plain flour
   (see page 206)*
450 g (1 lb) rashers streaky bacon, rinded and boned
1 large onion, peeled and chopped
450 g (1 lb) sausage meat
1 × 400 g (14 oz) tin Italian tomatoes
1 teaspoon soft brown sugar
Worcestershire sauce
Plenty of freshly ground black pepper
A little salt, if necessary
4 tablespoons brown breadcrumbs
4 tablespoons chopped fresh sage
4 large eggs
4 tablespoons chopped fresh parsley
100 g (4 oz) strong Cheddar cheese, grated

Pre-heat oven to gas mark 6, 200°C (400°F) and grease the spring-clip cake tin well.

Roll out the pastry and line the tin, pressing in to the sides and particularly into the join of the base with the sides. Line the pastry base and sides with most of the streaky bacon.

Cover the base with a layer of chopped onion, then press out the sausage meat to cover the onion. Strain the tomatoes without pressing them. Place them on the sausage meat and spread them out. Sprinkle the tomatoes with brown sugar, Worcestershire sauce, pepper, salt and a layer of brown breadcrumbs and sage. Reserve a little of the egg yolk for glazing then beat the eggs and pour them over the breadcrumbs. Add the parsley, a layer of cheese and the remainder of the bacon. Roll out the pastry lid. Wet the edges of the pie tin, place the lid on top and crimp together. Paint the pie lid with the reserved egg yolk and then cut a slit in the top.

Stand the pie on a baking-sheet and place in a hot oven for 30 minutes. Lower the temperature to gas mark 4, 180°C (350°F) and cook for a further 1½ hours. Put a skewer into the slit to make sure the onions are soft. Turn off the heat and allow the pie to cool in the oven. When cool, place in the fridge overnight. Next morning, run a sharp knife round the edge of the pie, and only then release spring clip. Either wrap in tin foil and refrigerate (or it freezes well, too) or serve cold with salad. It may also be re-heated.

3. Untouchables

Offal used to be the bits of the animal that were sold cheaply. Unfortunately, as you will have found if you have tried to buy calves' liver recently, that is no longer strictly true. But most offal is still a bargain considering its taste and nutritional value.

All these recipes should persuade the most die-hard opponent once the flavour hits the taste buds. The big difficulty can be getting some of the ingredients when so much meat comes pre-packed. Given a little notice, supermarkets will often get an item. But proper butchers are a better bet and it is often worth looking in ethnic butchers. They still start with the whole animal.

Australian-style tripe

This dish is inspired by a recipe from one of Australia's leading cooks. You can simmer this rich autumn stew on top of the stove or cook it in the oven. Serve it with plenty of potatoes and cabbage, broccoli or kale.

Serves 4

4 tablespoons olive oil
2 cloves garlic, peeled and sliced
225 g (8 oz) onions, peeled and sliced
900 g (2 lb) cleaned and blanched tripe
2 tablespoons balsamic or red wine vinegar
3 tablespoons tomato purée
1 teaspoon freeze-dried oregano
1 teaspoon freeze-dried thyme
2 bay leaves
Salt and freshly ground black pepper
2 tablespoons chopped fresh parsley

If you are cooking the dish in the oven, pre-heat the oven to gas mark 4, 180°C (350°F). Heat the oil in a flameproof casserole and fry the garlic and onions gently until translucent. Cut the tripe into walnut-sized pieces, add it to the onions and cook over a high heat till most of the liquid the tripe gives off is gone. Pour in the vinegar, let it come back to the boil and add all the other ingredients except the parsley. Season with salt and pepper, stir and simmer for 45 to 60 minutes on top of the stove or place in the oven. Check for seasoning and serve sprinkled with the parsley.

Stout was the old-fashioned partner and would make an equally good marriage today.

Venetian-style liver

An incredibly quickly cooked dish that is a favourite in the eastern part of Italy where the Po river comes down to the Adriatic sea. As with a lot of Venetian dishes, the style and flavours are reminiscent of the Levant, that part of the Middle East that the galley fleets of the 'serene republic' dominated for so long. Be ready to serve it instantly with rice and green peas.

Serves 4

2 tablespoons oil
675 g (1 ½ lb) large onions, peeled and very thinly sliced
1 clove garlic, peeled and crushed
Salt
½ teaspoon freshly ground nutmeg
½ teaspoon freshly ground black pepper
450 g (1 lb) calves' or lambs' liver, very thinly sliced
4 tablespoons cider or white wine vinegar
1 tablespoon butter

Heat the oil in a large frying pan and fry the onions and garlic until they are completely soft but not brown. Season with salt, add the spices, and put on a warmed oval serving plate. Turn the heat up and flash-fry the liver for only 30 seconds a side then add it to the onions. Swill the pan out with the cider or wine vinegar, allowing it to bubble, then add the butter. When it melts pour all over the liver and serve immediately.

WINE tip To complement the positive flavour, I'd go for the unlikely sounding partner of New Zealand Sauvignon Blanc.

Tongue

Tongue almost always in Britain means ox tongue, although you can sometimes buy fresh lambs' tongues. It also tends to mean salted or cured ox tongue. It is possible to cure your own, the problem is finding fresh ox tongue with which to do it. So, if you do find one and want to, the method for curing silverside of beef on page 169 will work equally well for tongue. Tongue is marvellous hot or cold, and the basic method of cooking is identical in both cases.

Rinse the tongue and trim off any particularly grim-looking bits with a sharp knife. If you're going to cook it in an ordinary saucepan, put it in with a couple of bay leaves, 6 peppercorns and 4 allspice berries, and enough water to cover the tongue completely. Bring it to the boil, turn the heat down, cover it with a lid and simmer gently for approximately 3 hours. If you're using a pressure cooker, add the same spices and herbs but only 2.5 cm (1 inch) of water, bring the cooker up to pressure, put on the control weight system and cook for 1 hour.

Whichever method you use, when the tongue has finished cooking, remove it from the pot, discard any remaining liquid, herbs, etc., and place on a secure board. With a sharp knife, split the skin, which will peel away from the basic meat. Wait till the tongue cools before you do this but don't let it get cold, after which the skin is harder to remove.

Cold

If you're going to eat it cold, curl the tongue round and put it into a soufflé or similar-shaped dish. Put a plate or saucer on it which will fit inside the soufflé dish and weight it with about 900 g (2 lb) of weight – a bag of flour, tins of tomatoes, or similar will do very well. Place it in the fridge with the weights on it and leave it to cool for at least 24 hours. You can then remove it from the soufflé dish and slice in the traditional way. Keep it refrigerated and use within 5 days.

187

Hot

To eat it hot, once you've skinned it, place it extended on a carving board and carve in slices across the grain. Serve it with a sauce made from 2 tablespoons of the cooking liquid, 175 ml (6 fl oz) of orange juice in which you have soaked a tablespoon of dried currants, a pinch of cinnamon, 2 teaspoons of cornflour slaked in 120 ml (4 fl oz) of water, and a teaspoon of butter. Put all these ingredients together into a non-stick saucepan, bring gently to the boil and stir until smooth. The resultant sweet and sour sauce is perfect with the hot, sliced tongue. Allowed to go cold and with the juice of half a lemon added, it makes an excellent accompaniment to the cold tongue as above.

WINE tip A light red Vin de Pays des Bouches-du-Rhône for cold tongue.

Gratin of sweetbreads

Sweetbreads are light and delicate. With this crafty technique they're also easy peasy and (as you will see) lemon squeezy. Serve this dish with tagliatelle and buttered spinach.

Serves 4

450 g (1 lb) sweetbreads
Juice of 1 lemon
40 g (1 ½ oz) butter
40 g (1 ½ oz) plain flour
300 ml (10 fl oz) milk
½ teaspoon ground bay leaves
½ teaspoon freeze-dried thyme
½ teaspoon freeze-dried sage
50 g (2 oz) Gruyère cheese
225 g (8 oz) button mushrooms
1 tablespoon grated Parmesan cheese
1 tablespoon fresh breadcrumbs

Pre-heat the oven to gas mark 6, 200°C (400°F).

Wash the sweetbreads, put them in a pan, just cover them with water and add the lemon juice. Bring to the boil, simmer 5 minutes, drain then press gently between two plates with a 225 g (8 oz) weight on top and leave to cool. When cold and firm, divide them into bite-sized pieces. Place the butter, flour and milk in a pan and gently bring to the boil, whisking 2 or 3 times until the sauce is smooth and thick. Add the herbs and the Gruyère cheese. Stir until smooth and melted.

Put a thin layer of the sauce in a large gratin dish, add the sweetbreads and mushrooms then cover with the rest of the sauce and sprinkle with the Parmesan and breadcrumbs. Bake in the oven for 20 minutes.

Kidneys in mustard and cream

Made with fresh lambs' kidneys, this dish has a flavour delicate enough for the most discerning of palates. This is a rich dish, though, so a small portion often goes a long way. It's also nice served in an individual pastry shell as a course on its own.

Serves 4

8 lambs' kidneys, trimmed and skinned
1 tablespoon oil
25 g (1 oz) butter
100 g (4 oz) button mushrooms, sliced
Salt and freshly ground black pepper
150 ml (5 fl oz) double cream (or 8 per cent fromage frais)
1 tablespoon made Dijon mustard

Cut the kidneys in half across into butterfly shapes. Melt the oil in a frying pan, add the butter and sauté the kidneys briskly for 3 minutes. Add the mushrooms, season with salt and pepper and add the cream and then the mustard. Stir until mixed, bring to the boil, and serve as quickly as possible. (Do not boil if using fromage frais.)

WINE tip If you prefer red – go for the buzzy style of French Minervois.

Kidneys in mustard and cream

Oxtail casserole

In the north of Italy, there's a famous dish made from shin of veal: osso buco. It is virtually impossible to obtain this cut in Britain, so the Milanese way of cooking it is adapted here to our own oxtail – a very delicious and nutritious cut that deserves far better than the ubiquitous soup. It's treated very differently in other countries. A French recipe involves cooking it with grapes, and there is a splendid Indian curry. This particular recipe has its special charm with the garnish traditionally added in Italy. A mixture of freshly chopped garlic, lemon rind and parsley, it's called a *gremolata*. Even if you're not a garlic-lover, you'll find that the combination of flavours and piquancy it adds to the long-simmered stew is really worth trying. Yellow rice is the traditional accompaniment to osso buco, but you could try mashed potatoes, or even pasta.

The majority of good butchers and supermarkets sell oxtail. For this recipe, ask the shop to slice it through the bone into slices approximately 2.5 cm (1 inch) thick.

Serves 4

2 tablespoons olive oil
900 g (2 lb) oxtail, in 2.5 cm (1 inch) slices
225 g (8 oz) onions, peeled and chopped
1 clove garlic, peeled and crushed
450 ml (15 fl oz) passata, or 1 × 500 g (18 oz) tin
    chopped tomatoes
½ teaspoon freeze-dried oregano
½ teaspoon freeze-dried thyme
½ teaspoon freeze-dried basil
Salt and freshly ground black pepper

For the garnish:
2 cloves garlic, peeled and finely chopped
Finely grated rind of 1 lemon
2 tablespoons chopped fresh parsley

Pre-heat the oven to gas mark 3, 160°C (325°F).

In a flameproof casserole, heat the oil and fry the oxtail pieces over high heat until browned. Add the onions, garlic, passata or chopped tomatoes, herbs and seasoning. Cover and place in the oven for 3 hours. Alternatively, simmer on the top of the stove, also for 3 hours. You will need to check at regular intervals to ensure it stays moist: if the casserole starts to dry out, add a little water. At the end of the cooking time, place the oxtail stew on an oval serving dish, or serve on a bed of long-grain rice coloured with saffron. Mix the garnish ingredients and sprinkle over the meat.

189

WINE tip Red Entre-Deux-Mers from Bordeaux, or if you want to go all Italian, go for the mighty Barolo, Spanna or Guttinara.

Oxtail casserole

Barbecues

Barbecuing isn't difficult but it's got its own rules, both for delicious results and safety. Here are a few of the most important do's and don'ts, plus a few recipe ideas as well. All of them are designed to feed about 10 people because barbecues always seem to be best when they're a real party. They're not too expensive either. Salmon and steak, can be quite reasonably priced. The idea is to feed the whole party for less than £25 – pretty good value when you think about it. There aren't many Sunday lunches indoors or outdoors these days you can get for £2.50 a head.

DO'S

1 Make sure your barbecue is in a safe place and steady on its feet, not near a passageway or a door.
2 Light it with a proper barbecue lighter – it's both safer and nicer smelling.
3 Light it in good time – at least 1 hour before you want to start cooking; that's at least 1½ hours before you want to start eating.
4 Wait until the charcoal is grey to the eye before starting to cook with it. That means it's properly alight and has enough heat to cook the food thoroughly (at night a dark, dull red colour may glow through the grey).
5 Have somewhere safe to put the food and tools within easy reach of the barbecue but not too close.
6 If you're cooking at night, make sure you have a good source of light so that you can see what you're doing and see how the food's cooking.
7 Have a bucket of water handy just in case things go badly wrong and you need to put the fire out in a hurry.
8 Have a water spray bottle handy (the kind you use for house plants). It will allow you to cool the coals down a bit if the food's starting to burn or cook too quickly.
9 Part-cook difficult things or food that takes a long time, like baked potatoes.
10 Have a fall-back position just in case it starts raining. Know what you're going to do and where you're going to put people indoors.
11 Grease the grid so that the food doesn't stick to it. This can be done with a little oil on a pastry brush. Do it before you put the grid to heat.

DON'TS

1 Don't use paraffin to light the coals. It will taint everything.
2 Don't economize on charcoal. You need enough to make sure that the food will cook thoroughly and quickly. You can always douse it afterwards, let it dry out and re-use it.
3 Don't use the grill as a work surface. If you need to cut food up or keep things warm, make sure you've got somewhere safe to put them that isn't too hot.
4 Don't put the barbecue up-wind of the guests, however delicious the steak's going to smell. Smoke gets in your eyes.
5 Don't put the food too close to the heat. Make sure the grid's at least 5 to 6 cm (2 to 2½ inches) away from the charcoal itself otherwise the food will burn on the outside before it's cooked on the inside.
6 Barbecued chicken is often known as 'Salmonella-on-a-stick'. Cook it gently, turning it often. Before serving, pierce it at its thickest point and ensure that the juices which come out are clear not bloody.
7 Don't leave preparation until the last minute. Try to get everything ready before you start to light the barbecue – that way you won't have to panic or perspire.
8 Don't forget long tongs and oven gloves – they make handling the food both safe and comfortable.
9 Don't forget appetites are much more keen outdoors so you'll probably need more food than you would indoors.
10 Don't wear your best clothes without a big apron.

THE BEST BANGERS
● **The legal minimum for meat is 65 per cent. But 'meat' covers a multitude of animal bits, so look at the label – the higher above 65 per cent the better (and, regrettably, the more expensive).**
● **'Premium' sausages are usually higher in meat but the term has no legal meaning. So, again, look at the label.**
● **Cheaper sausages with the legal minimum of meat tend to have lots of rusk (a biscuity filler) and fat to bulk them out, plus pink colouring to make the whole melange look like meat. Avoid.**
● **'Low-fat' sausages are a bit of a nonsense. Sausages are high in fat anyway and good flavour depends on a healthy dose of the stuff. If you want to eat less animal fat eat fewer, good quality sausages.**

So – your barbecue's lit, the coals are perfect, the party's in full swing – what are you going to eat? We've got three main course choices for you – Herbed Salmon Steaks, Sirloin Sizzlers, and South Seas Chicken with the most delicious peanut sauce.

Any normal-sized barbecue will cook enough for any of these main courses for 10 people. We suggest a choice of salads to go with them and my special magic potato bundles. For a dessert there's also a clever idea for cooking bananas in their skins.

Herbed salmon steaks

Serves 10

1 tablespoon soy sauce
1 tablespoon Worcestershire sauce
6 tablespoons lemon juice
6 tablespoons olive or salad oil
10 salmon steaks, cut across the fish approximately 2.5 cm (1 inch) thick
4 tablespoons chopped fresh or freeze-dried dill
150 g (5 oz) butter, softened
½ teaspoon salt
Grated rind of 2 lemons
Juice of 1 lemon

Mix together the soy sauce, Worcestershire sauce, lemon juice and oil and whisk thoroughly. Marinate the salmon steaks in the mixture for at least 2 hours and up to 12 (overnight in the fridge is fine), covered with foil or cling film. Mix the chopped dill into the softened butter with the salt, lemon rind and juice; mix well with a fork or in a food processor. Form into a long sausage shape, about 2.5 cm (1 inch) across, roll in foil and chill in the fridge.

Place the salmon steaks on the greased grill about 5 cm (2 inches) from the heat. Cook for 5 minutes a side, basting occasionally with the marinade. When they are cooked so that the meat flakes away from the bone, place them on warm plates. Cut the butter sausage into 10 pieces and place a round of herb dill butter on each golden grilled salmon steak.

Sirloin sizzlers

This uses an old-fashioned barbecue sauce in the style that's eaten in the southern states of America. It's a perfect accompaniment for steaks and you can keep a little saucepan of it warm on the corner of the barbecue to serve as an extra appetizer. Passata is thick, sieved, tomato purée, available in all supermarkets.

Serves 10

10 × 2 cm (¾ inch) sirloin steaks, fat trimmed and snipped in 3 places to prevent them curling
For the sauce:
1 tablespoon olive or salad oil
1 large onion, peeled and finely chopped
2 cloves garlic, peeled and finely chopped (or 2 teaspoons garlic purée)
½ teaspoon chilli powder
500 ml (½ litre) passata
1 red pepper, de-seeded and chopped
1 teaspoon salt
1 tablespoon brown sugar
1 tablespoon cider or white wine vinegar

To make the marinade, heat the oil and fry the onion, garlic and chopped pepper gently until softened. Add the chilli powder and fry for 1 minute. Add all the other sauce ingredients and stir until thoroughly mixed. Bring to the boil then turn down the heat and simmer for 20 minutes.

Brush the marinade thickly on to one side of the steaks and grill that side down, with 3 minutes for rare, 4 minutes for medium, 5 minutes for well done. Before turning, brush the uncooked side, turn and cook for the same length of time again. Brush the cooked side with marinade and when you serve, put a second coat on the other side. Serve the marinade separately for people to add more to the steaks as they eat them if they care to.

South seas chicken

This is a marvellous dish with a sauce that everybody seems to adore. It comes from the Spice Islands below the Malay Peninsula and is eaten there with meat on skewers like kebabs. We've suggested chicken breasts here to make an even more luxurious treat.

Serves 10

4 tablespoons soy sauce
4 tablespoons soft brown sugar
3 tablespoons lemon juice
10 chicken breasts (part-boned)
175 g (6 oz) crunchy peanut butter
1 tablespoon garlic salt
2 tablespoons tomato ketchup
1 teaspoon chilli powder (or to taste)
300 ml (10 fl oz) water

Mix the soy sauce, sugar and lemon juice together, pour over the chicken and leave to marinate for about 1 hour. Put the rest of the ingredients into a saucepan and bring to the boil over a gentle heat. At first this is going to look pretty unspectacular but don't worry – suddenly it will start to go smooth and shiny. Add the marinade and stir thoroughly till the whole sauce has gone glossy and light chocolate brown. Put the sauce to one side and grill the chicken breasts over the coals for 5 minutes skin side down, and 5 to 6 minutes, depending on how thick they are, bone side down.

Place the chicken breasts skin side up on to plates and pour a tablespoon of the sauce over them. Serve the rest of the sauce separately for guests to help themselves. In the unlikely event of you having any sauce left over, it makes the most wonderful peanut butter on toast.

Potato parcels

Serve any of the main courses with potato parcels. I think these are much better than traditional baked potatoes at a barbecue, not least because they cook much more easily and much more quickly. They're a bit of a cheat in a way in that the potatoes are pre-cooked before you bring them to the barbecue, but the final flavourings come through because of the heat from the coals, so it's not too naughty really.

Serves 10

1.65 kg (3½ lb) new potatoes, well scrubbed
Salt
100 g (4 oz) butter
1 handful chopped fresh parsley
1 handful chopped fresh chives or 2 tablespoons freeze-dried chives

Make sure the potatoes are all approximately the same size, bring them to the boil in salted water and cook for approximately 10 minutes until just starting to be tender. Drain them, and in the same saucepan melt the butter and add the herbs. Roll the potatoes in the buttered herbs till thoroughly coated and pack into 10 squares of foil with 3 or 4 potatoes in each and do up the top with a twisting action like giant packets of salt in crisp bags used to be. Do this while the potatoes are still hot and they will finish cooking in the parcels.

To serve; bring them out and place them on the barbecue coals for about 5 minutes to heat through and acquire the slightly smoky flavour. Each guest unwraps his own parcel of delicious herbed new potatoes to go with our main course.

St John's rice salad

A green salad with French dressing is highly recommended as a barbecue accompaniment. But there's another delicious salad that always seems to go down well, particularly with the more exotic main courses. It's named after the town on the east coast of Africa where they have wonderful barbecues in their velvety summer nights. Do believe us about the dressing, it may seem a bit peculiar at first but it works wonderfully.

Serves 10

450 g (1 lb) long-grain rice
1 teaspoon salt
A few drops of oil
225 g (8 oz) frozen peas
1 large bunch spring onions finely chopped
1 red pepper, de-seeded and finely chopped
100 g (4 oz) button mushrooms, finely chopped

For the sauce:
4 tablespoons tomato ketchup (really!)
2 tablespoons cider or white wine vinegar
2 tablespoons sugar
6 tablespoons water

For the garnish:
Cucumber slices
Cherry tomatoes, quartered

Mix all the sauce ingredients together and stir until the sugar has dissolved. Rinse the rice in a colander under some running water until the water flows clear, having washed the starch away. Put it into a saucepan with at least 10 cm (4 inches) of water to cover and add a teaspoon of salt and a drop of oil. Bring to the boil and simmer for 10 to 11 minutes until the rice is thoroughly cooked but not soggy. Drain it and tip another saucepan full of warm water from the tap or a kettle through the rice. Allow to drain thoroughly. Boil the peas for 2 minutes until hot but not khaki. Stir all the vegetables into the rice and pour the dressing over the rice while it is still warm. Mix thoroughly; it will go a pale and extremely pretty colour. Pile it into an attractive serving dish, cool then chill in the fridge. Before serving, decorate the salad with thinly sliced rounds of cucumber and quartered baby tomatoes.

Baked barbecue bananas

The best barbecue pudding of all – it's easy to do, exciting to watch and tastes scrumptious. Have a jug of cold single cream or yoghurt, a bowl of soft brown sugar or demerara and some lime or lemon quarters ready to go.

Serves 10

10 bananas, unpeeled
Cream or yoghurt, brown sugar and lime or lemon quarters as above

When you are cooking the savoury foods, leave a little room on the grill. Towards the end of the barbecuing, place the bananas on the grid close to the heat and packed closely together. Let them cook until the side nearest the charcoal is black, turn over and cook again on the other side. It should take about 10 minutes each side. When the skins are thoroughly black and the banana inside really hot, put one on each plate. Carefully peel one section of the skin back all the way along the banana so that you have a canoe of skin full of banana. Sprinkle brown sugar along the open section and a squeeze of lime or lemon, pour a little cream or yoghurt over it and eat with a teaspoon. The hot sweet banana, crunchy sugar, sharp citrus and cool cream are an unforgettable combination.

193

The basic principle for bread-making is to choose a flour with a good gluten content – this is what makes the bread spongy and elastic. They're often designated as 'strong' flours. Self-raising flour and ordinary cake-type flour don't make good bread.

bread and pizza

Key types of flour

White flour

This comes in a number of different grades, all of them containing approximately 70 per cent of the milled grain with the brown parts and the wheatgerm removed. There are two main types.

- **Bleached** This is white flour that has been treated so that it is as pure white as possible. It's not in any way unwholesome but does tend to lack flavour. It can produce spectacularly risen bread, though.
- **Unbleached** This is white flour which has not been treated in any way except to remove the part of the grain that would make it brown. It's a creamy colour and experts believe it makes the best white bread. It has a better flavour and a more substantial texture than bleached white.

Wholemeal flour

This is wheat flour that has been ground without the wheatgerm or bran being removed. It comes in two main categories.

- **Standard wholemeal** Produced in modern factories using high-speed steel rollers, standard wholemeal flour has a very even grain from which it is possible to produce reliable, high quality bread.
- **Stoneground** When wholemeal grain has been processed through the traditional millstones, the flour is less heated in the milling process and it is held by some to

produce a bread of better flavour. It is often produced in small batches by specialist millers. It can be coarser and larger grained than standard wholemeal.

Malted flours

There are two branded types of malted flour:
- **Granary** This is a wholemeal-style flour with malted (i. e. sprouted) grains ground into it and included in pieces. It makes a chunky bread with a sweetened flavour.
- **Cobber** Another malted, branded flour, mostly used by professionals to produce very crisp crusted rolls and bread. It's slightly finer ground than Granary but similar in most other respects.

Rye flour

Rye flour comes in both light and dark forms. Both are usually added to wheat flour for a satisfactory rise in the bread.

Barley

Barley bread was a staple in medieval Europe but it's very difficult to rise. A small proportion of barley flour is sometimes incorporated into wheat bread to give a rustic flavour and texture.

* * *

All the above flours, with the exception of the two brand malted flours, come in both normal and organic form. In addition to these, a range of specialist flours is emerging, often of a very traditional kind. One example is Spelt, used to make varieties of wholemeal bread with a particularly rich flavour.

195
....

Above: *Light wholemeal bread* (page 198). Below: *Farmhouse white bread* (page 197)

VITAMIN C – THE GREAT IMPROVER

Vitamin C, or ascorbic acid, is a plain white powder that's often added to bread flour – it's the only ingredient permitted as an additive in France. It's not done for health reasons – vitamin C has a spectacularly helpful effect on rising bread. The bread not only rises up to three times faster, but often rises higher too. It is debatable whether it should be used as a matter of course. But whatever the purists may say, it can certainly improve the quality of home-made bread.

Seven key points for making bread

1. Time

You have to allow enough time for making bread. It doesn't take *you* long. But the bread has one or two natural rising periods. During this time you can get on with anything else. Different loaves and different mixtures vary but allow at least 2 hours from start to finish. However you will only need to spend about 15 minutes *actively* making the bread.

2. Warmth

It is possible to get bread to rise in cold conditions, in larders or even in fridges, but it's a very long and slow process. Steady, draught-free warmth is ideal if you can arrange it. Such conditions can be achieved inside a bowl covered with cling film, if nowhere else. Warm your hands and equipment – even your flour – before starting.

3. Yeast

There are a wide range of dried yeasts on the market, many of which can be mixed straight into the dough as you make it without any pre-preparation. While they're very convenient, none of them provides the same rise as *fresh* yeast. Fresh yeast looks like fudge and can be bought from bakers and most supermarkets with baking sections. It is inexpensive and keeps well in the fridge for up to a fortnight. You need about 25 g (1 oz) of yeast or a packet of dried yeast for 1–1.5 kg (2¼–3¼ lb) of flour. To work the yeast when it's fresh you need to mix it with half a teaspoon of sugar and a little of the water you're using for the bread, preferably at finger heat. It'll foam in about 10 to 15 minutes at which point it's ready to use.

4. Kneading

All bread needs to be kneaded. Good food mixers or food processors with kneading blades attached take some of the work out of it. It can also be a very satisfying process by hand. But you must be prepared to devote at least 5 to 6 minutes continuous hard work for the first kneading and another couple of minutes second time round.

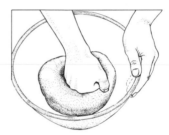

The best way to knead by hand is in a large bowl using the heel and clenched fist of your hand. Don't try to do it by squeezing with your fingers

5. Shaping

Bread benefits from shaping before it's baked. When you've finished the two rises and are about to put it into tins don't just cut off a lump and drop it in but try and roll it round itself into a sort of cushion shape. This will help it to rise more uniformly and more attractively.

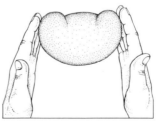

For bread, roll into a cushion shape before baking

Rolls should be rolled between the palms of your hands like plasticine marbles in order to achieve a good round and cohesive shape

6. Proving

Proving is the formal word for making the bread rise. Most recipes require you to do this twice, knocking it down, (i. e. kneading it again) in the middle. The first rise will normally take between 45 minutes to 1½ hours depending on whether you're using vitamin C and whether your kitchen is warm and draught-free. It's important to let bread rise enough but not too much. The best indication is that when it's fully proved the first time: 1.4 kg (3 lb) of flour will fill a standard-sized mixing bowl when fully risen. If it overproves the first time it's not a catastrophe.

For the second rising you put the dough into tins, normally leaving about 4 cm (1½ inches) of tin still showing. When it's proved the second time the bread should have risen above the edges of the tins but not have flopped over into a kind of dead mushroom shape. If it has, sprinkle a little more flour over it and knead it again. Then put it back into the tins and allow it to prove once more. Otherwise when you bake it, it will just produce soggy and unpleasant bread.

7. Baking

To make good bread you need a hot oven with plenty of pre-heating time. For most bread and rolls the right temperature is gas mark 7, 220°C (425°F), 190°C in a fan oven and the roasting oven of an Aga. But check with the manufacturers' recommendations as well, particularly for fan ovens. Some recipes recommend that you turn the oven down after putting in the bread, but if you're putting in several loaves (as most of our recipes allow for) the oven temperature will be lowered pretty effectively by the addition of the bread itself. If you find it's cooking too fast and burning on the top, turn the oven down to about gas mark 4, 180°C (350°F) or 160°C in a fan oven. In the Aga put in the baking sheet above the bread to produce a cooler area. Bake for about 45 to 55 minutes.

The way to tell if bread is cooked is to tip it out of its tin (or pick it up from the base if it's not tinned) and tap it. If it sounds hollow, like knocking on a door, it's ready. If not, it needs another 5 minutes or so, possibly upside down. Always allow bread to cool completely on a rack before eating it. It will smell delicious but not have a good texture if you cut it or try to eat it before it's properly cooled.

Five great loaves

Farmhouse white

This is the traditional, big, crusty loaf of English high tea. Made from unbleached flour, it's one of the most attractive and delicious loaves there is.

Makes 2 × 1.1 kg (2½ lb) loaves

25 g (1 oz) butter, softened
1.4 kg (3 lb) unbleached white flour
1 heaped teaspoon salt
½ teaspoon sugar
25 g (1 oz) fresh yeast (or 1 sachet dried yeast)
900 ml (1½ pints) warm water
¼ teaspoon vitamin C (optional)
1 tablespoon sunflower oil

Mix the soft butter into the flour with your fingertips or in the food mixer then add the salt. Mix together the sugar and yeast, add a cupful of the warm water and leave to ferment for 10 minutes until it's frothy. Add the vitamin C, if using, to the flour. Add the frothy yeast and the rest of the water and knead thoroughly for 5 to 6 minutes until the dough becomes elastic. Oil the bowl and turn the dough in it so it doesn't stick. Cover the bowl with a damp tea towel or cling film and leave it in a warm place for approximately 30 minutes if using vitamin C or for 1 hour if not. The dough will rise to the top of the bowl.

Grease 2 × 1.1 kg (2½ lb) farmhouse-sized loaf tins. Punch down the dough and knead it again for 1½ minutes. Divide it in half and use to fill the prepared loaf tins. Cover with a tea towel and leave the bread to rise in a warm place until it is proud of the tins.

Pre-heat the oven to gas mark 7, 220°C (425°F).

With a sharp knife, cut a slit along the length of the loaf to a depth of 5 mm (½ inch), slightly offset from the centre. Sprinkle with a little more flour and bake as above for 45 to 55 minutes. The bread will rise and open along the cut, providing the classic farmhouse design.

197

Light wholemeal bread

This is a loaf with many of the qualities of wholemeal bread – a strong, wheaty flavour and firm texture – but minus the heaviness which is sometimes associated with it. You can substitute all wholemeal flour for the mixture of wholemeal and white I recommend, in which case it will be a pure wholemeal loaf and a little heavier than the original version.

Makes 2 × 900 g (2 lb) loaves

25 g (1 oz) fresh yeast (or 1 sachet dried yeast)
½ teaspoon sugar
900 ml (1½ pints) warm water
900 g (2 lb) wholemeal bread flour
450 g (1 lb) unbleached bread flour
1 teaspoon salt
¼ teaspoon vitamin C (optional)
1 tablespoon sunflower oil

Place the yeast in a small bowl, add the sugar and a cupful of the warm water and stir until smooth. Leave it to stand for 10 minutes until it's frothy. Mix the two flours, the salt, the vitamin C if using, and the oil in a large, warm bowl and stir in the yeast mixture and the remaining warm water to form a soft dough. Knead it thoroughly (using a machine or by hand) until the dough is elastic. Oil the bowl with a little extra oil, turn the dough in it so that it doesn't stick, cover with a damp tea towel or cling film and leave it to rise for approximately 45 minutes in a warm place.

Grease 2 × 900 g (2 lb) loaf tins. Knead the dough again, either by hand or by machine, for a few minutes. Divide it in two and place it in the loaf tins. Put them in a warm place, cover with a tea towel or cling film and allow to rise again until the bread is about 2.5 cm (1 inch) above the edge of the tins.

Pre-heat the oven to gas mark 7, 220°C (425°F).

Bake in the oven as above for 45 to 50 minutes. If they are not quite hollow sounding, leave them out of the tin to bake a further 5 minutes, preferably on their sides.

Three seed bread

This is an unusual bread which is enormously appealing. As well as the nuttiness of the flour there's a range of seeds in the bread itself which add crunch and flavour. The seeds are available in supermarkets and health food shops. It's important to note this bread must cool thoroughly, preferably overnight.

Makes 1 × 750 g (1½ lb) loaf

Generous 15 g (½ oz) fresh yeast (or 1 sachet dried yeast)
1 tablespoon golden syrup
200 ml (7 fl oz) warm water
¼ teaspoon salt
1 tablespoon sunflower oil
350 g (12 oz) wholemeal flour
50 g (2 oz) peeled sunflower seeds
25 g (1 oz) sesame seeds
25 g (1 oz) peeled pumpkin seeds

Mix the yeast with a teaspoon of the golden syrup and a little of the warm water and stir. Leave it to stand for 10 minutes until it is frothy. Put the rest of the syrup, the salt, oil and flour together in a mixing bowl. When the yeast is frothy, add it to the flour with the warm water and knead thoroughly. Put a little oil in the bowl, turn the dough in it, cover with a damp tea towel or cling film and leave to rest for about 1 hour, until it has risen well.

Grease a 900 g (2 lb) loaf tin. Knock the dough down with the back of your hand, add the seeds and knead thoroughly until they are mixed in. Put the dough into the loaf tin, cover and leave it to rise for about another 35 to 40 minutes.

Pre-heat the oven to gas mark 7, 220°C (425°F).

Bake the bread for about 45–50 minutes as above until the bottom sounds hollow. Turn out of the tin to cool.

From top: *Three seed bread*; *Rye bread* (page 200); *Italian bread* (page 201)

Rye bread

Despite the name, rye bread contains a significant proportion of wheat flour; this makes it rise satisfactorily. Without it, the bread would be extremely flat and dense. This is a light rye loaf with a pleasant fresh, slightly sour, flavour.

Makes 1 × 900 g (2 lb) loaf

20 g (¾ oz) fresh yeast (or 1 sachet of dried yeast)
A pinch of sugar
250 ml (8 fl oz) warm water
350 g (12 oz) unbleached white flour
175 g (6 oz) wholemeal rye flour
1 teaspoon salt
A pinch of vitamin C (optional)
2 tablespoons natural yoghurt

Cream the yeast with the sugar and a little of the water and leave for about 10 minutes until frothy. Mix the two flours together with the salt and the vitamin C, if using. Stir the yoghurt into the remaining warm water, add it to the dough with the yeast mixture and knead thoroughly. The dough may be a little moist, or too dry, so you may need to add a little more water or flour to correct it (flours vary in moisture content). Lightly oil the bowl, turn the dough in it so that it doesn't stick, cover with a damp tea towel or cling film and leave to rise for about 1 hour. It will not rise as much as wholewheat bread dough.

Grease a 900 g (2 lb) loaf tin. Knead the dough thoroughly again for 2 to 3 minutes by hand then place it in the loaf tin. Turn the tin upside down on to a baking sheet and allow the dough to fall out of the tin in the rough loaf shape. Cover and leave to rise like this in a warm place for about 40 minutes.

Pre-heat the oven to gas mark 7, 220°C (425°F).

Bake the bread in the oven for about 50 minutes. The bread will take on the characteristic shape of rye bread which is a long, plump roll.

Additions and Decorations

There are a number of additions and decorations you can make to alter the appearance, texture and sometimes the flavour of bread. Here are the basic ones:

Washes

- **Salt** A mixture of a tablespoon of salt dissolved in 4 tablespoons of water brushed over a loaf before baking produces a salt glaze, a very shiny appearance that doesn't alter the colour of the bread very much.
- **Milk** Brushed over the bread just before baking, milk produces a more golden colour with a matt finish.
- **Beaten egg** Brushed over the loaf, egg produces a bright golden colour and a very shiny finish.

Sprinkles

- Before baking the bread you can sprinkle it with some flour to produce a farmhouse dusty appearance.
- Cracked wheat, particularly good with wholemeal bread, gives it a crunchy and rustic appearance.
- Sesame seeds make for a Mediterranean-style bread.
- Coarse salt, used sparingly, produces a rough texture and crunchy taste.

DELICIOUS ADDITIONS
Try mixing the following into the bread at the last kneading before baking:
● **a tablespoon or two of herbs, freeze-dried or fresh;**
● **stoned, chopped olives;**
● **walnut pieces (particularly good as a replacement for some of the seeds in Three Seed Bread on page 198);**
● **100 g (4 oz) mixed dried fruit, 50 g (2 oz) butter and a tablespoon of brown sugar to make a white loaf turn into a currant loaf.**

Italian bread

Italian bread has become very popular in Britain in recent years (although the loaf that's led the way, Ciabatta, is a speciality loaf even in Italy). Italian bread is almost inevitably white bread but has a denser texture and is chewier than the white bread that we're used to in Britain. Partly this is the flour – they often use flour with a surprising amount of quite coarsely ground semolina in it. But with or without that, the crucial ingredient tends to be the addition of a substantial amount of olive oil. It's a very similar dough to that which is used to make Focaccia and pizza bases. However, it makes a pleasant loaf and even better rolls.

Makes 2 × 400 g (14 oz) loaves

15 g (½ oz) fresh yeast (or ½ sachet dried yeast)
A pinch of sugar
300 ml (½ pint) warm water
4 tablespoons olive oil
1 teaspoon salt
¼ teaspoon vitamin C (optional)
450 g (1 lb) unbleached white flour

Cream the yeast and sugar with a little of the warm water and leave to stand for 10 minutes until frothy. Mix the oil, salt and vitamin C, if using, into the flour. Add the yeast mixture and knead for a minute or so. Gradually add the remaining water, making sure that the dough doesn't become too moist to handle. You may not need all of it, it depends on the flour. Add another tablespoon of oil to the bowl, roll the bread dough in it, cover with a damp tea towel or cling film and leave to rise for 45 to 50 minutes (25 to 30 minutes if using vitamin C).

Knock down the dough and knead again thoroughly, making sure all the oil from the bowl is incorporated into the dough. Divide into 2 pieces of dough and roll each out to about 23 cm (9 inches) long. Press to flatten a little (about 1-inch thick) on to a baking sheet, cover and leave to rise for 35 to 40 minutes at the most. If you prefer you can make them into 8 rolls, usually of a slightly elongated shape.

Pre-heat the oven to gas mark 7, 220°C (425°F).

Bake the bread in the oven for about 40 minutes for loaves or 25 minutes for rolls.

Pizza from Italian bread

If you want pizza, at the second kneading of Italian bread add another tablespoon of olive oil and knead the dough thoroughly. Divide into two and spread out on baking sheets, Swiss roll tins or suitable pizza bases, using your hands rather than a rolling pin to spread it out until it is about 5 mm (½ inch) thick all over. You can then use any of the pizza toppings below. Allow the dough to rise once it's been topped for 15 to 20 minutes and then bake at gas mark 7, 220°C (425°F) for about 15 to 25 minutes depending on the toppings.

201

Focaccia

Pizza toppings

Focaccia

This is the simplest form of flavoured bread, eaten with anti-pasti, hors d'oeuvres or sometimes on its own with nothing more than a few olives or radishes and a glass or two of something. It's nicest fresh out of the oven.

Sprinkle the dough with a teaspoon of coarse salt for each piece of bread and either a tablespoon of finely chopped onion, or 4 to 5 sage leaves torn up, or 2 teaspoons of rosemary crumbled through your fingers. Bake at gas mark 7, 220°C (425°F) for 15 to 20 minutes.

Pizza Margherita

This is perhaps the most famous of all Italian pizzas, named after the first queen of United Italy. It represents the colours of the Italian flag. You can buy garlic purée in the supermarket or make it yourself by crushing some garlic cloves with a little salt.

For each pizza base

1 teaspoon garlic purée
1 tablespoon tomato purée
100 g (4 oz) tinned chopped Italian tomatoes
100 g (4 oz) Mozzarella cheese, chopped or coarsely grated
4 fresh basil leaves or 1 teaspoon freeze-dried basil
1 teaspoon olive oil

Pre-heat the oven to gas mark 7, 220°C (425°F).

Spread the garlic purée all over the pizza base. Spread the tomato purée on top of that, making sure it reaches the edges. Spoon over the chopped tomato and spread that evenly as well. Top with the Mozzarella and sprinkle with the basil and oil. Bake in the oven for 15 to 20 minutes until bubbling and golden.

Pizza margherita

Sicilian seafood pizza

Mozzarella and mushroom pizza

Sicilian seafood pizza

A cheese-less pizza this time, but one which is greatly enriched with a variety of seafood favourites and ingredients.

For each pizza base

1 tablespoon tomato purée
100 g (4 oz) tinned chopped Italian tomatoes
100 g (4 oz) tuna in oil
50 g (2 oz) prawns
6–12 anchovies (to taste)
1 teaspoon olive oil
½ teaspoon chopped fresh or freeze-dried thyme
½ teaspoon chopped fresh or freeze-dried oregano

Pre-heat the oven to gas mark 7, 220°C (425°F).

Spread the tomato purée over the pizza base and top with the chopped tomatoes. Finely flake the tuna in its oil and spread that as evenly as possibly over the tomato mixture. Arrange the prawns on top and arrange the anchovies radiating out from the centre like the spokes of a wheel. Sprinkle with the oil, thyme and oregano and bake in the oven for 15 to 20 minutes until bubbling.

Mozzarella and mushroom pizza

This tomato-less pizza has a lovely chewy texture to the topping.

For each pizza base

225 g (8 oz) Mozzarella cheese, chopped or coarsely grated
100 g (4 oz) button mushrooms, finely sliced
50 g (2 oz) Parmesan cheese, finely grated
1 teaspoon chopped fresh or freeze-dried oregano
1 tablespoon olive oil

Pre-heat the oven to gas mark 7, 220°C (425°F).

Spread half the Mozzarella on the pizza base, top with the mushrooms then a second layer of Mozzarella. Sprinkle on a layer of Parmesan, followed by oregano and oil. Bake in the oven for 15 to 20 minutes until golden.

In general a young red Chianti is a good bet. And for the Sicilian Seafood Pizza a Sicilian red (or white). Or, as a refreshing mouthful, how about Italian beer?

CHAPTER FOURTEEN

Shortcrust, pâte brisée, choux, hot water paste pastries to make at home, and puff and filo pastry to buy.

pastry

Three key facts about pastry

1. Flour

One common thing about all pastries, is a standard form of flour – plain flour, finely ground and preferably white. It is possible to make pastry with wholemeal flour but it has the texture and very often the appeal of soggy shoe leather.

2. Fats

It's possible to use a variety of different fats for making pastry. Most low-fat spreads, however, won't do. Butter or one of the vegetable fats designed for pastry-making (like Trex or Cookeen) are preferable.

3. Cooking utensils

Although fluted china tart dishes look good, the best pastry is normally cooked in tinware, non-stick or unlined. It produces a crisper result, does not need baking blind and the pastry is easier to remove, especially with loose-based kinds. The exceptions are the old-fashioned pie dishes which use no pastry lining and are only lidded by pastry – these are perfect for big savoury pies.

FACT FILE

MIXING
You can make pastry by hand or use a food processor. If you're making it by hand you need to rub the fat into the flour with your fingertips until it's the texture of fine breadcrumbs. Make a well in the centre of the pile of flour and fat, pour in the liquid and draw flour in over the top until it's all mixed together. If you're using a food processor put in everything except the liquid and process for 10 to 15 seconds. Then add the liquid and process until the mixture balls up around the knife. Don't overprocess the pastry or it will go hard.

205
· · · · · · · · · · · ·

Rub the fat into the flour with your fingertips until it's the texture of fine breadcrumbs

Make a well in the centre and pour in the liquid

Above: *Strawberry tarts* (page 211). Below: *Smoked salmon quiche* (page 208)

Four pastries to make

1. Shortcrust pastry

The traditional British pastry, which can be made either savoury or sweet, has a pleasant, flaky texture. This is the basic savoury version. For sweet Shortcrust Pastry, add a tablespoon of icing sugar to the original flour mixture.

175 g (6 oz) plain flour
A pinch of salt
75 g (3 oz) butter
2–3 tablespoons water

Mix the flour, salt and butter together by hand or in a processor until the mixture resembles fine breadcrumbs. Add the water a tablespoon at a time until the pastry binds together. Knead it carefully, wrap it in cling film and place it in a fridge to rest for 30 minutes.

2. Pâte brisée (French-style shortcrust pastry)

This is a rather tougher pastry than our shortcrust, more crumbly and less flaky to eat, and can usually be rolled more thinly. To make a sweet version, Pâte Sablée, add 50 g (2 oz) caster sugar and reduce the flour by 25 g (1 oz).

150 g (5 oz) plain flour
65 g (2½ oz) butter
½ teaspoon salt
1 egg yolk
1–2 tablespoons cold water

Mix together the flour, butter and salt until the mixture resembles fine breadcrumbs. Add the egg yolk and then the water, ½ tablespoon at a time, until the pastry binds together. If you're making it by hand it may need a little less water than if you're using a food processor. Either way, when it's made, give it a set of firm compacting pressures with the heel of your hand, wrap it in cling film and leave it to rest for 30 minutes before using.

3. Choux pastry

This is the pastry that is used for profiteroles and éclairs (which of course can be filled with savoury creams like haddock mousse as well as sweet creams). You can make it by hand, but it's easier and quicker to use a food processor.

250 ml (8 fl oz) water
50 g (2 oz) butter
150 g (5 oz) flour
3 eggs

Pre-heat the oven to gas mark 7, 220°C (425°F), and grease a baking sheet.

Bring the water to the boil in a small saucepan, turn off the heat, add the butter, and leave it to melt. Put the flour into the food processor and, with the motor running, pour the boiling water and butter mixture in through the feed tube; it will instantly form a paste. Return the paste to the saucepan and cook, stirring gently, for 3 to 4 minutes. Break the eggs into a jug. Put the mixture back in the food processor bowl and, with the motor running, add the eggs one at a time. The pastry will now be pale gold and look like very sticky, thick cream.

Place tablespoonfuls of the pastry on the greased baking sheet in dollops for profiteroles or in long sausage shapes for éclairs. Or you may use it to fill an icing bag with a 5 mm (½ inch) nozzle and pipe fancier shapes directly on to the tray. Bake in the oven for 25 minutes. The buns will rise so make sure there's enough space for them to do so. When they're cooked and golden brown, take them out of the oven and prick a hole with a skewer in the top of each one to let the steam escape. This will keep the shell crisp and firm. Split and fill to taste.

4. Hot water paste

This is used for the old-fashioned and delicious British raised pies or game pasties. It's easy to make and extremely durable. It used to be made with lard but in these rather more enlightened days one of the vegetable-based cooking fats is probably a better bet.

200 ml (7 fl oz) water
175 g (6 oz) white fat
1 teaspoon salt
450 g (1 lb) plain flour

Put the water, fat and salt in a non-stick saucepan and bring gently to the boil. Turn off the heat and tip the flour all at once into the saucepan. Stir thoroughly until you have a firm but soft paste. This should be used while it's still warm and pliable. It can be rolled out but is usually moulded by hand into appropriate shapes in tins or over a mould made from glasses or casseroles to achieve the right shape.

Two pastries to buy

1. Puff pastry

Puff pastry, can of course, be made by hand but it's a long, skilled and, frankly, tedious process that only produces good results once you've acquired much expertise. As this takes ages to achieve, it is a good idea to buy one of the many excellent butter or vegetarian-based puff pastries, fresh or frozen.

2. Filo pastry

Filo pastry is the very thin sheets of pastry used to make things like apple strudel and baklava. Once again, it can be made by hand but requires skill, time and dedication. It's much better bought – either frozen or fresh.

Five sweet and five savoury recipes for your pastry

Cheese and onion quiche

This is a classic French combination to make in a shell of Pâte Brisée. It's a rich filling that makes an excellent first course or a splendid light lunch with a salad.

Serves 4

1 tablespoon butter
225 g (8 oz) onions, peeled and very thinly sliced
1 quantity Pâte Brisée (see page 206)
150 g (5 oz) Gruyère or Leicester cheese, finely grated
2 eggs
1 egg yolk
200 ml (7 fl oz) milk
A pinch of freshly grated nutmeg

Pre-heat the oven to gas mark 7, 220°C (425°F).

Melt the butter and fry the onions gently for about 5 minutes until they're soft but not brown. Use the pastry to line a 20 cm (8 inch) metal flan dish and spread the onion mixture on that. (If you prefer a china quiche dish, bake the pastry blind. Line the pastry with tin foil and dried beans and bake in a pre-heated oven for 10 to 15 minutes at gas mark 6, 200°C (400°F).) Cover with the cheese. Beat the eggs and milk together and pour over the top. The mixture should come to about 5 mm (¼ inch) below the rim. Sprinkle with nutmeg and bake in the oven for about 25 minutes. Reduce the temperature to gas mark 5, 190°C (375°F) for another 10 minutes until the top is brown and the pastry cooked through. Serve it hot for maximum lift. It's still delicious cold but does sink a little.

WINE **Eggs murder a wine so the wine**
tip **should match the other ingredients – and don't spend too much on it. A good off-dry French Vouvray or spicy Gewürztraminer for the cheese and onion (it would match the Smoked Salmon Quiche as well).**

Smoked salmon quiche

A luxury quiche that can be made either in one big dish or in individual mini quiches for a first course. If you're doing the latter you will need to reduce the cooking time by about 10 minutes.

Serves 4

1 quantity Pâte Brisée (see page 206)
175 g (6 oz) smoked salmon (off-cut pieces will do
   perfectly)
200 ml (7 fl oz) milk
2 eggs
1 egg yolk
2 teaspoons cornflour
1 tablespoon grated Parmesan cheese

Pre-heat the oven to gas mark 7, 220°C (425°F).

Use the pastry to line a 20 cm (8 inch) metal flan dish. (If you prefer a china dish, see instructions for baking blind on page 207, Cheese and Onion Quiche.) Take 50 g (2 oz) of the smoked salmon and purée it with the milk in a liquidizer. Add the eggs, egg yolk and cornflour and process again for a moment until thoroughly mixed. Put a layer of smoked salmon into the quiche, pour in the egg mixture then decorate with the remaining pieces of smoked salmon and the cheese. Bake in the oven for 25 to 30 minutes. Serve hot.

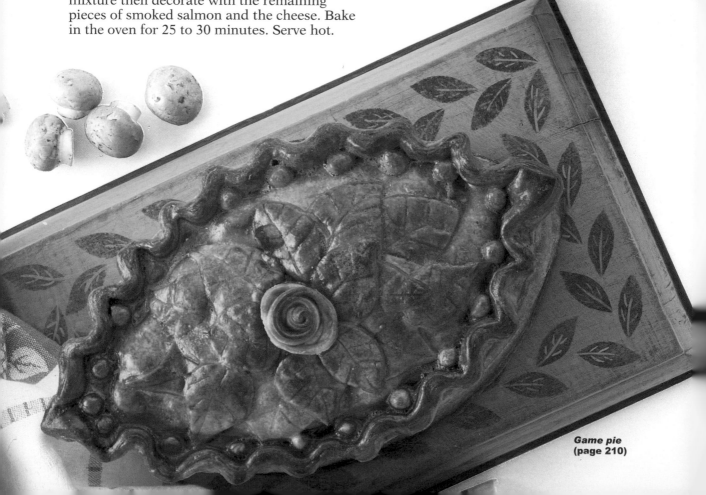

Steak and kidney pie

Game pie
(page 210)

Chicken pie (page 210)

Steak and kidney pie

One of the great traditions of British cooking, this dish goes back almost as far as the pudding of the same name. You can make it with shortcrust pastry but it's perhaps most exciting of all cooked with puff pastry. In either case the pastry normally only makes a lid. An old-fashioned pie dish is ideal for this, as is any solid earthenware casserole. It's delicious served with plenty of mashed potatoes and crispy cooked cabbage (see page 114).

Serves 4

25 g (1 oz) beef dripping or sunflower oil
675 g (1½ lb) braising steak
4 lambs' kidneys
25 g (1 oz) plain flour
225 g (8 oz) button mushrooms, halved
1 large onion, peeled and finely chopped
1 tablespoon Worcestershire sauce
Salt and freshly ground black pepper
600 ml (1 pint) beef stock
1 quantity Shortcrust Pastry (see page 206)
or 175–225 g (6–8 oz) puff pastry
Egg or milk for glazing

Heat the dripping or oil in a frying pan. Cut the stewing steak and trimmed kidneys into 2.5 cm (1 inch) squares and toss them in the flour. Put the meat into the oil or dripping and fry until lightly browned. Add the mushrooms and onion and sprinkle over the remaining flour. Allow this mixture to go pale golden brown, add the Worcestershire sauce, season generously with salt and pepper and add enough stock just to cover the meat. Simmer for 30 to 45 minutes until the beef is almost tender. Pre-heat the oven to gas mark 2, 150°C (300°F).

Transfer the mixture to a pie dish and check for seasoning. Roll out the pastry to fit the top of the dish and leave enough to make a thin sausage of pastry to put around the edge. Moisten the edge of the dish, place the sausage of pastry around it, moisten again and put the lid on top of that. Trim the edges, cut slots in the middle and, if you like a fine finish, brush with beaten egg. If you're using puff pastry or shortcrust you can use off-cuts to decorate the lid; traditionally leaves and flowers are the pattern. Glaze with a little beaten egg or milk. Bake in the oven for 1 hour. If the pastry is browning too quickly, put a piece of greaseproof paper over the top to allow the meat to cook through properly.

Chicken pie

A lovely, simple farmhouse recipe for a very substantial and delicious pie, this is the sort of pie that used to be made, and perhaps still should be, with a boiling fowl rather than a roasting bird. If you can find one, you'll need to cook it for about 30 minutes longer than a roaster.

serves 4

1 × (1.4 kg) 3 lb chicken
225 g (8 oz) carrots
225 g (8 oz) leeks
A good stalk of parsley
1 bay leaf
225 g (8oz) button mushrooms
2 hard-boiled eggs, quartered
1 tablespoon plain flour
Salt and freshly ground black pepper
1 tablespoon chopped fresh parsley
1 quantity Shortcrust Pastry (see page 206)
1 egg, beaten

Put the chicken (and giblets if you have any) into a saucepan big enough to hold them comfortably. Cover them with water, bring to the boil and skim off any scum. Peel the carrots and clean the leeks thoroughly in running water. Cut them into 2.5 cm (1 inch) pieces. Add the washed leek trimmings, the parsley stalk and the bay leaf to the chicken and simmer until it is tender – 35 to 40 minutes for a roasting chicken, about 1¼ hours for a boiler. Take the chicken and the flavouring ingredients out of the stock, add the leeks and carrots and continue to simmer for 5 minutes.

Pre-heat the oven to gas mark 7, 220°C (425°F).

When the chicken is cold enough to handle, skin it and remove the flesh from the bones. Drain the leeks and carrots and assemble them, the chicken and the button mushrooms in a 1.2 litre (2 pint) pie dish or casserole. Place the hard-boiled egg quarters on top.

Pour 300 ml (½ pint) of the stock into a separate pan and whisk in the flour. Season it generously, sprinkle the chopped parsley into the sauce and pour over the chicken, leek and vegetable mixture. Use a little of the pastry to make a thin sausage which you press on to the moistened rim of the pie dish or casserole. Roll the rest of the pastry out thinly and use to cover the casserole, trimming the edges and decorating the pie. Glaze with egg, cut a couple of slots in the top and bake in the oven for 25 minutes until the pastry is browned.

Game pie

This can be eaten hot or cold, sliced and out of a fancy mould or a loaf tin.

Serves 4

900 g (2 lb) game (stewing venison, the saddle and legs of a hare, a cut-up pheasant, or a combination)
2 tablespoons oil
225 g (8 oz) onions, peeled and quartered
2 tablespoons plain flour
4 tablespoons redcurrant jelly
½ tablespoon dried thyme
½ tablespoon dried marjoram
½ tablespoon ground bay leaves
Salt and freshly ground black pepper
1 quantity Hot Water Paste (see page 207)
100 g (4 oz) button mushrooms
1 egg, beaten
175 ml (6 fl oz) jelly stock (or tinned jelly consommé)

Clean and trim the game and remove as many bones as you can. Put the meat in a saucepan and cover with water. Bring to the boil, skim off any scum and simmer for 30 minutes. Meanwhile, heat the oil and fry the onions for 3 to 4 minutes. Process until smooth. Add the flour and 3 cups of the stock in which the game has been cooking and process again until it makes a smooth sauce. Take the meat from the stock and remove the bones. Mix with the redcurrant jelly, onion sauce and herbs and season.

Pre-heat the oven to gas mark 5, 190°C (375°F). Use two-thirds of the pastry to line a loaf tin or pie mould. Using hot water paste you'll find it easiest to do this by hand, pressing the pastry into shape while still warm. Fill with the game and sauce mixture and place the mushrooms in an even pattern along the top. Roll out the remaining pastry and use to cover the tin, crimping the edges. Brush the pie with a beaten egg, make two deep slits in the centre and bake in the oven for 55 minutes to 1 hour until the filling is cooked through and the pastry well browned. A piece of foil over the top prevents the pastry browning too quickly. Take out of the oven and allow to cool. If eating cold pour a little of the consommé through the slits in the top until the pie is full. Chill for 24 hours in the fridge before slicing.

 WINE tip — French Côtes du Roussillon – full and fleshy to cope with all the complex flavours – or South African Pinotage.

French fruit flan

This is the classic open French fruit tart that adorns restaurant tables throughout the year. You can make it very simply with this recipe or, to make it grander, add a measure of Crème Pâtissière (see page 213) between the pastry and the fruit.

Serves 4

900 g (2 lb) fruit (pears, peaches, apricots, plums or apples)
1 quantity Pâte Sablée (see page 206)
4 tablespoons apricot jam
4 tablespoons water

Pre-heat the oven to gas mark 6, 200°C (400°F) and grease a 20 cm (8 inch) round flan tin or Swiss roll tin.

Core or stone the fruit as appropriate but don't peel it; slice it thinly. Line the flan tin with the pastry. Fill the centre with a piece of foil or rice or beans to weigh it down and bake in the oven for 15 minutes. Take it out, remove the foil and beans and put it back into the oven for 5 minutes to dry out the centre. It should be pale biscuit-coloured gold all over. Remove and cool. If you're using Crème Pâtissière, fill the base of the flan with a layer at this point, then, with or without the cream, arrange the fruit in neat overlapping rows. Melt the apricot jam and water together and glaze the fruit with them. Return to the hot oven for 15 to 20 minutes, making sure that the pastry doesn't burn at the edges. It can be served hot but is more usually served cooled. If it looks a little caught at the top, don't worry, this is the glaze caramelizing and is quite authentic.

WINE *tip* | **Essencia or Orange Muscat from California or Monbazillac from Bergerac in France – not as sweet as Sauternes.**

Strawberry tarts

These are quite the most delightful fruit tarts in season and, in the form of small, boat-shaped pastry shells, the prettiest. The moulds for these can be bought in most kitchen shops.

serves 4

1 quantity Pâte Sablée (see page 206)
½ quantity Crème Pâtissière (see page 213)
450 g (1 lb) strawberries, hulled
125 g (4 oz) strawberry jam
4 tablespoons water
1 tablespoon lemon juice

Pre-heat the oven to gas mark 6, 200°C (400°F) and grease the mini tart tins.

Line the tart tins with the pastry, put a little crumpled foil in each one to keep them in shape and bake them in the oven for 7 to 8 minutes. Take out the foil and bake for 5 minutes or so, making sure that they don't catch but are a good biscuit gold all over. Remove from the oven and allow to cool. Fill to within 1 cm (½ inch) of the top with Crème Pâtissière. Reserve an unblemished strawberry to decorate each tart then pile in as many strawberries as they will conveniently hold.

Melt the strawberry jam with the water and lemon juice and beat until smooth, getting rid of as many of the lumps as you can. Trickle it over the top of each tart from a tablespoon so it runs down in the crevices between the strawberries. Make sure none of the strawberries is left uncovered by the glaze. Allow to cool and set. It's not a good idea to refrigerate the tarts as everything goes a bit soggy but they will keep in a cool place for about 6 hours.

211

Walnut and lemon tart

An old English combination of flavours for which the sweetened Shortcrust is a perfect pastry. It's best eaten warm rather than hot and it's equally good the next day when thoroughly cooled down.

Serves 4

1 quantity sweet Shortcrust Pastry (see page 206)
100 g (4 oz) unsalted butter
175 g (6 oz) golden syrup
2 eggs, beaten
Grated rind and juice of 1 lemon
225 g (8 oz) chopped walnuts

Pre-heat the oven to gas mark 4, 180°C (350°F) and grease a 20 cm (8 inch) flan or tart tin with 2.5 cm (1 inch) high sides.

Roll out the pastry and line the tin. Cover it with kitchen foil and bake blind for about 10 minutes. Take it out and allow to cool slightly. In a non-stick saucepan, mix the butter, syrup, eggs, and lemon rind and juice. Put the pieces of walnut into the pastry case, pour the syrup mixture over the top and bake in the oven for 40 to 45 minutes until the top is brown, bubbling and risen.

Walnut and lemon tart

WINE tip | Portuguese Verdelho Madeira – rich, nutty and medium sweet. Perfection.

French fruit flan (page 211)

Apple baklava

An adaptation of the classic Turkish nut-filled confection, this has a slightly different and fruitier filling which makes it more of a dessert than a sweetmeat.

Serves 4

350 g (12 oz) eating apples
175 g (6 oz) slivered almonds
3 tablespoons caster sugar
A pinch of ground cloves
450 g (1 lb) filo pastry
100 g (4 oz) butter
For the syrup:
Juice of 1 lemon
100 g (4 oz) sugar
½ teaspoon ground cinnamon

Pre-heat the oven to gas mark 4, 180°C (350°F) and lightly grease a 25 cm (10 inch) pie dish.

Core but don't peel the apples and chop them up roughly. Mix them with the almonds, sugar and the cloves. Unfold the filo pastry and cover it with a damp tea towel to stop it drying out. Melt the butter in a saucepan. Brush a piece of the filo with the butter, place it butter side down in the tin, brush the pastry with some more butter and add another sheet of filo, making sure that the whole of the tin is lined with four pieces, each buttered in turn, and letting the edges spill over. Put in half the apple mixture and spread it evenly. Put in 3 more layers of buttered filo, put the rest of the apple mixture in and put 2 more layers of filo on top, now fold the edges in and under so that the pie is neatly covered. Cut the last piece of filo so that it fits the shape of the tin and add that, buttering it completely. Cook in the oven for about 30 minutes. Remove the pie and turn the oven up to gas mark 6, 200°C (400°F). Cut the baklava through the top with a sharp knife into diamond patterns or fan-shaped slices and put back into the oven for 10 minutes or until golden on the top. Remove from the oven.

Make the syrup by heating the lemon juice, sugar and cinnamon in a non-stick saucepan until well blended. Pour over the pie and leave to cool. Purists make the syrup in advance, let it cool and pour it cold over the hot pie. It's still best eaten cold.

Crème Pâtissière

This is the simple recipe for Crème Pâtissière that the French use in profusion to make their pies and tarts creamy and plump-looking. It's easiest made with a food processor or liquidizer. A delicious, tangy addition to Crème Pâtissière is a little grated orange or lemon rind.

Makes 300 ml (10 fl oz)

2 eggs
75 g (3 oz) caster sugar
50 g (2 oz) plain flour
150 ml (5 fl oz) milk
½ teaspoon vanilla essence

Break the eggs into the food processor or liquidizer. Add the sugar and process for about 15 to 20 seconds until smoothly blended. Add the flour and process until mixed. Bring the milk to the boil in a non-stick saucepan. With the motor running, pour the milk carefully through the feed tube into the food processor bowl. Add the vanilla essence and process for a further 5 seconds. Return to the saucepan and cook over a very low heat for about 5 minutes, stirring regularly until the mixture thickens completely. Leave it to cool, stirring occasionally to stop a skin forming on the top. A layer of cling film laid directly on to the liquid will also prevent a skin forming. It will keep in the fridge, covered, for up to a week.

213
....

Apple baklava

• •

CHAPTER FIFTEEN

From lemon to
chocolate, coffee to
banana, marmalade to
Christmas fruit, here
are a wide variety of
delicious cakes with
biscuits, meringues and
other recipes for the
sweet-toothed.

cakes and biscuits

Four keys to crafty cakes

1. Easy mixing

Although it's possible (and sometimes
therapeutic) to make cakes by hand, by far the
craftiest way to approach cake-making is with
a food processor or a mixer. All the recipes
below can be made by hand. But all are,
frankly, better made by machine.

2. Simple baking

There are a number of ideas that make baking
much easier than it used to be.
● **Always use metal tins** They transfer heat
better, are easier to clean and provide a
crisper finish on the cake or biscuits.
● **Non-stick tins are ideal, if not essential**
They are widely available and are the easiest
thing of all to keep clean.
● **Loose-fitting bottoms to cake and flan
tins** These are a great boon. Some cake tins
have a spring system to tension them
around the bottom, preventing leakage.
● **Silicone paper** Silicone paper (or baking
parchment as it's sometimes known) has a
modern non-stick surface and is far better
than greaseproof paper. You can thus line
tins, non-stick or otherwise, for effortless
removal of cooked cakes or pies.

3. No icing

Icing seems, with the exception of set-piece
cakes like wedding cakes, to be merely a
complicated decoration which adds large
quantities of sugar to your diet. And it makes
the cake more difficult to slice. Don't use icing
unless you feel absolutely compelled to. Some
melted chocolate on top of a chocolate cake, a
little fromage frais or whipped cream, a light
sifting of icing sugar, or the judicious
distribution of nuts before or after baking are
all much more attractive and often healthier
alternatives.

4. Good eating

The pattern of lighter and more healthy eating
may now be well-established. But it's yet to
influence most forms of cake-making. Cakes
should look and taste good, but in order for
them to do some good it's worth using
polyunsaturated oil instead of saturated fat
for some recipes. There are a number of
recipes here which take this new approach.
You'll find that they're all totally delicious in
their own right, not merely a healthy option.

215
....

Above: *Chocolate cake* (page 216). **Below:** *Lemon
sponge cake* (page 216)

Nine special cakes – four plain and five fancy

The crafty sponge

This is a modern version of the Victoria sponge, extremely easy to make and virtually foolproof. It is best made in a food processor or with a mixer in the 'one go' method – everything is put into the machine in one go and then blended.

Makes 1 × 18–20 cm (8–9 inch) sandwich cake

150 g (5 oz) soft margarine, softened butter or polyunsaturated oil
150 g (5 oz) caster sugar
3 medium eggs
150 g (5 oz) self-raising flour, sifted

Pre-heat the oven to gas mark 4, 180°C (350°F) and grease and/or line 2 × 18–20 cm (8–9 inch) sandwich tins.

Put all the ingredients into the mixing bowl of your food processor or mixer. Blend together for 15 seconds, scrape down the sides, then blend together for another 10 to 15 seconds. It's important not to overbeat this mixture. Spread the mixture into the prepared tins, making sure the tops are even. Bake in the oven for about 25 minutes.

Towards the end of the time, check the cakes. You can test whether a sponge is done by gently pressing it in the middle with your fingertip. If your fingermark vanishes as the sponge rises and fills the gap, it's cooked. If it isn't, leave it for another 4 to 5 minutes. Turn the sponges on to a wire rack and leave them to cool.

They're delicious sandwiched together with jam and with a little icing sugar sprinkled over the top. There are also easy variations.

Variations

● **Lemon sponge** Add the grated rind of a whole lemon and the juice of ½ a lemon into the other ingredients before you start to blend them together. Otherwise proceed as above. Lemon curd or marmalade in the middle is a nice touch.
● **Orange sponge** You can make an orange version by using the rind of a whole orange and the juice of ½ an orange in the same manner.

Chocolate cake

This is the ultimate crafty chocolate cake, a recipe repeated without shame because it is quite the nicest and easiest-to-make-cake of all. It improves with keeping (if this proves remotely possible in your household). Up to three days helps the cake become even moister, darker and more handsome!

Makes 1 × 18 cm (7 inch) sandwich cake

175 g (6 oz) self-raising flour
4 tablespoons cocoa powder (not drinking chocolate)
1 heaped teaspoon baking powder
100 g (4 oz) caster sugar
1 tablespoon black treacle
150 ml (5 fl oz) sunflower oil
150 ml (5 fl oz) milk
2 eggs (size 1)

Pre-heat the oven to gas mark 3, 160°C (325°F) and grease and/or line 2 × 18 cm (7 inch) cake tins.

Put all the ingredients together in a food processor or mixer and blend well for 10 to 15 seconds. Scrape down the sides to make sure all the ingredients are mixed thoroughly together and blend together for another 10 to 15 seconds. Don't overbeat! Pour (the mixture will be runny) into the prepared tins. Bake in the oven for 45 minutes. Test the cakes for done by pressing with your finger – they should be firm to touch. Take them out of the tins and put them on a rack. Let them cool and then sandwich them.

My favourite mixture is black cherry jam in the middle and some well beaten fromage frais with a little double cream added to give it stiffness as a coating, arguably a healthier version of the black forest gâteau.

Coffee gâteau

A simple and quite light cake with a good coffee flavour, this has the addition of some hazelnuts which give it a marvellous grainy texture. Once again it uses sunflower oil, reducing the saturated fat level.

Makes 1 × 18 cm (7 inch) sandwich cake

75 g (3 oz) hazelnuts or hazelnut pieces
75 g (3 oz) caster sugar
100 g (4 oz) self-raising flour
3 eggs (size 3)
2 tablespoons sunflower or soya oil
1 teaspoon baking powder
2 teaspoons instant coffee
2 tablespoons boiling water

Pre-heat the oven to gas mark 4, 180°C (350°F) and grease and/or line 2 × 18 cm (7 inch) cake tins.

Put the hazelnuts into a food processor or liquidizer and grind them to a fine powder. Then put them with the sugar, flour, eggs, oil and baking powder into the mixing bowl of your mixer or processor. Dissolve the instant coffee in the boiling water and add to the bowl. Process thoroughly in 2 bursts of about 10 seconds, scraping the bowl down in between. Pour into the prepared tins, smoothing down the top. Bake in the oven for about 25 minutes until the cake is brown and has shrunk a little away from the sides of the tin. Check that it's done by pressing with your finger – it should rebound and fill the gap immediately. When it's cooked, turn it on to a rack to cool.

You can sandwich it with a variety of fillings including coffee butter cream if you fancy it. Decorate it with whole hazelnuts before serving.

Streusel cake

Streusel is an Austrian-style cake with a crumbly topping, traditionally eaten whilst drinking coffee covered in whipped cream. But it's a delicious cake in its own right and a nice pudding when eaten with a spoonful of fromage frais or thick yoghurt.

Makes 1 × 18 cm (7 inch) cake

175 g (6 oz) plain flour
50 g (2 oz) cornflour
2 teaspoons baking powder
100 g (4 oz) soft margarine or softened butter
100 g (4 oz) caster sugar
2 eggs, lightly beaten
175 ml (6 fl oz) milk
For the topping:
25 g (1 oz) plain flour
40 g (1½ oz) demerara sugar
1 teaspoon ground cinnamon
25 g (1 oz) butter

217

Pre-heat the oven to gas mark 5, 190°C (375°F) and grease and/or line an 18 cm (7 inch) cake tin. If you have one, the German Kuglhopf-tin with the funnel in the middle would be the most authentic.

Start by making the topping. Put the flour, sugar, cinnamon and butter into a food processor or liquidizer and process until they resemble very fine, dry crumbs. Keep these aside. Put all the cake ingredients into the bowl and blend or process those for about 15 seconds. Scrape the sides down and process again for another 10 seconds. Turn the mixture into the prepared tin, smooth the surface and sprinkle the crumble topping mixture on the top. Bake in the oven for about 1 hour. Check the cake is cooked with a skewer – it should run into the middle and out again and emerge clean. If the skewer is still smeary, the cake needs another 5 to 10 minutes. You may need to cover the top to make sure it doesn't burn while the cake finishes cooking. Lift it out carefully, making sure you don't spill the topping which will still be slightly loose. If you papered the tin, use it to ease the cake out. If you greased the tin, you will need to use appropriate implements such as meat forks to keep the cake upright. It's possible to eat this cake warm with yoghurt or fromage frais, or to allow it to cool.

Cherry cake

The great debate with cherry cakes is how to prevent the cherries sinking. There are all sorts of ideas as to the best solution and none are a guaranteed method, but glacé cherries that don't have too much sugar on them do seem to help. It is possible to rinse them in warm water and dry them thoroughly before using them, as well. This cake is so good that even with cherries at the bottom it's certainly worth making.

Makes 1 × 20 cm (8 inch) cake

50 g (2 oz) ground almonds
200 g (7 oz) self-raising flour
1 teaspoon baking powder
150 g (5 oz) caster sugar
150 g (5 oz) soft margarine or softened butter
3 eggs
90 ml (3 fl oz) milk
½ teaspoon almond essence
225 g (8 oz) glacé cherries

Pre-heat the oven to gas mark 3, 160°C (325°F) and grease and/or line a 20 cm (8 inch) cake tin.

Put all the ingredients except the glacé cherries in a mixer or food processor and blend together. Scrape the sides down and blend together for another 5 to 10 seconds. Remove the mixture from the machine and stir in the cherries. Pour into the prepared tin, cover the top with a piece of foil or baking parchment, not touching the cake mixture itself, and bake in the centre of the oven for 1¼ to 1½ hours. Check with a skewer to see that it's cooked – it should come out without any smears on – if not leave for another 5 to 10 minutes. To brown the top of the cake, remove the covering for the last 15 minutes. Turn out on to a wire rack and cool thoroughly before eating.

Banana cake

This is a favourite family cake. It is a wonderful way of using up the odd over-ripe banana. It's best cooked in a loaf tin. If you are feeling extremely self-indulgent you can lightly toast and butter the odd slice. It's delicious, however, as a cake in its own right.

Makes 1 × 900 g (2 lb) cake

225 g (8 oz) self-raising flour
½ teaspoon salt
100 g (4 oz) soft margarine or softened butter
175 g (6 oz) caster sugar
2 eggs
450 g (1 lb) ripe bananas, peeled
175 g (6 oz) mixed dried fruit

Pre-heat the oven to gas mark 4, 180°C (350°F) and grease and/or line a 900 g (2 lb) loaf tin.

Put everything except the dried fruit into your mixing bowl or food processor and process until thoroughly mashed up. The bananas should be chopped very finely through the mixture.

Remove the bowl from the machine and stir in the dried fruit. Pour the mixture into the prepared tin, spread it out evenly and bake in the oven for about 1½ hours. Test it with a skewer, which should come out clean. You may need to cover the top for the last 15 minutes or so with a piece of foil or paper to make sure it doesn't burn. Let the loaf cool before you tip it out of the tin. It will keep for 2 to 3 days and, if sealed airtight, will keep in a fridge for up to a week.

Streusel cake (page 217)

Marmalade cake

This is one of those wonderful store-cupboard cakes that can be made very rapidly for unexpected guests, although you do need to let it cool enough to be sensible to slice. You probably have all the ingredients ready to hand. It's another cake to cook in a loaf tin. Don't be tempted to add more marmalade, it won't help and will only sink to the bottom.

Makes 1 × 450 g (1½ lb) cake

225 g (8 oz) plain flour
1 teaspoon baking powder
100 g (4 oz) soft margarine or softened butter
90 g (3½ oz) sugar
2 eggs (size 1)
3 large tablespoons orange marmalade
Grated rind of 1 large orange
Grated rind of 1 lemon

Pre-heat the oven to gas mark 5, 190°C (375°F) and grease and/or line a 900 g (2 lb) loaf tin.

Put all the ingredients into a food processor or mixer bowl and mix together for 15 to 20 seconds. You will probably have bits of marmalade rind still left whole but don't let that worry you. Scrape down the sides and process for another 5 seconds or so. Tip into the prepared tin and smooth the top. You may, if you wish, sprinkle with a little caster sugar just before baking. Bake in the oven for 45 minutes to 1 hour. If the tin is particularly narrow and deep you may need to bake it for a little longer and protect the top as you do so with a piece of foil or baking parchment.

Test with a skewer which should come out absolutely clean. Tip out to cool on a wire rack before slicing like a loaf.

Golden fruit cake

A light Dundee-style fruit cake that's extremely easy to make, this is lighter than many traditional fruit cakes and is therefore more popular with children.

Makes 1 × 18 cm (7 inch) cake

175 g (6 oz) self-raising flour
75 g (3 oz) soft brown sugar
75 g (3 oz) soft margarine or softened butter
1½ tablespoons milk
2 eggs (size 3)
225 g (8 oz) mixed fruit
1 teaspoon ground allspice
50 g (2 oz) almonds

Pre-heat the oven to gas mark 3, 160°C (325°F) and grease and/or line a 18 cm (7 inch) deep cake tin.

Put the flour, sugar, margarine or butter, milk and eggs into the processor mixing bowl. Mix together for about 15 seconds, scrape down the sides and mix again, making sure the whole mixture is thoroughly blended. Remove the bowl from the machine and stir in the fruit and spice. Pour the mixture into the prepared tin and top with the almonds in a ring pattern. Bake in the oven for 2 hours. Test by running a skewer into the centre. It may need an extra 30 minutes cooking. If the top starts to brown before the centre is finished, cover it with a little foil to keep it from going too crisp. It needs to cool on a rack for at least 3 to 4 hours and then be stored in a tin for at least 3 days before you eat it.

220

Golden fruit cake

Marmalade cake

Christmas cake

Here is the original one-bowl-mix, crafty, Christmas cake. It's not the low-fat version that's become extremely popular in recent years but an old-fashioned, traditional, dark, rich, fruity cake. It is a cake that can be made as easily in a mixing bowl without a machine as with a mixer or processor.

Makes 1 × 25 cm (10 inch) cake

350 g (12 oz) self-raising flour, sifted
350 g (12 oz) soft brown sugar (not demerara)
350 g (12 oz) softened butter
100 g (4 oz) ground almonds
6 eggs (size 3)
2 teaspoons baking powder
½ teaspoon salt
175 ml (6 fl oz) milk
1 tablespoon dark treacle
100 g (4 oz) glacé cherries
100 g (4 oz) cut mixed peel
350 g (12 oz) raisins
350 g (12 oz) sultanas
350 g (12 oz) currants
Grated rind and juice of 1 lemon

Pre-heat the oven to gas mark 4, 180°C (350°F) and grease and/or line a 25 cm (10 inch) deep cake tin.

Put all the ingredients except the cherries, peel and fruit into a bowl and either blend or beat well until thoroughly smooth. Even by hand this only takes 2 or 3 minutes. Mix in the peel and fruit and put the mixture into the prepared tin. Bake in the oven for 1½ hours. After that time, have a look and if the top is already going brown, cover it with greaseproof paper. Bake for a further 1 hour. Check when it's done by running a skewer into the middle.

If it doesn't come out completely clean, the cake needs another 15 to 20 minutes. Leave it to cool in the tin for 30 minutes before turning on to a wire rack to cool thoroughly. You can marzipan and ice it or eat it as it is. Either way it stores well for up to 3 weeks.

Christmas cake

Biscuits

Home-made biscuits are an enormous treat.
The flavours and textures are simply more
subtle than shop-bought biscuits. They are
quite time-consuming to produce in large
quantities. But here are four biscuit recipes
that are as economical on time as possible.

Traditional shortbread

**This is simply not worth making without real
butter as that's where the flavour comes from.
But even if eaten just occasionally it reminds
you vividly why shortbread has always been held
to be the queen of biscuits.**

Makes about 15 biscuits

200 g (7 oz) plain flour
50 g (2 oz) cornflour
75 g (3 oz) caster sugar
175 g (6 oz) softened butter
½ teaspoon real vanilla essence

Pre-heat the oven to gas mark 2, 150°C
(300°F) and grease and flour a baking sheet,
shortbread mould or Swiss roll tin.
   Knead all the ingredients together or
process in a food processor or in a mixer until
the ingredients turn into a cohesive ball of
dough – this will be very soft. You can then
roll it with a well floured rolling pin to about
1 cm (½ inch) thickness and cut it into fingers
and arrange them on a baking sheet, or press
it into a shortbread mould, or put it in a
prepared Swiss roll tin. Prick gently all over
the surface with a fork, mark into biscuits and
bake in the oven for 30 to 35 minutes until
pale gold. Keep an eye on it! Leave to cool on
the baking sheet or in the dish you've cooked
it in.

Variation

Almond Shortbread There is a variation
made in Scotland which substitutes 50 g (2
oz) of ground almonds for 50 g (2 oz) of the
flour. It produces a very crumbly and delicate
shortbread that has a wonderful almondy
flavour. You can also substitute the vanilla
essence for almond essence to increase this
flavour. Otherwise cook it as above.

Lemon thins

**A very simple biscuit to make, this is especially
nice to eat with other things such as ice-creams
or fruit fools. You can make them with orange as
well, simply substituting the orange rind and
juice for the lemon.**

Makes about 24 biscuits

225 g (8 oz) self-raising flour
50 g (2 oz) icing sugar, sifted
150 g (5 oz) soft margarine or softened butter
Grated rind and juice of 1 lemon

Pre-heat the oven to gas mark 5, 190°C
(375°F) and grease a baking sheet.
   Mix the flour and icing sugar together and
then mix in the butter and lemon juice and
rind. In a food processor this needs to be
mixed for about 10 to 15 seconds. By hand
you have to rub it in until it's thoroughly
amalgamated. Turn the mixture on to a
floured surface, squeeze it with the heel of
your hand until it's well blended, then roll it
out very thinly indeed, about 5 mm (¼ inch)
thick is the intention. Use a pastry cutter or a
thin glass to cut circles of about 5 cm (2
inches) in diameter. Gather up the remaining
pastry, roll it out again and go on doing it
until you have none left. Put these on to the
prepared baking sheet and cook in the oven
for about 8 to 10 minutes until they're lightly
golden. Allow them to cool for a moment
before lifting off with a spatula or food slice
on to a wire tray. Let them cool completely
before eating them as they won't go crisp until
then.

Digestive biscuits

**These are not the sweet and rather smooth
version you find in the shops but a slightly
coarser and more rustic style of biscuit.**

Makes about 24 biscuits

100 g (4 oz) wholemeal flour
50 g (2 oz) oatmeal or porridge oats
25 g (1 oz) soft brown sugar
1 teaspoon baking powder
½ teaspoon salt
75 g (3 oz) soft margarine or softened butter
2 tablespoons milk

Pre-heat the oven to gas mark 4, 180°C
(350°F) and grease a baking sheet.
  Mix all the dry ingredients together and rub
in the margarine or butter – you can do this in
a processor in about 5 to 10 seconds. Add the
milk a spoonful at a time until the mixture
becomes cohesive, like a dough. Using a well-
floured rolling pin and plenty of flour on the
work surface, roll it out until it's about 5 mm
(¼ inch) thick. Cut into 5 cm (2 inch) biscuits
using a pastry cutter or thin glass. Re-roll the
remaining dough and cut again until you've
used it all up. Arrange on the prepared baking
sheet, prick the top with a fork and bake in
the oven for 10 to 15 minutes until brown.
Don't let them start catching at the edges.
Cool on a wire rack.

Above: *Fudge brownies* **(page 224). Below:** *A simple
pavlova* **(page 225)**

Fudge brownies

These really aren't a biscuit at all, more half-way between fudge and a cake. They are extremely popular in America and quick to make, but very sticky. The silicone paper mentioned on page 215 is thus a huge help. These can be eaten warm almost straight out of the oven so they make a good instant standby as well.

Makes about 12 brownies

175 g (6 oz) soft margarine
50 g (2 oz) cocoa powder (not drinking chocolate)
50 g (2 oz) self-raising flour
50 g (2 oz) chopped nuts (not peanuts)
2 eggs
175 g (6 oz) soft brown sugar (not demerara)

Pre-heat the oven to gas mark 4, 180°C (350°F) and grease and line a 20 cm (8 inch) square cake tin.

Melt one-third of the margarine in a non-stick saucepan then stir in the cocoa. Reserve the nuts and put the rest of the ingredients into a food processor or mixer and beat together until smooth. Add the melted margarine and cocoa, and stir in the nuts.

Pour into the prepared tin and bake in the oven for 35 minutes. Leave them for 5 minutes then mark into squares or diamonds. The mixture is too gooey to be cut before then. You can glaze them with chocolate or a fudge mixture, sift a little icing sugar over them, and eat them warm or cold.

Meringues made simple – three crucial preparations

When making meringues there are three things that have to be right and then they're one of the easiest things in the world to make.

● **Separating the eggs** Make sure you do this carefully. There are gadgets on the market that will help you. I always use a bowl, a cup (for the egg yolks), and the shells themselves. But either way it's essential that the whites contain no yolk at all or they simply won't beat properly.

● **The bowl should be spotlessly clean** A glass bowl is ideal, though experts use copper bowls because they believe the effect of the copper helps the egg white to build a bigger foam.

● **Getting the right whisk** If you've got an electric whisk your problems are over. Some food processors now incorporate specially designed whisks which also work very well. If you're whisking by hand the traditional chef's balloon whisk is a possibility but the best of all can only be described as a bed-spring-round-a-coathanger whisk (actually called a 'coil' whisk – see p. 304). It produces an extremely high peaking mixture very easily by incorporating the maximum amount of air.

Simple English meringue

This is the ideal meringue for eating as a biscuit with pudding or splitting and filling with cream and strawberries (or whatever else takes your fancy).

Serves 4

4 egg whites
A pinch of salt
175 g (6 oz) caster sugar

Pre-heat the oven to its lowest setting or to gas mark 2, 150°C (300°F) (see method) and line a baking sheet.

Beat the egg whites until foamy and thick but not completely stiff. Add the pinch of salt and continue to whisk, adding a tablespoon of the sugar at a time and whisking until it is completely beaten in. The egg white should beat up to a peak after about the third tablespoon of sugar. Add all but one tablespoon of sugar, by which time the mixture should be absolutely firm – the traditional test is to turn the bowl upside down. Fold in the last tablespoon of sugar without whisking to add a certain texture to the meringue. You can put this mixture into a piping bag and pipe shapes, use tablespoons to make individual-sized portions or, using a dampened palette knife, spread it out on the parchment paper to make meringue cake.

You can cook meringues in two different ways. One – at a low gas mark 2, 150°C (300°F), 130°C in a fan oven or the bottom of the simmering in an Aga – will produce a golden-coloured meringue after about 35 to 40 minutes. If you want a totally white meringue, you have to dry the mixture out at a much lower temperature. The bottom of the lowest oven in the Aga is ideal and fan ovens have trouble with this. But the lowest setting on your gas or electric oven should produce, over a period of 2 to 3 hours, a completely crisp but still white meringue.

A simple pavlova

This uses an Australian adaptation of a technique known as Italian meringue. It's a meringue which cooks crisp on the outside but has a slightly chewy centre. It can be used for recipes other than Pavlova but this fruit-filled confection is its most famous incarnation.

Serves 4

3 egg whites
½ teaspoon salt
150 g (5 oz) caster sugar
2 teaspoons cider or white wine vinegar

Pre-heat the oven to gas mark 2, 150°C (300°F) and line a 20–25 cm (8–10 inch) flan ring.

Beat the egg whites until they are foamy and thick. Add the salt and continue to beat, adding a tablespoon of the sugar at a time and beating until each is fully incorporated. After 3 tablespoons of sugar, add the cider or wine vinegar and continue to add the last 2 tablespoons of sugar, whisking as you go. The mixture will become glossy and smooth and should be thick enough to turn the bowl upside down. Using a spatula, pile the mixture into the prepared tin and smooth around so that it has an indentation in the centre rather like a pastry case for a tart. The indentation need not be too deep. Bake in the oven for about 45 to 50 minutes until the meringue is cooked. It will be pale gold on the outside and, when allowed to cool, slightly marshmallowy and chewy in the middle. You can, if you prefer, dry the Pavlova out in an extremely slow oven for 2 to 3 hours to get a totally white effect.

When ready to serve, whip some cream and fromage frais together (about 3 tablespoons each), fill the indentation and add a variety of seasonal soft fruit: strawberries, kiwis, mangoes, raspberries, currants, or a judicious mixture, all make a wonderful pudding. Do not allow the filling to be put into the Pavlova more than an hour before you wish to eat it or the whole thing will start to go a little soggy. It's best not refrigerated before eating.

CHAPTER SIXTEEN

A fabulous farandole of
fruit – with ideas and
recipes for each

fruit

Apples

Britain has some of the best apples in the
world with a very long season stretching from
August to January. This country is unusual in
that it has apples specially bred for cooking as
well as for eating. The most popular eating
varieties grown in Britain are led by the Cox's
Orange Pippin. But recently up to twenty
other varieties have become available every
autumn in supermarkets, greengrocers and
pick-your-own farms. Buy them! Eat them!
Otherwise the shops will slip back into their
bad old habits of just stocking a few varieties,
normally imported.

Eating apples

These are often very good for cooking as they
don't break up into a soft mush. They're
therefore ideal for things like Pheasant Vallée
d'Auge (see page 99) and for baking, where
they provide a fragrant alternative to cooking
apples. Here's an apple tart that calls for sweet
eating apples – you could mix Cox's Orange
Pippins, Egremont Russets and Spartan for a
lovely flavour combination.

Apple and almond tart

Apple and almond tart

Serves 6 to 8

For the pastry:
225 g (8 oz) plain flour
A pinch of salt
2 tablespoons caster sugar
100 g (4 oz) unsalted butter, diced
2 egg yolks
4 tablespoons cold water

227
• • • • • • • • • • •

For the filling:
10 sweet eating apples, peeled, cored and grated
Juice of 1–2 lemons (depending on tartness of the apples)
4 tablespoons caster sugar
1 heaped teaspoon ground cinnamon
50 g (2 oz) flaked almonds, toasted

To make the pastry, sift the flour and salt into
a bowl and mix in the sugar. Using your
fingertips, rub the butter into the flour until
the mixture resembles fine breadcrumbs.
Blend the egg yolks with the cold water and
mix into the pastry with a knife, then form the
pastry into a small ball with your hands. Or
blend the dry ingredients in a food processor,
add the eggs and water and process until the
mixture forms a cohesive ball. Cover and chill
for about 40 minutes. Pre-heat the oven to gas
mark 6, 200°C (400°F). Sprinkle the grated
apples with the lemon juice, sugar and
cinnamon and mix well. Carefully roll out the
pastry and line a 30 cm (12 in) flan ring or
loose-bottomed tart tin. Sprinkle with the
almonds and spoon in the apple mixture,
packing down well. Bake for 50 to 60 minutes
until golden and soft. Serve hot or cold with
Greek strained yoghurt or fromage frais. This
tart looks exceptionally pretty decorated with
almonds on the top as well.

Welsh blackberry tart **(page 231)**

Scandinavian apple cake

**Use traditional English apples for their more
intense flavour. This cake is more like a pudding
– serve it in a glass bowl so that everyone can
appreciate the attractive layering.**

228

Serves 4 to 6

*900 g (2 lb) eating apples, peeled, cored and roughly
    chopped*
¼ teaspoon whole cloves
50 g (2 oz) sugar
Juice and grated rind of 1 lemon
100 g (4 oz) unsalted butter
350 g (12 oz) fresh white breadcrumbs
100 g (4 oz) light muscovado sugar
¼ teaspoon ground cinnamon
Fromage frais or whipped double cream, to serve

Place the apples, cloves, sugar and lemon
juice in a pan with just enough water to
prevent them from sticking. Simmer for about
15 to 20 minutes until soft and puréed,
stirring occasionally – they do not need to be
completely smooth. Melt the butter in a pan
and fry the breadcrumbs until golden.
Remove from the heat and stir in the light
muscovado sugar, the cinnamon and the
lemon rind. Place one-third of the apple
mixture in the bottom of a glass bowl and top
with a third of the breadcrumbs. Continue
layering in this way until you have used all the
ingredients. Tap the bowl gently on the work
surface to settle the layers. Chill for at least 2
hours. Serve with fromage frais or cream.

Cooking apples

The most common variety – Bramley – cooks
to something of a mush. Grenadier and
Howgate Wonder are firmer varieties. But all
varieties ought to be baked in the same way:
core them, fill with a mixture of dried fruit,
brown sugar, and top with butter or honey.
Run a sharp knife around the equator of the
apple to stop the skin splitting untidily and
bake in a medium oven, gas mark 4, 180°C
(350°F) for about 40 to 45 minutes. A little
water or juice in the bottom of the pan while
they cook makes a delicious sauce.

Apples make wonderful pies but you can
also try making the following pudding by
cutting an apple into twelve segments like
unpegging an orange. There's a wonderful
device called an apple corer that does this
perfectly.

**Apricot fool
(page 230)**

**Gooseberry fool
(page 231)**

Apple sauté

Serves 4

2 tablespoons butter
2 large cooking apples, pegged
2 tablespoons apricot jam
25 g (1 oz) slivered almonds

In a non-stick frying pan, heat the butter till it sizzles and add the apples. Turn until they're hot but not soggy. Add the apricot jam, stir for 1 minute and serve sprinkled with the slivered almonds.

Apricots

In the short season that they have, fresh apricots are best eaten as they are, or perhaps in a tart (see page 211). Dried apricots are a wonderful year-round ingredient and make a tremendously rich, highly flavoured fool.

Apricot fool

Serves 4

Soak 225 g (8 oz) of dried apricots just covered in tea, preferably Earl Grey, for 4 to 6 hours and then simmer them until soft. Purée them in a liquidizer or food processor with enough of their cooking liquid to make a mixture the thickness of double cream. Whisk 150 ml (5 fl oz) of double cream until it's thick and add the same quantity of plain yoghurt, whisking as you add it. Stir in the apricots, check for sweetness and balance (add sugar if necessary) and pour into wine glasses. Chill in the fridge for at least 2 hours before serving. You can put it into one large dish and serve it from that if you prefer.

230

Bananas

Although most of us think of bananas simply as something to peel and eat, they also cook remarkably well and bake equally well (see page 193 for Barbecued Bananas). In New Orleans there's a famous dish called Bananas Forster which mixes bananas and some of the other favoured local ingredients.

Bananas Forster

In the restaurant in which it was invented this is used as a covering for home-made vanilla ice-cream!

Serves 4

4 large ripe bananas
2 tablespoons butter
2 tablespoons soft brown molasses sugar
Juice of 1 lime

Peel the bananas and cut them in half lengthways and then acrosswise so you have 4 pieces for each banana. In a non-stick frying pan, melt the butter and sauté the bananas gently for 2 to 3 minutes. Add the sugar and stir, being careful not to break the bananas. When the sugar and butter have amalgamated to a thick toffee-like mixture, squeeze on the lime juice and serve immediately.

Blackberries

One of the great free foods of Britain, blackberries can still be picked from hedgerows and waste ground in cities and throughout the countryside. They're supposed to be picked before the first frost, but the important thing is to look for blackberries that are fully ripe as green ones or ones with bits of green on them don't make for settled stomachs. When fully ripe they have a wonderfully fragrant flavour and are delicious eaten like strawberries with a little sugar and cream. But they also make a marvellous tart in the Welsh style.

Welsh blackberry tart

Serves 4 to 6

Roll out a measure of Sweet Shortcrust Pastry (see page 206) and use it to line a wide, shallow tart tin. Put in 450 g (1 lb) blackberries and cover with a thin layer of pastry, crimping the edges. Bake in a hot oven, gas mark 6, 200°C (400°F) for 25 to 30 minutes until the tart is browned. To serve, sprinkle two or three tablespoons of caster sugar over the top of the hot tart, directly on to the pastry. (Or, in the Welsh tradition, lift the lid off and sprinkle it directly on to the cooked blackberries.) Eat the tart hot with pouring cream.

Cherries

Another fruit that it seems almost a waste to cook, as the season is so short and the fresh fruit so delicious. However, bitter cherries make a marvellous sauce for duck and are often available, particularly in fruit-growing areas.

Duck sauce

To make a store-cupboard sauce which can be used with duck when you wish, boil clean cherries in a little water for about 10 minutes until they are softened. Add three-quarters of their weight in sugar and, for each 450 g (1 lb) of cherries, a tablespoon of cider vinegar. Simmer for about another 10 to 15 minutes until the mixture goes clear and bottle in sterilized jars. This, of course, will have stones in. Stoning bitter cherries is not a crafty idea, but warn your guests so they don't crack their teeth!

Sauce montmorency

Sweet cherries also make an excellent sauce for ice-cream (Montmorency). It can be stored. To 450 g (1 lb) of cherries add 350 g (12 oz) of vanilla sugar or caster sugar, a cup of water and a teaspoon of vanilla essence. Simmer together gently until the cherries are on the edge of disintegration. Many of the stones will float to the surface at this point and can be skimmed off, or you can use stoned cherries if you're willing to undertake the labour. Bottle in sterilized jars and store in the fridge for up to 3 months.

Gooseberries

Gooseberries are a most English fruit, indeed they're hardly grown in Europe and banned in America (they harbour a virus that attacks certain kinds of American timber trees). In Britain there are two main varieties of gooseberries: 'dessert' gooseberries and 'cooking' gooseberries. The former tend to be large, often pinkish in colour and quite sweet. The latter are green and rather bullet-like. Both require the ends to be nipped off and arguably both are better cooked.

Gooseberry fool

They make an excellent fool cooked to a purée with enough sugar to sweeten them to your taste and mixed with either the Vanilla custard, chilled, on page 62, or whipped double cream. The cooking gooseberries make a very good tart or crumble.

Grapefruit

Grapefruit now come in both old-fashioned yellow and modern pink versions. The pink ones are much sweeter and slightly more fragrant. Both grill well. Cut and loosen the grapefruit halves as you would for eating raw, sprinkle with a little demerara or caster sugar and if you like, a couple of drops of Angostura Bitters. Put under a pre-heated grill for 4 to 5 minutes until the sugar has melted completely and the top of the grapefruit is just singeing. It makes an excellent light first course for a substantial meal.

231

Grapes

We now benefit from having first-class grapes
available in Britain all year round. The
flavours and styles vary, with the autumn
being the time for the highly flavoured Muscat
or Italia grapes and the spring for the seedless
varieties that tend to come from south of the
equator. There are few better ways of eating
grapes than from a bowl of chilled, indeed,
iced water, with some good fresh (preferably
soft) cheeses and crispy French bread – the
combination is magical. But they are used
occasionally in cooking. The most famous
dish is Sole Véronique. This is best made with
the Italia-style white grapes and is a
marvellous, delicate and quite grand dish.

Sole véronique

**Serve this dish with mashed potatoes and keep
other vegetables for a second course.**

Serves 4

450 g (1 lb) sole fillets
25 g (1 oz) butter
300 ml (10 fl oz) white grape juice
Salt and freshly ground black pepper
150 ml (5 fl oz) double cream
2 teaspoons cornflour
175 g (6 oz) white muscat grapes, halved and de-seeded

Pre-heat the oven to gas mark 4, 180°C
(350°F).
  Put the sole into a buttered baking dish.
Pour over the grape juice and season
generously with salt and pepper. Place in the
oven for about 15 minutes until the fish is just
cooked. Place it carefully on to individual
warm serving plates. Mix together the double
cream and cornflour, add that to the juice in
the pan and stir it in a small saucepan over
heat until it thickens. Season to taste, add the
grapes and pour over the sole fillets, grouping
the grapes at one end.

Kiwi fruit

A furry brown fruit with a jellied sweet
interior. Peel and slice across for pretty,
decorative effects. Nice in Pavlova or fruit
salad. Formidably full of vitamin C and fibre.

Lemons and limes

These fruits are indispensable in all kinds of
recipes, to add sharpness, flavour and colour
as well as, with their peel, some texture. They
are too powerful and idiosyncratic to make
dishes of their own, with the possible
exception of a fruit sorbet.

Lemon or lime sorbet

Serves 4

300 ml (10 fl oz) lemon or lime juice or a mixture
225 g (8 oz) caster sugar
2 egg whites

Heat the juice and the caster sugar together
gently until the sugar has completely
dissolved. Test for sweetness and adjust,
adding more sugar if necessary. Pour the
mixture into a plastic container and put in the
freezer (or pour into an ice-cream making
machine and follow the directions). After 3 to
4 hours when the mixture is pretty well
frozen, put into a food processor and process
until it is a mush. Beat the egg whites in a
separate bowl until they're firm and add to the
mush. Put back into the container and freeze
for another 3 to 4 hours. The mixture should
be solid but have quite a soft texture. To serve,
allow to stand in the fridge for 20 minutes or
so before scooping into individual glasses or
bowls.

232

Melon fruit basket (page 234)

Mango

An exotic fruit that's become almost commonplace in Britain, a ripe mango is not mushy to touch but still firm. Avoid those that are squashy as they will be rotten and inedible. If you have bought one that's not quite ready to eat yet, it can be ripened quite quickly in a paper bag in a dark drawer. Like many exotic fruit they're best eaten raw, by cutting the cheeks off, scoring them finely in criss-cross lines and turning them inside out. It's known as making 'a hedgehog'.

Mango fool

You can, if you have a profusion of mangoes, purée the flesh of one or two with a spoonful of sugar and use it as the basis for a fruit cream or fool. It's best beaten together with equal quantities of whipped cream and plain yoghurt – the yoghurt balances the acidity and sweetness of the mango perfectly. About 150 ml (5 fl oz) of cream and an equal quantity of yoghurt to 1 large mango and a tablespoon of caster sugar are the right proportions.

234

Melon

Melons come in all shapes and sizes, from the tiny golden Ogen right up to the large dark green water melons with their bright red flesh. Most of them are best eaten in large slices, well chilled, without sugar or ginger. With a big melon, preferably one of the round-shaped water melons that are now appearing, make an exotic fruit basket. It is ideal as a container for a grand fruit salad or a centrepiece for a buffet party.

Melon fruit basket

Serves at least 4

Cut a flat base for the melon and cut 2 wedge-shaped pieces out of the top quadrants, leaving a solid handle running over the top. The incision around the edge can be flat or crinkled. Scoop out the centre of the handle thus, creating the basic basket shape. Then, using a sharp spoon helped by a grapefruit knife, remove as much of the flesh from the inside of the melon as possible. If you're using a water melon, cut up the seedless parts into neat cubes and use it with other suitable fruits such as strawberries, peaches or apricots to fill the basket with a fruit salad. Use the remaining melon to make a melon sorbet having removed the seeds and puréed the melon flesh (follow the lemon sorbet instructions on page 232). Or keep it in large slices and use it as a dessert in its own right.

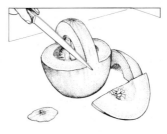

Cut 2 wedge-shaped pieces out of the top, leaving a solid handle

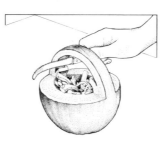

Scoop out the centre of the handle creating a basket shape

Remove as much of the flesh from the inside of the melon as possible

Oranges and their relatives

Citrus fruits now come in the most amazing range of types and varieties from giant ugli fruit (a cross between orange and grapefruit) right the way down to kumquats, which are about the size of a marble and are eaten peel and all. Oranges are one of the most versatile fruit, but don't forget to eat them on their own (chilled with a small container of caster sugar for each person to dip the end of the pegs in).

An outstanding way of eating oranges (or one of the variants – miniolas, satsumas, etc.) is in the Middle Eastern style.

Middle Eastern oranges

Serves 4

Peel four oranges and slice them across the grain carefully into 1 cm (½ inch) slices. Place these in an attractive pattern in a bowl. Remove all the pith from some of the peel, and cut the peel into matchstick slivers – the more you can manage to cut the better. Blanch these in boiling water then discard the water. Measure the peel in tablespoons. Put it into a non-stick saucepan, add an equal number of tablespoons of caster sugar and a little water. Bring it to the boil and let the peel begin to caramelize with the sugar and water. Don't let it go dark brown or it will burn – pale toffee is about right. Very carefully add about a cup or so of cold water, making sure you do not scald yourself with the sudden boiling effect from the pan. When this mixture has cooled slightly pour the caramelized orange peel and its liquid over the sliced oranges in the bowl and leave to marinate for at least 2 hours before serving.

Vitamin C is a so-called anti-oxidant vitamin, now thought to help prevent some cancers and heart disease (along with vitamins A and E). All citrus fruits are particularly high in vitamin C. Its chief role in the diet is in the prevention of scurvy, and without it our bodies suffer from poor healing of wounds. Smokers have particularly low levels of vitamin C and are advised to take supplements.

Above: *Middle Eastern oranges*. Below: *Peach melba* (page 236)

Pawpaw

This is the fruit also known in tropical countries as papaya. It's like a tropical melon with very hard grey and black seeds. Its skin is particularly useful to help tenderize meat – most commercial meat tenderizers are made of papaya. There are few recipes for it although it's delicious eaten fresh and chilled. In Thai cooking grated unripe papaya is used as a salad ingredient with a dressing made of sugar, lemon juice, crushed peanuts and a little fish sauce. It's an acquired taste but with Thai meals is very refreshing.

Peaches and nectarines

Despite mythology to the contrary, peaches and nectarines are first cousins and can be treated by and large in the same way. As with so many fruit they're at their best for a short season, and during that time are best eaten raw. Most peaches in Britain, and almost all nectarines, are clingstone varieties from which it is quite difficult to free the stone. White versions of both are freestone varieties and much easier to use when cooking, if you can find them. Peaches and nectarines make an excellent fruit salad in their own right, unmixed with anything else except a little raspberry juice or coulis of raspberries (see page 239) to flavour them and bring out their sweetness. They also are excellent in the fruit tart you will find on page 211.

236

Peach melba

The classic Peach Melba calls for half a peach per person, skinned and poached gently in sugar syrup for about 10 minutes. The peach is then cooled and, to serve, placed on a helping of vanilla ice-cream topped with some of the raspberry coulis (see p. 239). It's both pretty and delicious.

Pears

Pears, like apples, come in a wide variety of sizes, flavours and textures. Although they are out of fashion now, there even used to be varieties of cooking pears. If you are going to cook with them, look for pears that are not yet ripe as the minute they start to go soft they will disintegrate in the cooking process. Pears make marvellous tarts and pies and bake very well, too.

Baked pears

Core and peel the pears but leave them whole. Bake them in a single layer in a casserole under a variety of flavouring liquids – grape juice and honey produce golden pears (try these with a pinch of cinnamon as well); red fruit juices like cranberry juice or red wine produce dark maroon-coloured pears.
Or try this great French favourite:

Pears belle Hélène

Peel, halve and core some pears and poach them in a little plain sugar syrup without any other flavourings. Allow them to cool slightly, place them on a bed of vanilla ice-cream and pour over a hot chocolate sauce – delicious.

Pear tart

Use firm, ripe pears, but not ones that have gone squashy. I think this tart is best eaten warm. It's delicious cold – but the filling will sink a little.

Serves 4 to 6

275 g (10 oz) Shortcrust Pastry (see page 206)
675 g (1½ lb) ripe pears, peeled, cored and sliced
Juice of 1 lemon
250 ml (8 fl oz) whipping cream
2 eggs
1 egg yolk
75 g (3 oz) caster sugar

Pre-heat the oven to gas mark 6, 200°C (400°F).

Roll out the pastry on a floured surface and use to line a 23 cm (9 in) flan tin that is at least 2.5 cm (1 in) deep. Prick the base all over with a fork, line with foil and then add rice or baking beans. Bake blind for about 12 minutes. Remove the foil and the rice or beans. Reduce oven temperature to gas mark 5, 190°C (375°F). Arrange the sliced pears neatly in the pastry case and sprinkle with lemon juice to prevent them from discolouring. Mix together the cream, eggs, egg yolk and sugar and pour over the pears. Bake for 20 to 25 minutes until the cream is just set. Allow to cool for 10 minutes before serving.

Pineapples

Pineapples are perhaps the most exotic of all fruit because of their exuberant appearance. They can be peeled and sliced in a wide variety of ways, some that leave the plume of leaves on and some that remove it. You can twist the plume out effortlessly with your bare hands if you want to remove it, you don't need to cut the pineapple at all. Indeed, only when the plume waggles is a pineapple ripe – a useful tip.

One of the most spectacular presentations is:

Hot pineapple salad

Serves 4

1 large pineapple
4 seedless satsumas or clementines
25 g (1 oz) butter
1 tablespoon caster sugar

Split the pineapple, plume and all, in half vertically. Cut round the edge and then, in a criss-cross pattern with a sharp knife, and using a strong spoon, pop the cubes out of the pineapple leaving 2 empty shells. Peel and peg the satsumas. In a large non-stick frying pan heat the butter, add the pineapple and cook rapidly for 2 minutes until heated through. Add the segments of orange and the sugar and turn together until the sauce forms a glaze. Pile quickly back into the pineapple shells and serve immediately. This is delicious hot and dreadful cold.

237

Plums and greengages

Another group of fruit with a wide range of sizes, textures and colours, the plum season, however, is comparatively short. Plums, and particularly greengages, make marvellous fruit tarts either in the open French style (as on page 211) or stoned and used to fill a shortcrust pastry base and covered in another layer of pastry. Make sure you don't add any liquid as plums give out a great deal when they're cooking. They benefit from being stirred with a tablespoon of cornflour before being put into the pastry case.

Plum compote

Plums also make an excellent compote, particularly the small, dark red ones known as Switzers or Czars. The way to make a good plum compote is to cut the plums in half and try to remove as much of the stone as you can – but don't worry too much about the stones at this stage. Place them in a saucepan with just enough water to keep them from burning and bring gently to the boil. When they're simmering, add caster sugar to taste – the quantity will depend entirely on how sweet the plums are and on the sweetness of your tooth. Add it bit by bit as you can always stop. When the plums are cooked the stones will loosen from the flesh and many will float to the surface and can be removed. Try not to break up the plums too much. You can stir in a teaspoon of vanilla essence at this point if you like. Allow to cool, having removed as many stones as possible. The mixture will thicken when you chill it but if you want a really thick, almost set, plum compote, to each 450 g (1 lb) of plums add, at the end of cooking, a dessertspoon of arrowroot mixed with a little water to a smooth paste. Stir this into the compote and continue cooking gently for 2 to 3 minutes until the mixture clears. Allow to cool and then chill and you will have a jelly-like consistency.

Quinces

Quinces are the original golden apples of the Hesperides, a mythical fruit that in reality has the most wonderful scent when fully ripened. They are grown in old gardens and occasionally available in greengrocers that specialize in supplying Mediterranean produce. They are inedible raw. Grated or thinly sliced and added to an apple pie they produce a marvellous aromatic flavour and make splendid jelly (see method on page 242) – they have a high pectin content that helps the mixture set. They can be peeled, cored and turned into a compote very much like plums but need slightly longer to cook.

Raspberries

Raspberries are a fruit that really do not need anything done to them (except consumption in significant quantities).

Raspberry coulis

If you are lucky enough to have a surplus, or wish to make Peach Melba (see page 236), take 450 g (1 lb) of them and crush them with a fork. Sprinkle over 225 g (8 oz) of caster sugar and leave overnight. Put the mixture into a saucepan and bring gently to the boil. Turn the heat down and simmer for 10 minutes – no more! Put the whole concoction into a food processor or liquidizer and process until thoroughly smooth. Put through a sieve and you will have the most delicious raspberry sauce or purée. It can be used as it is, thinned down to make drinks or jellies, or thickened with arrowroot, 2 teaspoons to 600 ml (1 pint), to make a Scandinavian pudding called Rotegrote: mix the arrowroot with a little water, stirring it into the purée while hot, and allow to thicken and clarify for 5 minutes.

Raspberry cream crowdie

To help them go further, make Raspberry Cream Crowdie. Whisk 150 ml (5 fl oz) of double cream with an equal quantity of Greek yoghurt, adding the yoghurt as the cream thickens. Stir in 2 tablespoons of runny honey and 1 tablespoon of toasted oatmeal (porridge oats tossed in a dry frying pan until pale gold). Pour this mixture into wine glasses and top with such raspberries as you have. Then sprinkle a little caster sugar over the top. So good it's almost worth a shortage.

239

Above left: Raspberry coulis. Above right: Plum compote. Below: Hot pineapple salad (page 237)

Rhubarb

Another classic English fruit, although it's really a vegetable, rhubarb makes delicious fools – about 450 g (1 lb) of rhubarb and 225 g (8 oz) of sugar to 150 ml (5 fl oz) of double cream and 150 ml (5 fl oz) of plain yoghurt. In America, it is traditionally mixed with strawberries to make surprisingly delicious open tarts.

Rhubarb and strawberry tart

Serves 4

The rhubarb is cooked first with a little sugar and then puréed and used as a bed in a pre-cooked pastry case for the sliced strawberries which are glazed with strawberry jam before being baked briefly to caramelize.

Star fruit

An attractive but flavourless melon-textured tropical fruit. Peel the corners of the 'star' before you cut it across.

240

Strawberries

It's almost impossible to imagine a surfeit of strawberries. To suggest that they should be cooked in any way (except the strawberry tarts on page 211) is regarded by many as sacrilege. However, even eaten raw their presentation can be varied quite considerably. Sugar and cream are the classic accompaniment. Some people prefer a little black pepper and a teaspoon of caster sugar sprinkled over them. Others like them sliced in half and marinated in fresh orange juice for an hour or so before serving with thin rather than thick cream. A particularly exotic favourite is to serve strawberries marinated in the raspberry coulis on page 239 with just a trickle of thin pouring cream to marble the surface.

The four crucial fruit salad rules

Most fruits mix well into a fruit salad but there are some rules that are worth remembering.

1 **Never more than four fruits in one salad** This is a good rule. The separate flavours will just vanish and the textures lose their contrast against each other.

2 **Balance the textures and flavours** One crisp thing – apples, pears; one soft thing – berries of some sort; one sharp thing – raspberries or pineapple; and one sweet thing – mangoes, peaches, ripe apricots – makes a good sort of base. It's arguable that exotic fruit are best kept separate from temperate fruits. But a number of fruits bridge these rules – like grapes. You'll have to make up your own mind.

3 **Liquid medium** All good fruit salads have a little liquid to bathe them. Sometimes this can be plain fresh fruit juice – orange, mango or pear nectar are all good in this respect. Equally a sugar syrup made quite thick, about 4 tablespoons of sugar to the same of water, and sometimes flavoured with spices. Make sure that the fruit has a chance to blend in the liquid medium. But the liquid should be no more than half-way up the fruit – don't drown the salad.

4 **Chilling** All fruit salads benefit from an hour or so in the fridge before serving. It allows the flavours and textures to balance out.

Rhubarb and strawberry tart

Preserves and pickles

Five steps to super jam

Most fruit makes satisfactory jam, some fruits make great jam. Experience suggests that temperate fruit make better conserves than the tropical exotics. The key thing in jam making is pectin. It's a chemical substance that helps the fruit set. It's available in abundance in some fruits, like apples and lemons, but some others are very short on it indeed. You can buy pectin from a chemist to add to your jam if you're worried about the set. Marmalade is jam made from citrus fruits either singly or in combination. The fruit is squeezed and the juices are used to make the jam with segments of the peel sliced in varying thicknesses depending upon your taste. Now for the steps:

1. **Use good quality fruit** It shouldn't be too ripe, whatever kind of fruit you're using, and it should be clean, firm and unblemished. If you're using citrus fruit to make marmalade some prefer fruit that hasn't had its skin waxed ('untreated'). Seville oranges, which are the basis for most marmalades, are never waxed. They're available in the months of December and January only.

2. **Use the right sort of sugar** Preserving sugar is available most of the year. It's a specially clarified sugar that produces preserves without much foam when they're cooked and a clear, crystal-like jelly. Much preserving sugar now comes with added pectin built in. This can be a great help in ensuring the jam sets. Failing preserving sugar, pure cane sugar is the best. Normally white sugar only is used in making jam though some of the darker marmalades in the Oxford style do use one of the soft brown sugars to achieve colour and depth of flavour.

3. **Cook the fruit before adding the sugar**

- Depending on what fruit you use, you should cook the fruit until it's just tender in as little water as will achieve this. With cut-up fruit you may need to add a little lemon juice to preserve the colour. (If you are making jelly, this is the time to strain the mixture.)

- Only when the fruit is translucent and cooked should you add the sugar. Use the same weight of sugar as cooked fruit. Stir until the sugar has thoroughly dissolved off the heat, bring to the boil and cook gently until the mixture sets when a spoonful is dropped on to a cold saucer.

- For marmalades, blanch the cleaned and sliced peel before adding it to the juice of the oranges or citrus fruit and cook that without the sugar until the peel is translucent. Then add the sugar and proceed.

- For jellies, strain the cooked fruit through a jelly bag without pressing the fruit; if you do press it, the jelly will be cloudy. Add 450 g (1 lb) of sugar to each 600 ml (1 pint) of juice and proceed.

4. **Bottling** Bottle into clean, sterilized jars. This can be achieved by chemical sterilization (as for baby's bottles) or with the use of boiling water. And don't forget to sterilize the lids and dry the jars out in a warm oven.

5. **Filling and closing** Use a jam funnel to fill the jars – it's safer and easier (see page 304). To seal, close the lids tightly. As the jam or preserve cools it will create a vacuum, thus ensuring long life and preservation. Most jams and marmalades improve by being kept for at least a week to a month before use. Properly made, they will keep in a cool store cupboard for 2 or 3 years.

ALUMINIUM
The cheapest preserving pans are aluminium. But acidic foods like fruit attack the metal and minute quantities of it leach into the food. There has been a suspicion that ingestion of too much aluminium can cause Alzheimer's disease. But the majority of the aluminium we consume comes from tea, coffee and drinking water. And experts now doubt that there is a direct link anyway. But if you wish to avoid this possible hazard, use non-stick or the much more expensive stainless steel pans. One other tip – don't store acidic foods like fruit or tomatoes in aluminium foil. The acid will attack the foil and the parcel will leak.

Chutneys and pickles

Here are three ways of making fruit preserves
to be eaten with savoury foods. The method
used to make the apple chutney is a basic one
which works well with most combinations of
fruit. The preserving method for the kumquats
works equally well, suitably adjusted, for
peaches, quinces and crab apples.

Basic apple chutney

Makes about 2.25 kg (5 lb)

1.4 kg (3 lb) cooking apples
450 g (1 lb) onions, peeled and diced
225 g (8 oz) raisins and sultanas mixed
900 ml (1½ pints) vinegar (for a lighter chutney use
  cider vinegar, if you prefer a full-bodied one brown
  malt vinegar is suitable)
450 g (1 lb) soft brown sugar
25 g (1 oz) salt
½ teaspoon ground cloves
1 small chilli pepper
450 g (1 lb) tomatoes

Peel and core the apples and cut them up into
marble-sized pieces. Mix with the onions,
raisins and sultanas. Put them into a stainless
steel or non-stick pan and add the vinegar,
sugar, salt, cloves and chilli pepper. Simmer
very gently for 1 to 1¼ hours until the mixture
thickens. Cut the tomatoes into marble-sized
pieces, add those and simmer for another 30
minutes, stirring regularly, until fully
thickened. Discard the chilli pepper, spoon the
chutney into hot, sterilized jars and seal at
once.

Above: *Pickled eggs* (page 245). **Below:** *Basic apple*
chutney

Christmas chutney

This very grand and quite expensive way to make chutney is wonderful at Christmas time with cold meats. In small pots tied with pretty ribbons it makes a nice home-made present as well. It's quite spicy so if you like a milder chutney cut down a little on the mustard seed and chilli.

Makes about 1.5 kg (3 lb)

600 ml (1 pint) cider vinegar
50 g (2 oz) soft brown sugar
25 g (1 oz) sea salt
450 g (1 lb) green grapes (preferably seedless)
50 g (2 oz) currants
50 g (2 oz) raisins
50 g (2 oz) sultanas
100 g (4 oz) cut mixed peel
100 g (4 oz) crystallized ginger
2 cloves garlic
25 g (1 oz) whole mustard seed
4 dried red chillies, chopped
450 g (1 lb) tinned mango, drained

Bring the cider vinegar, sugar and salt to the boil. Add all the other ingredients except the mango and cook for 25 to 30 minutes until the mixture has thickened. Chop the mango and add it, cooking for another 5 to 10 minutes. Make sure that the chutney is fully blended. Pour it into sterilized jars with rubber seals and seal immediately while it's hot. It needs at least 2 weeks before you can eat it; 3 to 4 months improves it magically.

Spiced kumquats

This is a preserve meant to be eaten with cold meats or cheese. It's made from the baby oranges known as kumquats which can be eaten whole, skin and all. It's a process that, adjusted for the ingredient, can be used for a variety of soft fruits to make spectacular spiced pickles.

Makes about 900 g (2 lb)

900 g (2 lb) kumquats
175 g (6 oz) caster sugar
2 tablespoons white wine or cider vinegar
4 star anise
10 coriander seeds
2 bay leaves
1 dried red chilli pepper
6 peppercorns

Place the kumquats in a stainless steel or non-stick pan, cover them with water and bring to the boil. Strain and discard the water, put the fruit back in the pan, and add enough water to come just below the surface of the fruit. Simmer gently for 35 minutes or so until the fruit is becoming translucent. Remove the pan from the heat, add the sugar and wine or cider vinegar to the liquid and stir continuously until the sugar dissolves. Bring the whole thing to a rolling boil for about 5 minutes. Take out the fruit and place in sterilized jars with the star anise, coriander seeds, bay leaves, chilli pepper and peppercorns divided up between them. Top up with the liquid until the jar is completely full. Cover but don't seal down tight until the fruit is cold.

Pickled onions

As the pickle part of a ploughman's lunch, these are perfect. Try sticks of three cheeses (Cheddar, Wensleydale and Stilton for choice) with a couple of crusty rolls to complete the meal. The quantities of onions and vinegar used in this recipe vary according to the size of jars.

Makes 2 × 1 litre (1¾ pint) jars

450 g (1 lb) pickling onions
50 g (2 oz) sea salt
600 ml (1 pint) light or dark malt vinegar
50 g (2 oz) light soft brown sugar
1 tablespoon pickling spice
Muslin and a little string to tie up the pickling spices

To peel the onions, drop them into boiling water for 1 minute, then run them under cold water to stop the cooking. Remove the skins, and put the onions in a shallow dish, sprinkle with salt and leave for 6 hours. Rinse and wait till they dry before proceeding. Boil the vinegar and sugar together until the sugar dissolves, add the bag of spices and simmer for 5 minutes. Put the onions in the jars and pour the hot vinegar over them. Close the lid and leave for 2 weeks before eating.

Pickled eggs

A traditional treat still sometimes to be found in old-fashioned pubs. Pickled eggs are a good addition to a ploughman's lunch and salads.

Makes 12 pickled eggs

12 hard-boiled eggs, shelled
600 ml (1 pint) cider vinegar
1 tablespoon white sugar
2 teaspoons pickling spice wrapped in muslin

Sterilize a 900 ml (1½ pint) preserving jar by placing in a saucepan of hot water, bringing to the boil and then placing in a hot oven to dry, or using a disinfectant suitable for sterilizing babies' bottles. Put the hard-boiled eggs in the jar. Boil the cider vinegar, sugar and spices together until the sugar dissolves. When both the eggs and vinegar are cool, pour the vinegar on to the eggs and seal the jar. Leave the eggs to pickle for 2 weeks before eating; they will keep for 2 months.

A key guide to spices

Allspice

Peppercorn-shaped spice originating in Jamaica supposed to contain the flavours of cinnamon, nutmeg, mace and cloves. Uses: pickling, beef stews, a general sweet spicing.

Aniseed

Star anise is the variety most available – a star-shaped shiny seed with a vivid flavour. Uses: Chinese cooking, carrots cooked in the French style.

Bay leaf

Edible leaf of the 'noble laurel'. Uses: essential ingredient in all bouquet garnis, most casseroles and marinades. It can be ground, to give food a mild bay flavour.

Caraway

Small pungent seed. Uses: in baking to flavour sweet cakes and in Middle European cooking for cabbage dishes and goulash.

Cardamom

Tiny black seed from a pea-sized fibrous pod. Fragrant and delicate. Uses: extensive in the Middle East and India and in traditional British biscuits and spice bread. Excellent with cinnamon and bay leaf for pilau rice.

Cayenne

Version of chilli pepper usually made from blend of chillies. Red or brown and extremely strong. Uses: light dusting on raw shellfish and pungent spice mixtures.

Chilli

Wide range of very hot peppers. Can contain various flavours. Available fresh and in dry and ground form. Uses: spice dishes from all over the world in quite delicate amounts. Also, dried whole, in pickling spice mixtures.

245

Cinnamon

Golden spice ground from the bark of a tree. Light, fragrant and sweet. Uses: baking, flavouring in puddings and apple dishes, with which it has a particular affinity. Also found rolled as cinnamon sticks.

Cloves

Small tack-shaped spices. Uses: whole in savoury dishes (often stuck into onions), pickling, sweets and puddings. Has a strong affinity for apples and pears.

Coriander

Coriander seed is pale golden and peppercorn-sized. Has a burnt orange flavour. Uses: an ingredient in curry and Middle Eastern food.

Cumin

Astringent seed with pungent, slightly bitter flavour. Uses: Mexican and Indian cookery. Basic spice in all curry mixtures.

246

Curry

Mixture of spices varying from region to region in the Indian sub-continent and South East Asia. Most people make their own. Here's a basic curry powder that can be kept in an airtight tin and used a tablespoon at a time:

4 tablespoons coriander seed
4 tablespoons cumin seed
3 tablespoons turmeric
2 tablespoons dried ginger
1 tablespoon chilli powder
2 teaspoons cardamom seed   *all ground*
2 teaspoons black pepper   *together*
2 teaspoons garam masala (a pre-mixed
  sweet spice blend)
2 teaspoons cinnamon

Ginger

A root like a dahlia tuber. Can be peeled and used fresh or bought ground and dried. Uses: essential in China, Japan and India. Also British cakes and biscuits and, in moderation, with fruit salad.

Juniper

Small, purple berries. Uses: gives gin its flavour. Also a flavouring for game.

Mace

Pale gold outer covering of nutmeg, similar in flavour but with a sweet note to it. Uses: baking and potted foods, particularly potted shrimps.

Mustard

Pungent spice which comes in a variety of strengths. English mustard seed, bright gold, is the strongest; German and French mustards, brown and black, are milder. Uses: traditionally as a meat condiment, also adds flavour to white and cheese sauces and in its milder forms for cream sauté sauces.

Nutmeg

Hard, grape-sized, fragrant spice. Uses: topping sweet puddings. Also it's added to mashed potatoes and cabbage dishes.

Paprika

Bright red, chilli-looking, powdered spice made from relatives of the hot chilli but mild in flavour. Uses: Hungarian and Austrian cooking for colour and richness.

Pepper

Black, green and white pepper are the same spice. Pungent white pepper is the core of black peppercorns. Green is the mild, unripe berry. Best freshly ground. Uses: general seasoning in British savoury cooking, and, exotically, to bring out the flavour of fruit such as strawberries.

Saffron

Stamens of the autumn crocus. Most expensive spice in the world. Uses: in extremely small quantities to produce a rich gold colour and delicate fragrance. Also in baking (particularly Easter cakes and breads), in pilau dishes and in exotic sweets from the Indian sub-continent.

Sesame

Tiny, pale, cream seeds. Uses: particularly in Greek-style breads and on biscuits. When ground, the basis of Tahini, one of the principal ingredients of the vegetarian dip Hummus. Also the basis of Middle Eastern sweetmeat, Halva. Used widely in Chinese cooking, particularly as a toasted oil for flavouring vegetable dishes.

Turmeric

Bright gold, mild spice. Uses: essential part of curry powder. Has a similar colouring ability to saffron for which it is occasionally used as a substitute. In Britain, it is a colouring agent for pickles and chutneys (as in piccalilli), and in mustards.

Vanilla

A sweet flavouring found in vanilla pods or beans – long, thin, black fruits. Pods can be ground up to powder, or kept in sugar to flavour it aromatically. May be bought as essence; a pale brown, clear liquid. Uses: for flavouring custards, cakes and biscuits. Best known in ice-cream, but also good in syrups for fruit salads and cooked dried fruit. Also goes well with chocolate.

247

1. **Curry powder**
2. **Whole chillies**
3. **Crushed chillies**
4. **Chilli powder**
5. **Vanilla pod**
6. **Ground cumin**
7. **Juniper berries**
8. **Cumin seed**
9. **Whole aniseed**
10. **Coriander seeds**
11. **Whole allspice**
12. **Ground allspice**
13. **Turmeric**
14. **Cardamom seeds**
15. **Nutmeg**
16. **Ground nutmeg**
17. **Caraway seeds**
18. **Sesame seeds**
19. **Mace blade**
20. **Ground cinnamon**
21. **Cinnamon stick**
22. **Ground bay**
23. **Bay leaf**
24. **Saffron**
25. **Black pepper**
26. **Mixed peppercorns**
27. **Mustard seed**
28. **Ground mustard**
29. **Whole green peppercorns**
30. **Whole white peppercorns**
31. **Cayenne pepper**
32. **Ginger**
33. **Paprika**
34. **Cloves**

CHAPTER SEVENTEEN

By dairy products we mean any milk-based foods. There's now a wider choice than ever before.

dairy products

Milk and its various forms

Dairies and most supermarkets now supply milk in a confusing variety of forms. Here is a simple guide to what they contain. All milk is pasteurized (heat-treated) before being sold. Unpasteurized, or green top milk, is virtually unobtainable unless you actually live on a farm.

1. Whole milk

This contains approximately 4 per cent fat and comes in plain and homogenized forms. Homogenized milk has been blended so that the fat is equally distributed throughout it, not collecting on the top as cream.

2. Channel islands or breakfast milk

This is whole milk produced by Guernsey or Jersey cows with a higher, 5 to 6 per cent, fat content. It adds a particularly rich taste to custards and other dishes cooked with it.

3. Semi-skimmed milk

Milk that has had half its fat removed, so it is approximately 2 per cent fat, is widely used for drinking and cooking in the same way as whole milk. Although it is significantly lower in fat, its perceived qualities are such that it makes a totally adequate substitute in almost all respects.

4. Skimmed milk

This is milk with the fat content below 1 per cent. It's valuable as a low-fat alternative to semi-skimmed or whole milk. But it's not ideal for cooking – it's so low in fat that it often leads to lumpy or stringy results.

5. Evaporated milk

This is a form of whole milk which has been heat-treated to sterilize it. It's a slightly old-fashioned method now and produces a milk with a degree of sweetness in it from natural milk sugars. **Condensed milk** is even sweeter.

6. UHT milk

This is milk that has also been heat-treated to preserve it but has no sweetener. It does have a slight flavour from the steam treatment but will keep unopened in its Tetrapack for the best part of a year and is therefore an excellent store-cupboard standby.

249

NUTRITIOUS MILK
Children under the age of five should not be given skimmed or semi-skimmed milk as they depend quite heavily on fat for their food energy. All milk is an excellent source of calcium. Most milks are a good source of riboflavin (vitamin B_{12}) and whole milk is the best source of vitamin A. (Evaporated and condensed milks have a much lower vitamin content). Milk left in direct sunlight will not only go off but also quickly loses its vitamins.

Above: *Stilton* (page 250). Below: *Cheddar* (page 250)

Cheeses

A quick guide to hard cheeses

Here is a selection of popular hard cheeses with their best cooking uses.

CAERPHILLY

Flavour Delicious fresh salty flavour. Can be nice cut in thick slices and grilled on bread to make a primitive form of Welsh rarebit.

CHEDDAR

This comes not only from the Somerset region of Britain but from all over the world in various guises.
Flavour Mild to very strong. The more mature, the stronger the flavour. Farmhouse is the best quality. Excellent from New Zealand and Canada as well as Britain.
Cooking uses Melts easily into cheese sauces. Good for grating. Makes fine Welsh rarebit.

CHESHIRE

250

Flavour Medium to strong. Some Farmhouse Cheshire is available. White and gold taste the same.
Cooking uses Crumbly texture, melts well as a topping but not good in sauces.

EDAM

Flavour Mild and waxy.
Cooking uses Only in its raw state as an addition to salads, grated or in cubes.

GOUDA

Flavour Rich and creamy. Gouda is an ideal alternative to Gruyère as a cooking cheese, especially the mature kinds which have a similar richness of flavour.
Cooking uses Good for gratins, soufflés, cheese sauces and fondues.

GRUYÈRE

Flavour Rich and complex.
Cooking uses This is almost exclusively a cooking cheese. Great for cheese sauces, topping gratins, cheese soufflés, fondues and any other culinary use where its flavour and texture contribute.

LANARK BLUE

Flavour Rich and salty.
Cooking uses This newly developed British cheese is an ideal alternative to Roquefort in dressings or blended into cheese pâtés or for blue cheese sauce.

LANCASHIRE

Flavour Slightly sour and sharp flavour.
Cooking uses Excellent cooking cheese for sauces, grates well for gratin toppings and excellent for rarebit.

MOZZARELLA

Flavour Mild but richer when cooked.
Cooking uses The cheese for pizza toppings – it melts superbly. Also eaten in salads with avocado and tomato (purists will tell you it has to be made with water buffalo's milk – but the cow's milk version is fine).

PARMESAN

Flavour Salty and strong, delicious eaten fresh in chunks, with ripe fruit.
Cooking uses Usually grated finely and used to top pasta dishes and pizzas. It's also used extensively to enrich and sharpen cheese sauces and other dishes where milder cheeses have provided the bulk of the content.

STILTON

Flavour Deep and rich, particularly the blue-veined variety.
Cooking uses Usually eaten as it is, it makes excellent blue cheese dressing and as a melted cheese on steaks. Also good with strongly flavoured soups, like celery.

WENSLEYDALE

Flavour Mild to medium, honeyed.
Cooking uses Not too good for cooking but particularly nice eaten with sweet foods such as apple pie or currant bread.

Parmesan

Gouda

Brie

Cambozola

Portcarreg

Gorgonzola

Camembert

Mozzarella

A quick guide to soft cheeses

There are more soft cheeses than there are pages in this book! But here are some of the more widely available ones.

BRIE

Flavour Mild, creamy and delicate.
Cooking uses Not often used in cooking, though excellent sliced thinly and made into sandwiches. Soft blue cheeses such as Blue Brie, can be used as a basis for a mild blue cheese sauce

CAMEMBERT

Flavour Strong and pungent when ripe.
Cooking uses Occasionally dipped in breadcrumbs or nuts and deep-fried, served with a sharp sauce such as gooseberry.

GOATS' CHEESES

Flavours Mild and strong flavours are available, creamy white in appearance and crumbly in texture.
Cooking uses Often preserved in oil and used in salads. They can also be cut in half and grilled on a croûton to make a *nouvelle cuisine* first course.

GORGONZOLA

Flavour Rich, creamy blue flavour.
Cooking uses This semi-hard cheese makes excellent pasta sauce mixed with a little cream and butter and melted until quite smooth.

LOW FAT AND FLAVOURED SOFT CHEESES

These come in an increasingly wide variety, many under brand names like Boursin or Tartin. Most brands have low or very low fat versions often labelled 'light'. They are flavoured with a variety of flavourings including garlic, herbs and pepper, though some, notably Philadelphia, can have no flavourings at all. All make excellent spreads on toast or bread and, beaten down with a little milk, make good dips for crisps or raw vegetables. The higher fat ones also are excellent used instead of herb butters on grilled steaks and chops.

PENCARREG

Flavour Mild to medium, creamy. A Brie-type cheese made organically in Wales.
Cooking uses Like Brie.

SOFT CHEESE AND LISTERIA
In Britain, the government have advised pregnant women to avoid soft, rinded cheeses, such as Brie, Camembert and goats' cheeses. Their low acidity can allow a bacterium called Listeria Monocytogenes to multiply. This would only cause mild flu symptoms in a healthy adult; but Listeriosis can give rise to miscarriages or even stillbirths in pregnant women.

The crucial guide to cream, fromage frais and yoghurt

- **Clotted cream** Fat content 60 per cent. **Uses** Normally used on scones for Devon cream teas with strawberry jam.
- **Extra thick double cream** Approximately 50 per cent fat. Spooning thick double cream. Best used when eaten directly on to fruit or puddings.
- **Standard double cream** 40 per cent fat. The best cream for whipping and as an enricher for sauces and puddings.
- **Crème fraîche** 40 per cent fat. French-style double cream, slightly soured. Will whip thick and is used a lot in *nouvelle cuisine* sauces.
- **Whipping cream** 30 to 35 per cent fat. Similar uses to double cream but harder work to get thick.
- **Single cream** 20 per cent fat. A pouring cream which can be used for thickening sauces with the addition of some cornflour to achieve a lower fat result.
- **Soured cream** 20 per cent fat. A classic Eastern European addition to the likes of Blinis (see page 61) and Borscht (see page 12) and Beef Stroganoff (see page 163).
- **Fromage frais** 8 per cent, 6 per cent and 0 per cent fat. A thick, mild, creamy product in various grades. Can be used as double cream on savoury and sweet foods but will separate if boiled. A teaspoon or two of cornflour mixed in first helps prevent this. An excellent low fat alternative.
- **Quark** A German version of fromage frais. Usually drier in texture with similar uses.
- **Greek yoghurt** 8 to 10 per cent fat. This is plain yoghurt which has been thickened by draining much of the liquid from it and concentrating the solids. Very creamy in texture. Ideal for cooking with curries and other Middle Eastern foods. Will separate if boiled vigorously.
- **Whole milk yoghurt** 4 per cent fat. Usually a set yoghurt made from whole milk and ideal when firm texture is valued. Often referred to as 'plain' or 'natural' yoghurt.
- **Skimmed milk or low fat yoghurt** 0 to 1 per cent fat. Low fat yoghurt is slightly thinner in texture than the whole milk variety. Often sold flavoured and sweetened with substantial amounts of sugar.
- **Drinking yoghurt** This is low fat yoghurt that has been thinned down and flavoured with fruit or other flavourings. Usually highly sugared.

Home-made milk shakes

These are simple, easy-to-make milk shakes that are a favourite with children. In adult versions they're popular with grown-ups too. They can be made taking advantage of the low fat milks and milk products that are listed above. All milk shakes need a high speed liquidizer or blender to achieve the necessary result. Make sure that yours is strong enough to manage ice cubes as well.

Children's milk shakes

Banana milk shake

Thick, creamy and a great favourite.

Serves 2

3 bananas, peeled and cut into 3
600 ml (1 pint) semi-skimmed milk
1 cup of ice cubes
2 tablespoons 8 per cent fromage frais
1 teaspoon vanilla essence

Put all the ingredients into the liquidizer and process, holding the whole system securely until the ice cubes stop rattling.

253

Chocolate milk shake

Serves 2

1 tablespoon drinking chocolate
2 tablespoons boiling water
600 ml (1 pint) whole milk
4 scoops chocolate ice-cream

Dilute the drinking chocolate with the boiling water and stir until smooth. Add to the milk, put in the chocolate ice-cream and blend until smoothly mixed and foamy.

Adult milk shakes

Avocado and pineapple milk shake

This is a sophisticated milk shake that, in small quantities, makes a delicious starter for an outdoor meal or brunch.

Serves 4

1 very ripe avocado
600 ml (1 pint) semi-skimmed milk
175 g (6 oz) pineapple cubes, fresh or tinned in their
*   own juice*
½ cup ice cubes
A pinch of salt

Scoop the avocado out of the skin. Discard the stone and place the flesh in the liquidizer. (If the avocado is very small you may need 2.) Add the milk, ice cubes, pineapple chunks and salt and process until the pineapple is thoroughly blended in and the whole mixture is foamy. Serve in medium-sized glasses with a swizzle stick of celery if you fancy it.

254

Breakfast in a glass

This is the ultimate pick-me-up which, for all kinds of complex nutritional reasons, really does help deal with the over-indulgence of the night before. For food safety advice on eating raw eggs see page 55.

1 whole orange, pips and stem removed (unwaxed is
*   best if you can find one)*
600 ml (1 pint) semi-skimmed milk
2 tablespoons runny honey
150 ml (5 fl oz) plain yoghurt
A pinch of salt
1 raw egg

Cut the orange into quarters and cut them once again crossways. Put them, the milk, honey, yoghurt and salt into the liquidizer. Break in the egg, put the lid on and blend thoroughly until the orange is completely blended into the mixture, which will be thick and foamy. Pour into tumblers and drink as required. It's very nutritious and you don't have to be feeling awful to enjoy it.

Crafty ice-cream

There is an extremely simple way of making ice-cream without a fancy machine or complicated beating in the middle of the freezing process. Technically it's known as a parfait and is a frozen mousse. The basic method can be flavoured in a number of ways. Both this and the frozen yoghurt recipe that follows contain raw egg. For advice on raw egg safety see page 55.

Vanilla ice-cream

Serves 4 to 6

150 ml (5 fl oz) double cream
4 eggs, separated
4 tablespoons icing sugar
1 teaspoon real vanilla essence

Whisk the cream until it's really thick. Take two of the egg whites and whisk them till they're really thick then add them to the cream. Beat the four egg yolks thoroughly with the remaining egg whites and whisk in the icing sugar tablespoon by tablespoon until it's thoroughly incorporated and the whole mixture is pale, lemon-coloured, and very frothy. Add the vanilla essence. Then add the egg mixture to the cream mixture, folding it in to lose as little beaten-in air as possible. Pour into a plastic container with a lid and place in a freezer for 4 to 6 hours until frozen solid. (You may use an ice-cream maker following its instructions if you have one.) The mixture does not need beating or processing while it's freezing.

To serve: allow to de-frost for 30 minutes in a fridge and serve in ice-cream glasses.

VARIATIONS

● **Chocolate** You may ring the changes on the flavouring by adding 100 g (4 oz) melted bitter chocolate to the egg mixture instead of the vanilla essence and stirring that immediately into the cream mixture.
● **Peach** Make the basic mixture. Simmer 225 g (8 oz) peeled peach slices in a little sugar syrup for about 10 minutes until they are translucent. Purée half of them and mix into the basic ice-cream mixture. Chop the remainder roughly and add those and freeze as above. The peach slices will be quite chewy but the *parfait* will be smooth.

- **Strawberry** To the above basic mixture without the vanilla essence, add 100 g (4 oz) puréed strawberries and another 50 g (2 oz) strawberries cut into slices and mixed with a tablespoon of icing sugar. Freeze as above.

Frozen yoghurt

It's possible, if you have an ice-cream machine with an electric or hand beater system, to freeze yoghurt in a similar way to the *parfait* mixture as above. But it's very difficult to do if you don't have the proper machine.

Serves 4

2 eggs
75 g (3 oz) icing sugar
1 teaspoon vanilla essence
600 ml (1 pint) whole milk set yoghurt (Greek yoghurt is fine for this, too)

Break the eggs into a bowl and whisk them thoroughly with the icing sugar, adding it a spoonful at a time until the mixture is lemon-coloured and very frothy. Mix in the vanilla essence. Beat the yoghurt thoroughly until smooth, add the egg mixture and stir until well blended. Pour into an ice-cream maker and switch on. This only makes satisfactory ice-cream if the system has a moving, stirring device that prevents the mixture setting into ice particles as it freezes. Frozen yoghurt can be flavoured with fruit as in the ice-creams above, peaches and strawberries both making an excellent basis.

Above: *Avocado and pineapple milk shake.*
Below: *Frozen yoghurt*

enjoying wine

The wines here are grouped in two ways. First, by grape variety, where they are teamed with their perfect food partners (although there are few hard and fast rules, the most important thing is to choose what you like) and second by country (see page 275).

White grape varieties

Chardonnay

Chardonnay is the buzz grape variety of our time and all over the world grape growers are planting it – or simply grafting it on to less fashionable rootstock – to try to get a slice of the action. The craze is a little difficult to understand, because likeable though the variety is, it doesn't really have a single, definable taste. It tastes different country to country and even wine-maker to wine-maker.

France

The grape has its origins in France (although that's not where the current fashion for it began). Burgundy is its home and it is responsible for virtually everything from Bourgogne Blanc *ordinaire* right up to the most splendid *Grand Cru* wines, taking in white Beaujolais, Chablis, and the sparkling Crémant de Bourgogne on the way. Curiously, white Burgundy is the model for all Chardonnay wines made throughout the world – but because standards in Burgundy are unreliable, its imitators, (at the cheaper end of things, certainly) can frequently surpass it. The other major French region for Chardonnay is Champagne, where it is the only white grape. All but a very few Champagnes include Chardonnay in the blend and the Blanc de Blancs wines are made exclusively from it. Neither in Burgundy nor Champagne does the grape declare itself on the label. It is to the newer areas – largely in Southern France – that you have to look to for this simplicity.

Italy

Chardonnay is now widely planted in Italy, although it is not a traditional Italian grape variety. The first Italian Chardonnays to cut a dash here came from the far north of the country in Alto Adige (alias Süd Tirol). They are streamlined, slim types, the antithesis of some of the voluptuous, oaked versions of Australia.

Germany, Spain and Portugal

Germany, usually resistant to introductions from *anywhere*, has permitted a little Chardonnay to be planted, and the generally idiosyncratic countries of the Iberian peninsula have also bent their usual resolve and allowed in this popular foreigner. Spain makes some excellent Chardonnays and Portugal, despite her wealth of local varieties and understandable pride in them, is also experimenting here and there.

Central Europe

Bulgarian Chardonnay (often heavily oaked) needs no introduction; there's lots of it about and at cheap enough prices for wine lovers to have the chance to make its acquaintance. It's planted in Czechoslovakia, Hungary, Romania, Slovenia and parts of the former Soviet Union to give label shoppers yet more chance to buy their favourite grape at affordable prices.

257

North and South America

California has really taken Chardonnay to its breast. It is the most important grape variety there, and some exceptional wines are being made – like white Burgundy with knobs on. Chardonnay is quite new to Chile, but such is the enthusiasm for the grape that a valley has been identified as being *perfect* for it and is now planted peak to peak.

Australia and New Zealand

Australia's Chardonnays are legendary – and were probably responsible for starting the big Chardonnay fad. To begin with they were sometimes altogether too much of a good thing, so voluptuous with their tropical fruit salad flavours topped off with creamy new oak. But now reticence has crept in and some marvellous mouthfuls are being produced (along with some very ordinary ones). New Zealand has to date made less of its Chardonnays; its acclaimed skills being seen to lie more with Sauvignon Blanc. But there are signs that this Garden of Eden for the vine is now turning the spotlight on Chardonnay.

South Africa

South Africa, having misfired in the Chardonnay game (mistakenly planting the wrong vines in the belief they were Chardonnay) has entered the Chardonnay bonanza late. The plantings are as yet very new, but wine-producers are working hard to bring the wines on stream.

What Chardonnay tastes like

Asked what Chardonnay tastes like, most wine lovers would describe the flavour of . . . oak, so many Chardonnays are garnished with wood these days. Unoaked types have broad (as opposed to piercing), if slight bouquets, with perhaps a hint of creamy *pâtisserie* and a tinge of lemon or green apple. Fruit flavours range from apple through melon to the richer peach and nectarine pulpy fruits, ending in exotic fruit medleys for the hotter-climate versions. The modern trend is for Chardonnay to be a vehicle for oak, introducing the familiar vanilla and oak notes to the flavour spectrum.

Foods it goes with

Classic white Burgundy, including Chablis goes with top quality fish dishes, preferably without rich sauces. It is also good with turbot, bass, salmon and sea trout, fish terrines, shellfish (prawns, lobster, mussels), soufflés, chicken, veal and pork.

New World Chardonnays go with highly flavoured fish and shellfish dishes such as fish soup, bouillabaisse, fish stew, dressed crab, garlic prawns and also with roast chicken, veal and pork chops, risotto, pasta with sauce and quiche.

Italian and Spanish Chardonnays go with grilled oily fish, shellfish, sea bream, red mullet, monkfish; all meaty types of fish.

Chenin Blanc

Though infinitely less well known than Chardonnay or Sauvignon Blanc, Chenin, in its quiet way, is as important a cog in the world's wine industry. And it has enormous range, producing sweet wines of high pedigree, famous sparklers and inexpensive white plonk.

France

The Loire is its historic homeland, where (anonymously) it's responsible for most white wines of Anjou and Touraine. If that doesn't mean much to you, the names Saumur, Vouvray and Anjou Blanc will; all predominantly Chenin wines, whether they be dry, medium, sweet or even sparkling. The classiest types are without doubt the long-lived sweet wines such as Vouvray, Coteaux du Layon, Moulin Touchais, Bonnezeaux and Quarts-de-Chaume.

North and South America

Chenin Blanc is massively planted in California, where it has few pretentions. Wine-makers use it to supply the country's big appetite for cheap and cheerful 'jug' wines, usually medium dry (and unexciting) in style. Chile and Argentina, meanwhile, also have lots of Chenin Blanc to play around with – again, they tend to go for the fruity, soft, medium style.

Australia and New Zealand

Australia tends not to take Chenin Blanc too seriously – it's a cheap and cheerful white producer for them, too, often blended with other grape varieties. The cool climate of New Zealand has prompted some of her wine-makers to try a bit harder with the Loire's classic type, to attempt to get it to perform some minor miracles. Meanwhile, it produces some pretty ordinary white plonk in NZ, too.

South Africa

Chenin Blanc, occasionally called 'Steen', is the mainstay of the Cape wine industry. It is her most popular grape, making well-priced, dry and off-dry whites and some good sweet types, too.

 CAN ALCOHOL BE GOOD FOR YOU? Millions of us drink more alcohol than is good for us. This is the most important point about alcohol – it can cause pain as well as give pleasure. Having said that, there is some evidence that a moderate intake of alcohol (no more than 2 units a day) protects from heart disease. Recent studies suggest that red wine in particular may have this effect.

What Chenin Blanc tastes like

Chenin has a peculiar (and it has to be said, not wholly attractive) bouquet. As well as seeming to smell sweet, no matter what the provenance of the wine, there's a sickly scent to it, like over-ripe soft cheese, coupled with the slightly frowsty smell you get from damp wool drying by a radiator. Damp straw is another association. On the palate, better examples usually have a honeyed taste and feel, with sometimes a suggestion of concentrated orange juice. Regrettably many French Chenins are treated with too much sulphur which gives off the whiff of a just-struck match.

Fashionable Chenin Blanc wines in the nineties
South Africa has to hold the cards here; not only are her Chenins refreshingly crisp, but they are attractively affordable as well.

The most expensive Chenin Blanc wine in the world
Sweet Loire Chenins can be very long lived. Examples of Moulin Touchais from the last century, for instance, are still considered to be in their prime. Were they to be sold, these would command the highest prices. Otherwise it has to be Vouvray.

---

260 *Foods it goes with*

Of the good quality Loire Chenins the 'medium' styles match well with unusually flavoured dishes such as sweetbreads, oriental fish with ginger, pork-based terrines, rillettes, veal and other white meats with cream sauces.

Sweeter Loire Chenins match well with rich pâtés and *charcuterie*, salty cheese, caramalized fruit pastry dishes, fruit tarts, crêpe suzette and lemon soufflé.

Cheap and cheerful Chenins – led by South African versions – make ideal barbecue partners for meat and fish and go with shepherd's pie, cauliflower cheese and salads.

Pinot Blanc

Unusually for a French-originating grape, Pinot Blanc tends to declare itself on the label.

France

In France this is explained by its concentration in the forward-thinking region of Alsace, where grapes do make themselves known on labels. Pinot Blanc is the commonest Alsace wine seen around.

Italy

Popular as Pinot Bianco all over the country, this import from France makes a pleasant change from the rather dull, characterless run of still Italian whites. It also provides a talented base for dry sparkling wines which may call themselves simply Pinot.

Germany

It is known as Weissburgunder in Germany, where it is increasingly seen making good dry (*trocken*) and off-dry (*halbtrocken*) wines as well as being capable of making the traditional, sweeter types.

Central Europe

The New Wave wine-makers who are turning around the old-fashioned wine industry in such places as Hungary and Czechoslovakia are working wonders with Pinot Blanc, making subtle, delicate wines at easily affordable prices. Austria also has a strong leaning to the variety.

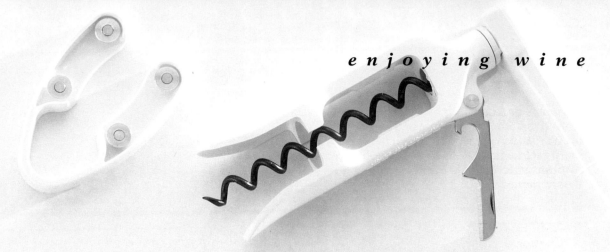

North and South America

California has a fondness for this soft, Chardonnay-style grape and uses it for simple, dry white wines (named after the grape), for wines with greater pretensions and more complexity, and for sparkling wine. The world's appetite for sparkling wine is being fuelled increasingly by Pinot Blanc. From South America, particularly Chile, you'll find good Pinot Blancs, soft and easy-drinking.

What Pinot Blanc tastes like

Never powerfully scented, if you work hard on the bouquet of a Pinot Blanc wine, you'll find it is essentially creamy, with perhaps a fleeting hint of apple. The creaminess continues into the flavour, which picks up good lemony acidity; kind of lemon and sugar at the same time. There can be pungent flavours, a suggestion of lavender or parma violet sweets. A soft, dry white wine, it is very easy to appreciate.

> **Fashionable Pinot Blanc wines in the nineties**
> *The newcomers from Czechoslovakia and Hungary.*
>
> **The most expensive Pinot Blanc wine in the world**
> *Alsace doesn't make much of a song and dance of her Pinot Blancs, so the honours must go to California, to Chalone Pinot Blanc.*

Foods it goes with

Pinot Blanc doesn't need food; it's a good wine to drink on its own. When it does partner grub, it isn't very assertive, so you have a wide choice. Here are some suggestions: rice dishes such as risotto and paella, shellfish (not oysters), pâtés and terrines, cold meats and pies, pasta with creamy sauces.

Riesling

An internationally popular grape variety that, for once, doesn't have its roots in France: Riesling, or Rhine Riesling as it is sometimes called, is strictly German by birth. There are all manner of Rieslings on the shelves but confusingly, they are not always related. Welschriesling, Riesling Italico, Laski Rizling and Vlassky Rizling are all names given to totally different grapes which usually make uninteresting medium sweet wines of little distinction.

Germany

All the best German wines are made from Riesling, whether they be dry(ish), medium, sweet, or extraordinarily luscious. It's not the most widely planted variety there (the Müller-Thurgau is), but it is certainly the most highly revered. There is a fashion for Germany to concentrate her energies on making dry wines, pandering to the worldwide fashion for 'crisp, dry white'. And certainly Riesling can make some deliciously attractive dry wines. But it is for the grape's ability to make sweet wines that it is most famous in Germany. The levels of sweetness are achieved by a harmless mould (called *botrytis cinerea*) which settles on the grapes and dries them up, so concentrating the sugar in the juice. The resultant wines are classified on a scale of sweetness (see page 283) and named accordingly. Although German wine labels are not exactly simple to understand, Riesling wines will all declare the grape on the label, and the official quality of the wine (Spätlese, Auslese, etc.) will suggest the sweetness. Look out for these two simple pieces of information.

France

Such is the rivalry between France and Germany that Riesling, that quintessentially German grape, is not permitted to be planted anywhere in France more than 50 kilometres from the German border. Happily, the beautiful wine region of Alsace lies within that band and here, too, Riesling is the most distinguished grape, making mostly dry wines with a haunting floweriness to them. A few, labelled *Vendange Tardive*, are sweet.

Italy

The far north of the country, Alto Adige, has adopted the grape with success, often making it into pretty, light whites with just a flash of fizz to them. Elsewhere in Italy, confusingly, the aristocratic 'Rhine' Riesling is known as Riesling Renano.

Central Europe

As well as the Welschrieslings, Rizlings and the like, most Central European countries – Austria, Czechoslovakia, Bulgaria, Hungary and the former Soviet Union – make wines from 'proper' Riesling too, although it must be said, not always with inspiring results.

262 USA

The California wine industry is devoted to its Riesling (calling it sometimes Rhine Riesling or Johannisberg Riesling). They use it to make dry wines in the main, but with more and more attempts to get it to perform the sweet miracles it does in Germany – sometimes by introducing the vital mould (which is normally airborne) by hand. These sweeter types distinguish themselves with the description 'late picked' (the direct translation of the German *Spätlese* and the French *Vendange Tardive*). Oregon and Washington State also have their fair share of the grape, and it weathers the chill winters on the East coast in upstate New York as well. Watch out for 'pretenders' to the name in the US, where there are inferior grape types calling themselves Emerald Riesling and Gray Riesling.

Australia and New Zealand

Rhine Riesling, as it is usually called down under, is a very important grape in Australia. It is widely planted over all regions now, though at first it was very much concentrated in the Barossa Valley, where there is a strong German influence. But here lies the problem; although it is the most widely planted white grape, its name has become unfashionable.

German wines have lost their grip on the market the world over, and there are attempts at disguising any Germanic origins, so sometimes Rhine Rieslings are called just 'dry white' or some such anonymous label. Sadly, the same is true in New Zealand, although there the grape has only a tiny share of the vineyard area.

South Africa

White or Weisser Riesling is how the South Africans identify the grape.

What Riesling tastes like

Dry or sweet, Riesling still has the same haunting characteristics. The most unusual, the most startlingly identifiable, is the smell of petrol. Deeply inhaling the bouquet of a glass of good Riesling – particularly a German or Alsace one – you'll get that whiff of kerosene you get sitting in an aeroplane revving up on the runway. It's a dead giveaway. There's also a sweet floral scent to Rieslings, overlaid with honey. The taste is delicate and almost scented-seeming itself, with a good thrust of sharp, limy acidity.

Foods it goes with

Top drawer, sweet delights such as *Beerenauslese* and *Trockenbeerenauslese* are best savoured on their own without the distraction of food, at the end of a meal.

Medium types, perhaps called *Spätlese*, *Auslese* or 'late picked', surprisingly go with some game-based dishes such as venison or hare terrine, capsicum pepper dishes and asparagus, as well as not-too-sweet desserts.

The driest styles from Germany, Alsace or the New World are good with freshwater fish, (salmon/trout/quenelles). Good mature Alsace is also a foil for smoked fish such as salmon, trout or mackerel.

Semillon

Semillon is a bit of a conundrum; few wine consumers rate it very highly, but it is in fact largely responsible for making the most expensive wine in the world. Semillon is extensively planted worldwide, rarely achieving very great things. But in Bordeaux, where it combines with Sauvignon Blanc (generally, for sweet wines, on the ratio of 80/20) it turns out such splendours as Château d'Yquem, with the crucial assistance of a peculiar mould called *botrytis cinerea*, which attacks the grapes, drying up some of the juice and so concentrating the sugar in the juice that is left.

France

Bordeaux is Semillon's home, and not only is it the main grape behind all the sweeties such as Sauternes, Barsac, Ste-Croix-du-Mont, etc., but it is largely responsible for the enormous quantities of (often dull) dry white Bordeaux as well. In the right hands, it is capable of making good dry whites in Bordeaux, too, freshened with a dab of Sauvignon Blanc. Too often, though, they are flabby and over-sulphured. It creeps south from Bordeaux into Bergerac, where it makes dry wines and sweet with its regular partner Sauvignon, and into Côtes de Duras. In none of these wines will you find Semillon boasted on the label. They go by place name instead.

Australia

The Australians have really made something of their Semillon. They don't wait for the airborne mould to transform it into a sweet

treat there, instead they consider it more like Chardonnay, often giving it oak ageing to fill it out. And Australia introduced the successful Semillon/Chardonnay blend.

South America

Semillon is an important grape in Chile and Argentina, turning out quantities of wine, sometimes blended with Sauvignon as in Bordeaux. They range from ordinary to the fatter, fuller, Antipodean style.

California

Semillon is being taken seriously in California, where it combines with Sauvignon to make both dry and sweet wines, the excitement on the sweet wine front being that *botrytis* is being artificially manufactured to be sprayed on to vines to produce a regular supply of high quality extra sweet grapes.

South Africa and Central Europe

South Africa and most of Central Europe have Semillon plantings and are beginning to capitalize on propitious climate and modern techniques for turning out some good Semillon wines.

What Semillon tastes like

In dry white Bordeaux, the answer is not much. Semillon, unaided by either care and attention *or* oak can have a dumb bouquet and be merely a vehicle for not-very-pleasant-tasting wine faults. Give it some attention, and some oak, and you get butter, straw and egg custard notes on the nose and rich mango and apricot-like fruit. It has a silky, almost a waxy feel in Australia, and you could be forgiven for confusing it with oak-matured Chardonnay. The unctuous sweeties, principally of Bordeaux, have a rich toffee, butterscotch character.

Fashionable Semillon wines in the nineties
Sweet wines are creeping back into fashion. Late harvest Semillon from South Africa and Australia is well worth investigating – and be adventurous, try sweet wines with rich, flavoursome savoury dishes, including the cheeseboard.

The most expensive Semillon wine in the world
Château d'Yquem (80 per cent Semillon), the most lustrous Sauternes, is the most expensive wine in the world. Dry Semillons lag far behind Bordeaux's extraordinary sweet repertoire on price.

Foods it goes with

Rich, dry Semillons from Australia go well with strongly flavoured white meat dishes and egg-based dishes; they are not good with red meat. Serve them with monkfish with strong-flavoured sauce, red and grey mullet, mackerel, lobster and crab.

'Lesser' sweet Bordeaux (not the arm and a leg jobs) are classically teamed with puddings, *fois gras* and Roquefort cheese, as well as liver pâté, liver and onions, and kidneys.

The top versions should be sipped on their own without food.

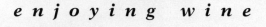
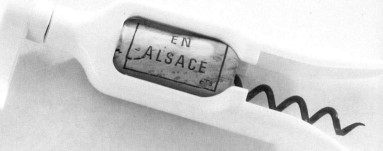

Sauvignon Blanc

Sauvignon Blanc effortlessly produces the type of wines that rocketed to fame in the eighties: lean, green, crisp, dry whites. They have reached a plateau in their popularity now, because there is a limit to the amount of astringence you can take. After a while even their most devoted fans cry out for something softer and more welcoming. Meanwhile, the grape has put down its roots all over the world, in some places managing to make wines in the fuller, more approachable nineties style.

France

The classic strongholds for the grape in the mother country are the Loire, where it masterminds those deeply fashionable 'crisp, dry whites' such as Sancerre, and in Bordeaux, where, working hand in hand with Semillon, it is behind most of the dry whites and all the rich and famous dessert wines of Sauternes and Barsac, etc. Further south in Bergerac, it is blended to make dry whites and the lush Monbazillac. It's also a key player in the Côtes de Duras.

Usually the grape is anonymously hidden behind labels such as the Loire's Menetou-Salon, Pouilly-Fumé, and nearly all white Bordeaux. But it is increasingly being mentioned on labels where it works on its own and has a whole rash of *Vins de Pays* in the south made from and named after it.

Italy

Northern Italy has taken a fancy to the grape and produces delicate, aromatic wines from it (and named after it, conveniently).

Spain

It is creeping over the Pyrenees into Spain, but is often used anonymously there in blends (such as Torres Gran Viña Sol).

Central Europe

It's a familiar grape on labels from Bulgaria, but the exciting new wines are coming from Czechoslovakia, Hungary and Moldavia – most interestingly, made with a helping hand from leading lights in the British wine industry. Watch this spot: we've only seen the tip of the iceberg where well-priced Eastern European Sauvignon Blancs are concerned.

South America

Chile's wine exports are in their infancy. When wine-makers were producing for the domestic market only, there was, shall we say, a relaxed view of grape varieties, and often other types would stray into the Sauvignon Blanc vineyards and their grapes into the crush. Chilean Sauvignon Blancs therefore had little varietal character – they were just another dry white wine. But things are looking up, and some good wines are emerging – made from the right grapes this time. Argentina has big plantings of the grape, too.

California

The dip in Sauvignon's popularity came earlier in California than in most places; in an attempt to win new customers in a falling market, Robert Mondavi dreamed up the idea of bastardizing the name Pouilly-Fumé (a very popular Loire Sauvignon in the States) and calling his Sauvignons Fumé Blanc. The name caught on. Now soft, even sometimes slightly sweet whites going by this name are being marketed.

South Africa

Sauvignon Blanc is big business down at the Cape, and we are only just starting to see what the country can do with the grape. So far, so good in the soft, rounded herbaceous style (and some good affordable prices, too).

Australia and New Zealand

Where Sauvignon Blanc is concerned, these countries can be linked only geographically. Australia hardly has any Sauvignon worth mentioning, whereas New Zealand is perhaps the most exciting producer in the world. In the Marlborough district, in the far north of South Island, she makes miraculous world class wines with a depth and breadth to them not found elsewhere.

What Sauvignon Blanc tastes like

Sauvignon Blanc (when it's not trying to be something else, which it often is in California) is a gift in a blind tasting, it has such a powerfully individual character. Nose in glass and instantly you know where you are. It has green associations, like just-cut grass and has an unmistakable whiff of gooseberries to it. The gooseberry aroma, if analysed, falls into the same scent spectrum as cats; take a deep sniff of a good Sauvignon and you'll see what I mean. There's a crisp, green apple flavour to these wines often with a squeeze of sharp grapefruit astringence; evident acidity is a trait of the grape. In some older New Zealand versions you can pick up a faint resemblance to asparagus. When it teams up with Semillon in Bordeaux, it produces broader, less streamlined dry whites sometimes with rather a blowsy, almost flabby character. When it teams up to make sweet whites, that's a different matter; good examples are rich as honey with a welcome dash of healthy acidity.

Fashionable Sauvignon Blancs
New Zealand holds most of the cards.
Cloudy Bay blazed the trail for
Marlborough Sauvignon Blancs and a
whole stream of honourable producers
followed. They can hardly go wrong. At the
cheaper end of things, Czechoslovakia,
Hungary and Moldavia are the countries
of the future.

The most expensive Sauvignon Blanc
wine in the world
Château d'Yquem (80 per cent Semillon,
20 per cent Sauvignon Blanc) is
Sauvignon's biggest claim to fame, being
the most expensive wine in the world.
Pouilly-Fumé commands the highest price
for a 100 per cent Sauvignon Blanc.

Foods it goes with

Inexpensive Sauvignon Blanc can act like a squeeze of lemon on simple grilled, battered or baked fish dishes, with its generous helpings of astringent acidity.

Good Loire Sauvignons go especially well with fish galantines and pâtés and surprisingly, mushroom omelette, pasta, cold buffets or goats' cheese dishes.

New Zealand Sauvignons deserve good fish, such as sole, bass or halibut, simply cooked.

Oak-fermented and oak-matured versions (sometimes blended with Semillon) are good for more complicated hot fish dishes with rich sauces.

Red grape varieties

Cabernet Franc

You'll almost never see the Cabernet Franc grape boasted on labels. Not that it's anything to be ashamed of – far from it. It just happens to star in the sorts of wines that tend to be named after places rather than grapes. It is also a key element in some important blends.

France

Although it's generally the Cabernet Sauvignon that you associate with claret (that's red Bordeaux), Cabernet Franc plays an important part in these world famous wines, too. And it's not just the poor relation in the blend, either. In the prestigious St-Emilion and Pomerol districts, it is more important than the much better known Cabernet Sauvignon.

In the Loire valley it's a key player among red wines, batting either on its own, or as the dominant partner with Cabernet Sauvignon. Delicious red Loire wines such as Anjou, Saumur, Chinon, Bourgueil and St Nicolas-de-Bourgueil rely either wholly or at least very heavily on Cabernet Franc, as does the soft, slightly sweet rosé, Cabernet d'Anjou.

Italy

The habit of naming Cabernet Franc/Cabernet Sauvignon blends simply 'Cabernet' is prevalent in northern Italy. When you see an Italian 'Cabernet' on the shelves, chances are it owes more to the zingy Cabernet Franc than to Cabernet Sauvignon; Cabernet Franc dominates the league of red grape varieties planted in the north-east.

New World

Because Cabernet Franc is an important ingredient in claret, the Holy Grail for many of the serious wine-makers of the world, you'll find pockets of it in California; in the recherché, so-called 'boutique' wine areas of Australia; and in Chile, where the wine industry has very classic French roots.

What Cabernet Franc tastes like

Wines made exclusively or predominantly from Cabernet Franc grapes from the Loire or northern Italy are often light in body for reds and lively with it, lending themselves to being chilled. They have a fresh, green, grassy character with a whiff of the herbaceous border to them. Another scent you may find conjured up by their bouquet is crumbly sponge cake. They can be splendidly fruity, reminiscent of ripe but slightly tart raspberries, with a direct, almost sharp acidity. As the more pricey, more substantial versions mature, they become richer with lush blackcurrant notes creeping in, and an earthiness, almost a leathery quality.

Fashionable Cabernet Franc wines
The exciting reds of the predominantly white wine region of France's Loire valley majoring on the Cabernet Franc grape are still little known in Britain and so have an unusual cachet. They come essentially in two styles – the young, vibrant ready to drink right away versions (with a recent vintage on the label) and the inkier, darker, more robust, older types. Look out for Saumur-Champigny and the easier-to-find Anjou Rouge.

The most expensive Cabernet Franc wine in the world
Château Cheval Blanc, one of the top two wines of Bordeaux's St-Emilion is 60 per cent Cabernet Franc; Château Ausone the other great St-Emilion is 50 per cent.

Foods it goes with

When Cabernet Franc is blended, as in claret, I suggest you team it with the same sorts of foods recommended to go with Cabernet Sauvignon (see page 269). On its own, as in Loire examples, it has a directness which would team well with roast lamb with redcurrant jelly, or other red meats accompanied by sweet sauces.

Cabernet Sauvignon

The most fashionable red grape variety in the world, Cabernet Sauvignon is the best known, best loved among all red varieties.

France

Its natural habitat is Bordeaux, home to that great red wine, claret. But great though claret's reputation may be, it's not the wine that put Cabernet Sauvignon so firmly at the top of the pops among red grapes. On Bordeaux labels, the identity of the grape keeps a very low profile; it's not even mentioned on the front label at all, and seldom on the back. It's only when it travels to other areas of France and off around the world that 'Cabernet Sauvignon' is boasted bold as brass on the label.

Although it is not a traditional grape in the south of France, it is increasingly being used in fashionable new wines. But Cabernet Sauvignon does not have legal blessing as a traditional grape in some of the new areas where it is now being grown. So wines including it have to sacrifice their right to the region's quality status, being known as simple *Vins de Table* (although being rather more pricey than your average run-of-the-mill table wines). In northern France, it is grown in the

Loire, playing second fiddle there, unusually to its cousin Cabernet Franc.

Italy

So-called 'Cabernets' from Italy are more often than not blends of Cabernet Sauvignon and Cabernet Franc.

Spain and Portugal

On the Iberian peninsula, although it is only a recent introduction, some modern wine-makers use it occasionally, either in tandem with local types or on its own.

Central Europe

Bulgaria was the trailblazer here; Bulgarian Cabernet Sauvignon, soon after it was introduced into Britain at mouth-watering prices, becoming the best-selling red wine. Bulgarian Cabernet has crept up in price but other countries, such as Hungary, are successfully coming into the frame to offer classic wine at tempting prices. Conveniently, the grape type is always declared on the label.

New World

The simple habit of naming the wine after the grape dominates the New World. Cabernet Sauvignon is the most prestigious red grape grown in California, South America, Australia, New Zealand and South Africa, and whenever it plays a part in a wine, sure enough, it'll announce its presence on the label loud and clear. New World Cabernet Sauvignons are generally softer, fruitier and easier to love than traditional French Cabernets. The grape is either vinified on its own or blended with Merlot (as in claret) or, breaking new ground here, with Shiraz in Australia.

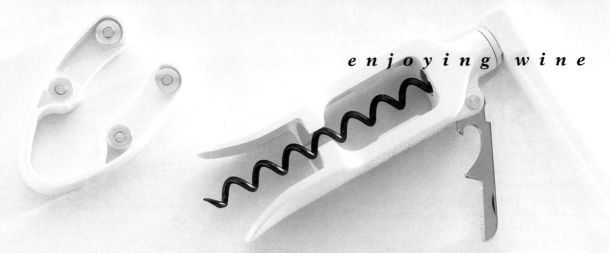

What Cabernet Sauvignon tastes like

'Shall I compare thee to a blackcurrant? Thou art more lovely.' Cabernet Sauvignon and the concentrated berry scents and flavours of currants share a lot in common. Add to the currants a hint of violets and the lovely, rich, aromatic scents of a cigar box and there you have ripe, mature Cabernet Sauvignon. In wines destined to mature for a while, tannins (the drying, mouth-furring elements contributed by the skins and the stalks) can be evident. But these soften in time. Youthful Cabernets intended to be drunk young have a piercing edge to them, a sharpness to the fruit which can even seem a little metallic.

Fashionable Cabernet Sauvignon wines in the nineties
Well-priced Cabernets from Chile. More expensive 'designer' wines made by dedicated wine-makers in southern France and northern Italy. Quinta da Bacalhôa from Portugal. Ridge Cabernet Sauvignon from California.

The most expensive Cabernet Sauvignon wines in the world
Mouton Rothschild (80 per cent CS); Opus 1, California (same grape mix). It is also an important part of Sassicaia from Italy and Vega Sicilia Unico, Spain's most expensive wine.

Foods it goes with

Being a versatile sort of grape, Cabernet Sauvignon can turn its fruit to making two different styles of wine. Serious, robust wines, made to last, are typified by claret. But in the same category I would include Australian Cabernets, Californian and South African Cabernets and the more expensive versions from Chile and Central Europe. Food partners for this type include steak and kidney pie, roast lamb, game pie, roast beef, well-hung game, goose and duck.

Lighter, slighter types are made in southern France, Italy, New Zealand and Chile. Suggested food partners are roast pork, roast beef, chicken, cold meat pies, cheese soufflé, and lasagne or cannelloni.

Gamay

Gamay is responsible for making one of the most famous wines in the world: Beaujolais, and it is remarkable for little else.

269

France

Beaujolais, true to form for a traditional French wine, is named after the area it comes from, a picturesque satellite of Burgundy, stretching south from Mâcon to Lyon. The only red grape grown there is Gamay, and it makes a juicy-fruity, light, red wine, generally enjoyed young, or even in its infancy (as in Beaujolais Nouveau). A special wine-making technique is used in Beaujolais to capitalize on the easy fruit flavours while keeping the bitter elements of tannin usually associated with red wines at bay. This method enables the new wines to hit the shelves only a few weeks after the grapes have been picked (whereas even the most youthful reds normally take six months minimum to appear in the shops). As well as Beaujolais Nouveau, the Gamay makes itself into Beaujolais plain and simple and Beaujolais Villages which is a step up the quality ladder. Top of the range are the *Cru* Beaujolais named after individual villages (see page 270).

Unusually for France, when Gamay is grown in areas other than Beaujolais, it often gives its name to the wine, as in Gamay de Touraine, Gamay de l'Ardèche and Anjou

Gamay. It may anonymously form part of the blend for Anjou Rosé and the Burgundian Mâcon Rouge is likely to be 100 per cent Gamay.

The rest of the world

Gamay hasn't been adopted by anywhere outside France on any significant scale. Although the name Gamay, expressed either as Gamay Beaujolais or Napa Gamay may crop up on labels of California wine, these are often not, in fact, true Gamay wines at all.

What Gamay tastes like

Gamay is ideal for making youthful, vibrant reds as easy to drink as white wine. It's not surprising that fruit – gorgeous, jammy, cherry and raspberry fruit – should lead the scent and flavour medley. If the fruit isn't obvious, you haven't got a very good Gamay in your glass. As well as fruit there is a haunting rubbery sort of aroma to this grape – combined rubber and tar, like gym shoes running on a sun-baked road. Acidity can be quite buzzy, giving the wine a slightly nervy, jumpy character.

270

Fashionable Gamay wines in the nineties
The Beaujolais Nouveau phenomenon injects enough fashion and fad into wine appreciation to last the whole year. It's less hyped now than it used to be, but because of our thirst for the novelty of it all in dank November, nearly as much Beaujolais Nouveau is produced as ordinary Beaujolais. It lasts until Easter (although shops feel hard done by if they haven't sold out in the first week). After that, drink the youngest ordinary Beaujolais you can find or, after July, look to better quality Beaujolais Villages or the Cru Beaujolais. The newest one to hit the shelves is the well-priced Regnié.

The most expensive Gamay wine in the world
Nothing startlingly expensive is made from Gamay. Of the Cru (that is single village) Beaujolais, Moulin-à-Vent always used to command the highest prices; now the more fashionable Fleurie has taken over the top spot.

Foods it goes with

With lots of fruit to boast, low tannins (the ingredient that makes your mouth feel dry) and high acidity, Gamay wines go with a wide range of foods – as well as on their own. All young Beaujolais is best slightly chilled. Try it with salmon (unusual for a red), white meats with white sauces, chicken, turkey, offal, *charcuterie* and cold meats, *antipasti*, savoury soufflés, pasta and macaroni cheese.

Merlot

Typical for a grape growing up in France, Merlot has historically played a low-key role, finding its name declared on few labels. But being easy to grow and easy to vinify into easy-drinking wine, not surprisingly it's spread into new areas where it is sometimes still anonymously included in blends, though more often making wines on its own in its own right.

France

The Merlot grape makes the biggest contribution to the most famous red wine in the world, claret – the biggest, though not the most prestigious. It is Cabernet Sauvignon which runs away with the glory, but the more widely planted Merlot, which provides the essential supporting act, softening out the harsh qualities of its more famous partner. Because it is soft, easy and succulent, it tends to dominate in affordable clarets (and in some highly prestigious, expensive ones, too). It doesn't restrict itself just to Bordeaux; it stretches down into Bergerac, Côtes de Duras and further south. It's also gaining ground over in south-east France where increasingly it gives its name to the soft, rich wines it makes in Languedoc.

Italy

Merlot's sites are set on inexpensive, young, simple sippers in north-eastern Italy, where it's name is seen so often on wine labels that it looks almost like a brand in its own right.

Spain

Certainly not a classic grape for the Iberian peninsula, Merlot is nevertheless creeping into vineyards planted by trendy 'designer wine-makers'. It also forms a small part of Spain's most expensive wine, Vega Sicilia.

Central Europe

Hungary does a good, inexpensive line in Merlots, while Bulgaria's versions range from cheap and cheerful up to the top *Controliran* quality, being sumptuous oak-aged wines in the middle price bracket. Romania grows the grape, too.

New World

Because early wine-making in Chile was heavily influenced by France, especially Bordeaux, Merlot is grown successfully there. It sometimes forms a typical Bordeaux-style blend but it can make good, frequently oak-aged wines in its own right. Merlot doesn't have the same opportunity to perform its traditional Bordeaux-inspired blending role in Australia. There it is the Shiraz grape (called Syrah in France) which marries most often with Cabernet Sauvignon, leaving Merlot to become a curiosity of the up-market 'boutique' wineries. It gets a better crack in New Zealand, where it is increasing its hold. California plants a bit – usually with the intention of aping Bordeaux again, while Washington State and Oregon are having a stab at turning it into serious wine on its own.

What Merlot tastes like

The taste of Merlot is most easily described in terms of its *feel*: it's a soft, velvety grape with a juicy succulence. Scents it's likely to remind you of are plums and red berry fruits with a pungent mintiness on some. Because it is soft and fruity, it's generally smooth and easy to enjoy. Although true to form, when it is grown in Italy, it can be jumpy and vibrant. It is a good candidate for ageing in oak, the oak making it seem even more velvety and resonant of vanilla.

271

272

Foods it goes with

Lighter Merlots from southern France, Italy and Eastern Europe go with simple pasta dishes such as cannelloni and lasagne (meat and vegetarian), napoletana sauce, simple pizzas, risottos and meat dishes.

New World Merlots and claret complement most red meats, fillet steak, beef sirloin, rack of lamb, steak and kidney pudding, navarin of lamb, casseroles, roast duck and Peking duck.

Pinot Noir

Pinot Noir is to red Burgundy what Cabernet Sauvignon is to claret. And there the parallel ends, because whereas Cabernet Sauvignon makes wine successfully all over the world, Pinot Noir presents many more difficulties when it travels. As yet, nowhere consistently rivals Burgundy where fine Pinot Noirs are concerned (although not for want of trying).

France

So, Burgundy is *the* place for Pinot Noir. It is the only grape allowed for the vast majority of red Burgundies and can weave astonishing magic in the finest examples . . . as well as putting out some pretty mediocre stuff under the name. Top Burgundies, the *Grand Cru*, are named after top vineyards; middle ranking wines, the *Premier Crus* are named after vineyard and village, hyphenated (such as Gevrey-Chambertin); lowlier wines being named after villages on their own, whole areas, or simply as Burgundy or Bourgogne. The second most important place for Pinot Noir in France is Champagne, this black grape surprisingly being an important part of most Champagne blends. Among cheaper Champagnes, it dominates most of those from the Aube area. Alsace has light, fruity reds made from and named after the grape and Pinot Noir is behind individual wines such as red Sancerre.

Italy

Italy tends to produce rather light, wishy-washy versions of this noble grape, which she does mainly in the north. They are not only called Pinot Noir, but Pinot Nero and Blauburgunder as well. As in Champagne, the grape turns its attentions, too, to making good sparkling wine.

Germany

Although Germany's great strength is in making white wines, her countrymen have an appetite for reds, too. And Spätburgunder (as they call the Pinot Noir) is a popular grape. Few examples travel; when they do you'll find them light and fragrant.

England

England's generally stronger on her whites, too, but she is doing surprisingly well with Pinot Noir, which can be turned into a fragrant but satisfyingly steely red. It also makes some rosé.

Central Europe

Probably the best Middle European examples of the grape coming to Britain are from Romania (although they are not consistently good). They have a sweet, strawberry scent and mirror palely the complex game-and-compost medley of good Burgundy. Hungarian and Czechoslovakian versions show promise; Bulgarian are, shall we say, 'untypical'.

New World

North America (that is, California, Oregon and Washington State) pursue the image of great Burgundy with great determination. Their results are patchy, but some great wines are being made (and unfortunately, being sold at great prices). Australia is having some success, as is New Zealand on a tiny scale, and Chile, too.

SAFE DRINKING
Safe limits for drinking are expressed in units. One unit is:

- a standard glass of wine
- a standard glass of sherry or port
- half a pint of beer or cider
- a single measure of spirits

For a man: 21 units a week
For a woman: 14 units a week

Men who drink 56 units a week and women who consume 42 units a week are well on the way to causing long-term damage to their health.

AVOID alcohol during pregnancy and NEVER drink and drive.

What Pinot Noir tastes like

Pinot Noir is the most extraordinary grape. At its feeblest, it makes a washed out, sugary sweet red with a faint aroma of cherries. At best, it combines scents and flavours you never dreamed of, with a characteristic smack of strawberries, the slight aroma of cooking cabbage and a faint twang of gamey meat in maturer versions. Great wines manage to be earthy while being supremely delicate and refined. In middle ranking Pinots, there is a delicious fragrance and refreshing fruit-and-acid balance.

273
....

> ### Fashionable Pinot Noir wines in the nineties
> All *Pinot Noirs* are fashionable; my particular soft spots lie with those from England, Alsace, and with red Sancerres.
>
> ### The most expensive Pinot Noir wine in the world
> *Romanée-Conti, a Burgundy emanating from a 2 hectare vineyard in the Côte de Nuits, fetches the highest prices of all Pinot Noirs. Among Champagnes, it's the 100 per cent Pinot Noir Bollinger Vieilles Vignes made from grapes grown on ancient vines.*

Foods it goes with

Serve it with coq au vin, simple roasts, especially pork, fancy sausages, pigeon, poultry (however cooked), sweetbreads, Christmas dinner, gentler-flavoured Chinese food and Thai flavours.

The lighter styles (from Alsace and German Spätburgunder) go with strong-flavoured fish dishes such as sea bass.

Syrah, alias Shiraz

This distinguished and distinctive red grape variety is concentrated almost exclusively in south-eastern France and Australia.

France

Among reds, Syrah is the aristocrat of the Rhône, particularly the northern Rhône. It makes superb, dense, earthy wines such as Hermitage, Côte Rôtie, St Joseph and Cornas, capable of turning heads and hiking prices. In the southern Rhône, it is part of the diverse blend going to make Châteauneuf-du-Pape, and assisted by EC encouragement to up the quality of ordinary wines, it is widening its influence to help along Côtes du Rhone and the like. It has a strong, distinctive character which brings a touch of class to rustic blends, although, true to form, you'll never see its name boasted on the front label of any of these wines.

Further south, it continues anonymously to improve the quality of blended wines (usually named after the place where they are made) but also occasionally gives its name to new wines made exclusively from it. Look out for southern French Syrahs, they're delicious.

Australia

The Shiraz, as the Syrah is known here, is Australia's most widely planted wine grape. Historically it has suffered from a bit of a work horse image, being easy to produce into thunderbolt reds. Planted all over the country, at the cheaper end of the scale, it can produce clumsy, jammily sweet wines that fade quickly. If poorly vinified they can suffer from the unmistakable aroma of high cheese and burnt rubber. But increasingly the grape is being given the respect it deserves by wine-makers who draw from it intense, ripe fruit flavours in modern-style, easy-drinking wines. It's also frequently blended in Oz, partnering Cabernet Sauvignon to make succulently fruity wines with backbone and staying power. The blend is generally stated on the label (unless other grape types are included as well). The first grape to be mentioned is the dominant variety in the blend.

The rest of the world

California is experimenting with Syrah grapes – not to be confused with their Petite Sirah which is completely different. And South Africa has quite sizeable plantations as well, generally used to make wines named conveniently after the grape. In Lebanon it is one of the grapes going to make the intriguing claret-like Château Musar.

What Syrah tastes like

In the Rhône and the south of France, Syrah makes dark red, earthy, spicy wines with rich, goulash flavours and a hint of pepper on the finish. There can be a haunting tar-like edge to the bouquet softened out by the scent of ripe raspberries. When used in a blend, as well as giving the wine guts and gubbins, it is the spice and most of all the pepper which shine through distinctively. In Australia, the fruit really comes to the fore with fruit-gum intensity, while you may find notes of leather and saddle soap as well. In both hemispheres it's possible to find a whiff of the cheesey foot – not, surprisingly, unattractive in a wine.

Fashionable Syrah wines in the nineties
Wines named after the Syrah in Languedoc give the grape a modern appeal. The Rhône's Crozes-Hermitage – the junior cousin of Hermitage is a good bet – especially on restaurant wine lists.

The most expensive Syrah wines in the world
Single property Côte Rôtie or Hermitage from the northern Rhône; Penfolds Grange Shiraz (formerly called Grange Hermitage) from the Barossa Valley north of Adelaide.

Foods it goes with

Rhône and southern French Syrahs can match powerfully flavoured dishes such as: venison, jugged hare, grouse, pheasant, *daubes*, beef, lamb, goose and wild duck.

Australian Shiraz is softer and needs simpler foods, likewise California Syrah. Try it with barbecues, plainly grilled meat, steak and kidney pie, cottage pie, moussaka, corn-fed chicken, guinea fowl and pork.

And now let's look at wines country by country.

Australia

Key facts about Australian wines

- Although wine-making in Australia is as old as the country itself, compared to Europe, that isn't very old. This is a plus rather than a minus, because wines are able to be made *how we like them*, not according to tradition and in keeping with outdated laws.
- Compared to most of Europe, Australia is HOT. In the past this meant it was committed to making big, overblown wines. Now, harnessing all the new wisdom and new technology they can get hold of, wine-makers are able to pick grapes when they are just ripe (usually, in hotter areas, in the cool of the night) and process them in artificially cool conditions to make rich but well-balanced wines.
- Only a few grape varieties dominate the class-act wines exported, and they are the predictable 'international classics'. Most wines are sold boasting the variety (or varieties) loud and clear on the label. If the wine is an unspecified blend of grapes, red varieties likely to be included are Cabernet Sauvignon and Shiraz. For unspecified white blends, the varieties are probably Riesling, Chenin Blanc, Muscadelle and perhaps Chardonnay and Semillon. The reason for the grapes being left undeclared is not because they are anything to be ashamed of, but because EC laws won't allow details of complicated blends to be specified.
- Vines are grown in all states of Australia, but the main concentration is in the south-east. There are regional differences between wines made with the same grape from region to region, but they are probably less significant than the differences from company to company.
- Sophisticated wine-box technology in Australia enables fresh, fruity wines to stay . . . fresh and fruity. Australian wine boxes are therefore worth looking out for.
- Australian sparkling wines, full bodied and genuinely fruit-flavoured, have overshadowed the skinny, wan offerings put out by European producers. They have even given cheaper Champagnes a jolt and are well worth the £5 to £6 they cost.

Key grapes and wines

Reds

Cabernet Sauvignon Claret's best-known grape is generous with its blackcurrant fruit scents and flavour in Oz, tending to make, at the cheaper end of things, come-onish, juicy-fruity reds. But not content with something so simple, the flavour medley is complicated sometimes by oak ageing and the fruit toned down by a serious edge of tannin. Cabernets increasingly tend to be more 'serious', less frivolous. The top spots for it are Coonawarra and Western Australia.

Shiraz The most widely planted red variety is known as Syrah in Europe. It used to parent big, beefy reds inspiring the Australian tasting term 'sweaty saddle'. The so-called sweaty character has been toned down now, giving way to raspberry fruit scents and flavours overlaid by leathery hints, a touch of spice and a suggestion of creamy saddle soap. It is often found blended successfully with Cabernet.

Whites

Chardonnay When we first saw what Burgundy's top white grape could do in Australia, it opened up new possibilities for the world. Instead of being shy and reticent, suddenly we saw the flavours could be so big and positive they almost jumped out of the glass to greet you. With a touch of oak (apart from the cheapest, most have some contact with oak barrels), ripe Australian Chardonnay comes to life with butter and honey and exotic fruit flavours. This is world-class wine.

Semillon The hidden star behind Bordeaux's sweet treats comes into its own in Australia, where it makes big, rich, ripe wines with a hint of straw on the bouquet and perhaps a whiff of egg custard. Ripe and succulent, they can be as inviting as the Chardonnays in all but label; Semillon is considered the less sexy grape. It is often successfully blended with Chardonnay which, like the Cabernet/Shiraz blend, is a peculiarly Australian combination.

Rhine Riesling Germany's top grape makes delicious flowery, delicate, dry whites with a hint of oiliness to them; shadows of their counterparts made in France's Alsace. They're not fashionable, but who cares about fad?

Muscat Often served up as 'late picked', meaning the grapes were picked very ripe to make a sweet wine, Muscat makes headily scented wines with juicy, grapey sweetness, delicious if you like sweet types. Try them with *charcuterie*, pâté or with the cheese board – the combination of flavours is dazzling.

The way ahead for Australian wines

Australia has established itself prominently on the wine shop shelves as a supplier of delicious, approachable, well-priced wines of all styles – everyone a winner . . . almost. But there is a glimmer of evidence that they may be becoming complacent, cutting corners here and there to produce slightly tough, rubbery reds at the cheaper end of things. Should they tarnish their record, we'll just have to vote with our shopping bags and look (let's hope only temporarily) elsewhere for our thrills. Meanwhile wines in the £5 and up bracket have hardly put a foot wrong.

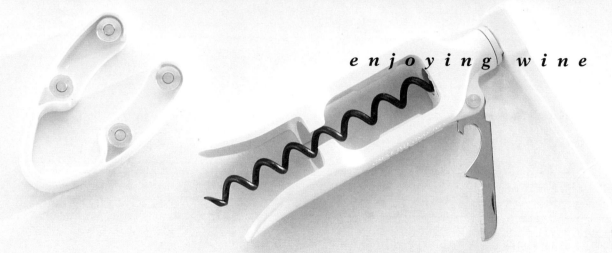

Central Europe

Austria

Key facts about Austrian wines

- Austria has a wealth of her own grape varieties, grown nowhere else and producing distinctive, individual flavours.
- Eighty per cent of Austria's wines are white.
- Having historically looked and sounded Germanic on the label, the new trend is for Austria to re-style her bottles, labels and even her wines to avoid any confusion.
- Austria claims to have the most exacting laws in the world relating to its production.

The two best-known grape varieties peculiar to Austria

- **Grüner Veltliner:** This white grape variety makes wines that taste like the name sounds: green and vibrant, leafy and, as they mature, becoming a bit spicy.
- **St Laurent:** A red grape variety, this makes juicy-fruity, light-style red wines with sweet, strawberry scents and flavours.

Quality classifications

Though Austrian wines may well be becoming less Germanic in style, the quality rating system used is strikingly similar:

Ordinary table wines are described as *Tafelwein. Landwein* is a step up, and must be made from recognized grape varieties. Neither of these lowly types is exported to the UK. Moving up into the quality area, *Qualitätsweins* must all come from a single region, from approved grape varieties. They are classified according to the amount of sugar present in the grapes when they are picked. The more sugar, the better the wine (although, the wines are not necessarily sweeter – remember fermentation consumes

sugar and turns it into alcohol, so high sugar levels don't necessarily result in sweet wines, unless you want them to). Climbing up the scale, the quality wines are classified as follows: *Kabinett, Spätlese, Auslese, Beerenauslese, Trockenbeerenauslese.*

Key wine terms on the label

- *Süss:* Sweet.
- *Halbsüss:* Medium sweet.
- *Halbtrocken:* Medium dry.
- *Trocken:* Dry.

The way ahead for Austrian wines

Even now, years after the great wine scandal, it's difficult to divorce Austrian wines from thoughts of anti-freeze. You'll remember that some wines were adulterated with an anti-freeze by-product in an attempt to put them in a higher (sweeter) quality category, with shocking results (some people even died). Now, looking on the bright side, the effects of the scandal have been to smarten up Austrian wine-making, subjecting all bottles to tighter controls. In an attempt to capture a new market for their wines, Austrian wine-makers have given them a new identity. Medium-style wines have largely been scrapped in favour of clean-cut, dry whites, giving the individual grape varieties the opportunity to show what they can do uncluttered by sugar. They are generally well priced. Fashionable light-style reds are creeping on to the shelves occasionally, too, and are worth looking out for.

Bulgaria

Key facts about Bulgarian wines

- Bulgaria, quite by accident, was in a strategic position in the eighties to pander to our thirst for the well-known, classic grape varieties, and she did so more cheaply than anyone, quickly becoming one of the most vigorous exporters of bottled wine.
- As well as supplying the 'right' grape varieties, Bulgarian wines were cheap, had easy-to-read labels declaring the grape varieties loud and clear, and offered likeable, easy-drinking styles. It's not surprising they were instant winners.
- Well-known so-called 'classic' grape varieties came to Bulgaria more by accident than by design. Although humble native varieties had traditionally been planted by poor farmers, after the revolution in 1944 smallholders were organized into huge co-operatives and efficient mechanization was introduced. To be able to use machinery in vineyards, you need well-ordered rows of tidily trained vines rather than the untidily sprawling local types. Enter the classic types we know and love; exit most of the local sorts that tended to crouch uncooperatively near the ground.
- As well as being some of the cheapest wines around, Bulgarian versions of the classics are generally very acceptable. Cabernet Sauvignon is perhaps the star grape. Chardonnays tend to be either over-oaked or musty, and rather uncharacteristic.

Quality classifications

There is a step-ladder of quality ascribed to Bulgarian wines, and you need remember only a few key words to cope with it. The bottom level of quality wines is generally described on the lable simply as 'Country Wines'. Next, 'Reserve' will be found on the label of better wines with some oak ageing. Top quality wines are described as *Controliran*.

Commonwealth of Independent States

- The various states of the former Soviet Union together form one of the biggest volume producers of wine in the world.
- What they call classic-style wines dominate, but so-called European-style wines (the kind we enjoy) are made, too.
- Some good old wines reserved for party chiefs sometimes become available. They are variable in appeal; the best being formidable and cheap (for what they are).
- As well as their own grape varieties, principally the white Rkatsiteli and the inky, dark red Saperevi, Cabernet Sauvignon, Merlot and Sauvignon Blanc are grown, too.
- Moldavia and Georgia are the focus of much attention from wine wizards of the West who see enormous potential for wine production. Their first efforts are starting to creep on to British wine shelves. Prices are very attractive.

Czechoslovakia

Key facts about Czechoslovakian wines (ie wines from the Czech Republic and Slovakia)

- Czech wines have only recently become available in the UK, and they are showing signs of potential excellence at good prices. UK wine importers have gone to Czechoslovakia and pointed the best-looking wineries in the right direction, with some delicious white wines resulting.
- Sauvignon Blanc and Pinot Blanc, among the classics, are looking good. But keep your eyes peeled for Irsay Oliver as well, a spicy, sweet-and-sour sort of wine in the dry Muscat style. All the wines are well priced.

Hungary

Key facts about Hungarian wines

- Only a decade ago, the only two Hungarian wines to have made any impact on the British market were Bull's Blood, a beefy red wine made from a cocktail of grape varieties, and Tokay, a historic, sweet wine made in degrees of richness, depending on how many wheelbarrow-loads of sweet grape paste (called *puttonyos*) had been added. There was a long-standing wine tradition in Hungary, but the apathy of communism hadn't done much to encourage experimentation or excellence.
- Hungary has taken longer than some of its neighbours to smarten up its act and to start to sell us marketable wines we want to buy. But in part due to advice and direction from UK corporate wine-buyers and some talented wine-makers, good, affordable red and white wines made from recognizable grape varieties are becoming available.
- Look out for some good, fresh Sauvignon Blancs and, inevitably, Cabernet Sauvignon at a good price.

Romania

Key facts about Romanian wines

- Even where wines are concerned, historic greatness has disintegrated into chaotic inconsistency.
- You'll find some recognizable grape varieties from Romania such as Traminer, pungent and spicy, and Pinot Noir – at its best, some of the best cheap Pinot Noir around, with good strawberry fruit and that characteristic hint of compost to the bouquet. Regrettably, even bottles which look identical may contain confusingly inconsistent wines, some excellent at the price, others downright poor.

Slovenia, Bosnia and Croatia

Key facts about wines from Yugoslavia-that-was

- Lutomer Laski Rizling was the trailblazer for Yugoslavia in the 1950s, a medium sweet wine with a little grapey fruit and a little spice. The grape isn't all that marvellous, but Lutomer is a good vine-growing area in Slovenia.
- Realizing this one-wine assault on the British market wouldn't get them very far, some canny importers introduced varietals in the 1980s, with Sauvignon Blanc and Gewürztraminer being the most successful.
- In future, 'Yugoslavian' wines will be labelled according to the republic of origin and it is hoped that, if peace is restored, healthy competition will encourage more striving for excellence, and more individual styles.
- 1992 produced an excellent vintage.

279

Cyprus and Greece

Key facts about Cyprus wines

● Being shut off from the world by the surrounding sea, Cyprus has fortunately never been threatened by the ravages of the dreaded vine louse, *phylloxera*. Vines in Cyprus (unlike those of most of the rest of the world, apart from Chile) have therefore not been grafted on to disease-resistant American rootstock; a much-coveted state for vines among the wine *cognoscenti*.

● Cyprus has been reluctant to introduce buzz European varieties in case the dreaded pest were to hitch a lift. Local varieties therefore prevail in the vineyards, although after a period in quarantine, experimental cuttings of Cabernet Sauvignon, Syrah, Chardonnay and Sauvignon Blanc are starting to be planted.

Key Cyprus wines

● So-called Cyprus sherry and Cyprus port used to dominate vinous exports to Britain, but happily less so since Cyprus joined the EC.

● Three wine companies dominate wine production, making rather old-fashioned, dull, flat reds, whites and rosés.

● Commandaria is Cyprus's most famous wine, a sweet, red or conker-coloured wine with an ancient past.

Key facts about Greek wines

● In Classical times, the finest wines of the world were Greek. Wine was central to the whole Ancient Greek culture, featuring prominently in art, literature and even religion.

● With an appetite for their own wines at home, early this century all wine was consumed domestically, most of it being taken home directly from the winery in *amphorae*. Now, as part of the European Community, steps are being taken to try to exploit the potential market. As yet, they haven't been very significant, wines remaining much as you might remember them from your Greek holiday. The trouble is, they seem to taste better there than here.

Key Greek wines

● **Retsina** A dry, white wine flavoured with pine resin, this is unusual and distinctive; an excellent foil (if you like that kind of thing) for oily Greek food.

● **Samos Muscat** A well-priced, sweet white, this is slightly orangey in character, very sticky and delicious.

● **Demestica** Anyone who has been to Greece will know this brand; it proliferates on menus, along with Retsina. It is the biggest brand of ordinary red and white table wine from mainland Greece; not very exciting.

● **Mavrodaphne** An indigenous grape variety, which produces sweet, luscious red wines which are high in alcohol and conveniently named after the grape.

● **Château Carras** This claret-like red is good but pricey.

France

Key facts about French wine

- Although there is evidence that grapes grew in stone-age France, it seems likely that wine-making vines were brought to France from Italy by the Romans in the second century BC.
- France vies with Italy for the position of the world's biggest wine-producing nation.
- There are six important regions producing quality wines. In the west the **Loire** makes mainly white wines. Further south there is the classic **Bordeaux** region, homeland of claret, white Bordeaux and the sweet treats of Sauternes. In the north-east there is **Champagne**, concentrating almost exclusively on the world's most famous sparkling wine. South of Champagne between Dijon and Lyon, you find **Burgundy**, making red and white wines, including Beaujolais and Chablis. Further south still there is the **Rhône** region which is predominantly a red-producing area. Right over in eastern France close to the Rhine, there is the small but important region of **Alsace** making mostly white wines.
- French wines are usually named after the place where they are made, and there are 800 *Appellations*, or designations for quality wines, each with its own precise name.
- All French wines are officially classified in terms of their quality.
- Apart from Riesling, all the internationally famous grape varieties, such as Cabernet Sauvignon, Pinot Noir, Merlot, Chardonnay and Sauvignon Blanc, originate in France where they make so-called classic wines, the blueprints for wines from across the world.

  Unfortunately the grapes themselves are seldom declared on the label so, for the record, Cabernet Sauvignon originates in Bordeaux, where it is the backbone of claret; Merlot likewise. Pinot Noir's home is Burgundy; almost all red Burgundy is made from this grape and it is an important player in most Champagnes. Chardonnay is Burgundy's first and foremost white grape, making all great white Burgundy and Chablis. It is also Champagne's only white grape. Sauvignon Blanc comes from the Loire where it stars in innumerable crisp, dry whites such as Sancerre.
- Hosts of grape varieties are used in France, especially in the south where their presence in the wine will not be declared on the label. Some modern wines, however, increasingly resort to the classic varieties and declare them boldly where they legally can.

Quality classifications

There are essentially two classes for French wine: Quality wines and Table wines. Quality wines are either *Appellation Contrôlée* or the slightly less lustrous *VDQS* (standing for the dreadful mouthful *Vin Délimité de Qualité Supérieure*). The more ordinary table wines are classified as either *Vin de Pays*, in which case they must come from a precise area and conform with the expected character of wines coming from that area, or they are *Vin de Table*, which means they may be any old plonk coming from any area or combination of areas.

Where *Appellation Contrôlée* wines are concerned, the general rule is that the more precisely identified the area controlled by the appellation, the better the wine is likely to be. So an *Appellation Bordeaux Contrôlée* is less lustrous than an *Appellation Margaux Contrôlée*, Margaux being a precise district within the Bordeaux region.

Key wine terms on the label

- **Blanc de blancs** Meaning literally 'white of whites', is a white wine made exclusively from white grapes.
- **Blanc de noirs** Literally, 'white of blacks', that is white wines made only from black grapes. They are quite unusual.
- **Brut** On sparkling wine labels, *brut* signifies the wine is very dry.
- **Cépage** Grape variety.
- **Château** The property where the wine is made – not necessarily a grand house, it could be a modest bungalow.
- **Claret** The English name for Bordeaux reds.
- **Demi-sec** Medium dry.
- **Domaine** Wine-making farm or estate.
- **Doux** Sweet.
- **Mis en bouteille au château** Bottled at source.
- **Nouveau, Primeur** A new wine from the latest harvest; very young.
- **Sec** Dry.
- **Supérieur** Not necessarily superior wine, simply more alcoholic.
- **Sur lie** Wine kept in contact with the sediment thrown by fermentation, which gives it more body and extra flavour.

The way ahead for French wines

France makes the most famous wines in the world, the classics which are often imitated in other newer wine-producing regions. The top wines (if you can afford the prices) are among the best wines made anywhere. But that's far from the full story. Being such a major player turning out such vast volumes of wine, the majority of wines made are considerably less lustrous. Having traded on the fame of the French name for so long, wine-makers all over France have become complacent and it is often the case that you can find more enjoyable wine, and more affordable alternatives, made elsewhere. Waking up to this shock, wine-makers are now starting to pull their socks up and standards are beginning to climb again. The key areas where the biggest improvements have been made are largely the unfashionable ones in the south. Alsace has never allowed her standards to slip, making deliciously well-priced, quality wines (mainly white). The Rhône makes some well-priced reds; try Coteaux du Tricastin and Côtes du Ventoux. The unusual reds of the Loire are light in style and a bit minty in character. Recent vintages can be chilled.

Germany

Key facts about German wines

- Germany is principally a white wine-producing country, known for slim, green or brown bottles, complicated labels and medium sweet styles.
- The best-selling German wine in the UK is Liebfraumilch. It is a blend of grape varieties from any one of four regions. Generally it is made as cheaply as possible and is undistinguished, flabby and suffers from the use of too much sulphur; rather unlovely, in fact. Liebfraumilch is unknown in Germany itself, being specially made for the British market.
- Liebfraumilch is only part of the tale. At the other end of the quality scale, Germany is responsible for some of the finest sweet wines in the world. In the mid-range of quality, she makes some exceptional varietal wines, usually medium sweet but sometimes dry (in most of the better wines, the grape variety is part of the information declared on the label).
- The top German grape variety is Riesling, responsible for most of the top wines. The most widely planted is Müller-Thurgau (alias Rivaner) which tends to make anonymous blends, soft, fruity and sometimes a bit spicy in style. Weissburgunder (alias Pinot Blanc) is increasingly found, making creamy, well-rounded, white wines. Morio Muskat makes pungent, heady, spicy wines with lots of obvious character for your money.
- Dornfelder is a lovely, juicy-fruity, red grape variety to look out for. It makes light, modern, easy-drinking red wines.
- Hock is a collective name for wines (usually just ordinary wines) from areas around the Rhine valley.
- Wines from eight of the major wine-producing areas are sold in Britain, and they are mainly clustered around the Rhine and Mosel rivers. You'll find the region declared on all bottles of quality wine (everything which isn't either *Deutscher Tafelwein* or *Landwein*, including Liebfraumilch). The areas are Ahr on the Rhine and the furthest north, known for good reds; Rheingau, the best Rhine area; Rheinhessen, a large 'volume' producer; Rheinpfalz, large, but producing some good new wines often from unusual grape varieties; and Nahe, surrounding a river of

that name, a tributary of the Rhine, which makes some interesting wines, including some reds. Franken and Baden wines are quite rare, they are often made in the dry style. And there is the Mosel, with its two tributaries the Saar and Ruwer, making the nervily acidic Mosel-Saar-Ruwer wines.
- Wines from the Rhine regions (that is the first five mentioned above) come in brown bottles, wines from Mosel-Saar-Ruwer in green.
- Watch out! Wines called simply *Tafelwein* – no matter how authentically German the label may appear – are blends of any old European wine, and are not worth buying.

Germany's quality rating system

All wines fall into one of four categories: *Deutscher Tafelwein* (the *Deutscher* is the important bit) is the ordinary table wine category; *Landwein* is a dry or off-dry country wine; and *Qualitätswein* is the bottom rank of the so-called quality wines (which includes Liebfraumilch). You then move into the precisely-defined, top quality wines (*Qualitätswein mit Prädikat*) which are classified according to the concentration of sugar in the grapes when picked. The more sugar, the better the resulting wine. In ascending order of quality, the classifications are: *Kabinett*, *Spätlese* (meaning late-picked), *Auslese*, *Beerenauslese* and the unctuously sweet *Trockenbeerenauslese*. You'll find the quality rating on the label.

Key wine terms on the label

- *Trocken* Dry.
- *Halbtrocken* Off-dry.
- *Deutscher sekt* German sparkling wine.
- *Sekt* Sparkling wine, which was probably made in Germany but from imported European grapes (any old grapes). It is not recommended.

The way ahead for Germany

Although Liebfraumilch and the like still sell well, Germany's image has fallen from grace. It's now considered fashionable to go for crisp, *dry* whites. Medium sweeties are far from chic. As customers have moved on from cheap German wines, so they have abandoned Germany altogether. The desperation of German wine-producers to woo back their public can be seen on the wine shop shelves.

There you have inexpensive German wines trying their very best to look anything but German. They're in French-shaped bottles, with English writing using international wine terms. They're even dry, or only just off-dry to boot.

The Germans themselves drink a lot of dry wines – they are easier to match with food than sweet wines. But sadly for them, we have quantities of dry wines to choose from in Britain. By making dry wines, Germany loses its identity altogether. But her good varietal wines with plenty of grape character and a bit of softness go down very well. Don't forget Germany *is* a great wine-producing nation with good things to boast. Splash out and try better quality examples. Riesling is usually a winner.

LAYING DOWN WINE
It sounds a bit fancy 'laying down wine'. But it can mean no more than keeping the occasional bottle lying about at home for a few months before you get round to drinking it. Ideal conditions for wine are cellar conditions. Few of us are lucky enough to have cellars so let's look at what the advisable conditions are.
● A cool, consistent temperature free from draughts.
● Dark – or at least no direct light source.

How do you recreate these conditions? Find a dark corner away from a heat source: under the stairs, perhaps, at the back of a cupboard, or in a garage. For short term storage, absolute cool isn't necessary. If you suspect temperature differences will be drastic, 'lag' the bottles with a thick cover to minimize the effect.

Always keep bottles lying down. It is important for the cork to be kept moist at all times or it shrinks and may let in air.

Italy

Key facts about Italian wines

● Italy vies with France as the world's major wine-producing nation. Unfortunately, although some marvellous wines are made, quality can be patchy, since historically quantity has been an important goal for wine-makers.
● The country claims the longest uninterrupted history of wine production in the world, and the persistence of some traditional wine-making techniques goes in part to explain the very Italianness of Italian wines. When you put your nose into a glass of red, particularly, the first striking feature is the unmistakable nationality of the wine: it shouts Italy at you with its vibrance, its obviously lively acidity.
● Most grapes used to make most Italian wines are peculiar to Italy. There are hundreds of them, many simply local and very few that have travelled outside the country at all.
● International varieties are scattered here and there – particularly Chardonnay, Merlot, and the two Cabernets (Sauvignon and Franc) which usually make wines named simply 'Cabernet'.

Famous wines and the regions they come from

North-west Italy: For red wines, the Nebbiolo grape – one of the world's aristocrats – is the linchpin. It goes to make the lusty, heavyweight **Barolo**, best enjoyed after a few years' maturation, and the lighter **Barbaresco**. It also makes the worth-looking-out-for **Gattinara** and the often well-priced **Spanna**. **Dolcetto** is a soft, plummy grape making good fruity wines named after it. The

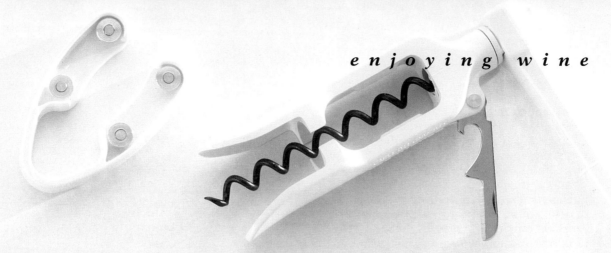

unfortunately over-produced **Barbera** is another grape which tends to make rather washed out reds, also named after it. Whites include the well-known (and often under-rated) sweet sparkler from the Muscat grape, **Asti Spumante** and the slightly fizzy, lightly alcoholic sweet treat, **Moscato Naturale**. Italy's most fashionable white wine is **Gavi** (overpriced); look out for other **Cortese** wines (that's the Gavi grape).

The north-east: There are old favourites such as the light-style reds **Valpolicella** and **Bardolino** (key advice is to drink them young and possibly chilled) and the generally dull white **Soave**. There are also the less well known, and consequently often preferable, juicy-fruity reds: **Teroldego Rotialiano**, for instance, and the white **Bianco di Custoza**. In the north, Alto Adige (called also Süd Tirol) does a fresh, streamlined wine from **Chardonnay**, while over in the far east, Friuli makes lovely, silky, nutty whites from French varieties such as **Pinot Grigio** (Pinot Gris) and **Pinot Bianco** (Pinot Blanc).

Central Italy: This area is dominated by Tuscany, with **Chianti** as its most famous wine. Young versions can do with a little chilling but, young or mature, all need food. **Sangiovese**, the core grape of Chianti, also makes the pricey **Brunello di Montalcino** and the not always so noble **Vino Nobile di Montepulciano**. **Lambrusco** comes from central Italy (near Bologna of Spaghetti Bolognese fame). It should at best be red and dry (rare in Britain); in general bottles stoppered by corks contain more genuine contents than those with screw tops. Among whites, **Orvieto** is now a squeaky clean, dry white (traditionally it was *Abboccato*, a bit sweet and honeyed) while **Frascati** from near Rome is (on the export market) usually disappointingly ordinary.

The south: From this region comes cheap

plonk, most of it consumed on the domestic market. Sicily, though, can make some well-travelled wines such as the ubiquitous **Corvo**, a reliable red and white. Sardinia has the white **Vermentino** grape which produces delicate, gentle wines.

Quality classifications

Vino da tavola is Italian for humble table wine, but watch out; a wine boasting this ordinary status with an ambitious price tag could be a new high quality 'designer wine', which breaks the rules and so fails to qualify for higher classification; usually worth paying extra for. *Indicazione Geografica Tipica* (or *Vini Tipici*) is a new country-wine-with-a-bit-of-character status, similar to French *Vin de Pays*. *Denominazione di Origine Controllata* is a fairly lax guide to higher quality; not entirely reliable.

Denominazione di Origine Controllata e Guarantita is supposed to be stricter and more selective than *DOC*.

Key wine terms on the label

- *Abboccato* Medium to medium sweet.
- *Amabile* Medium sweet.
- *Cantina* A winery.
- *Classico* The heart of the production area, usually making top wines.
- *Dolce* Sweet.
- *Frizzante* Slightly sparkling.
- *Invecchiato* Aged.
- *Liquoroso* High strength wine, usually sweet and fortified.
- *Riserva* Better wine that has usually been aged for longer.
- *Secco* Dry.
- *Spumante* Sparkling.
- *Superiore* Not necessarily superior, just higher in alcohol.
- *Vecchio* Old.

The way ahead for Italian wines

Che sarà sarà has tended to be the Italian attitude, wine-makers tending to ignore wine laws and do what they like. But with world demand, for wine on the decline, the authorities have started to try to put their *villa* in order in an attempt to secure reliable markets for their enormous volumes of wine; about a quarter of the world's wine output. If stricter controls have a good effect on standards, hooray, but as important is the injection of energy and zeal of serious wine-makers no longer content with mediocre standards. To date, the well-known wines coming over to Britain have been little more than mediocre. So far the most exciting new things are coming out of Tuscany (mainly reds) and the Friuli Giulia area, for fresh but characterful whites. Sparkling wine is booming, too.

SERVING TEMPERATURES
A lot of hoo-ha is made about getting the *temperature* of wine right before serving it. But what is right?

- It's all very well knowing that white wines, sparklers and rosés should be 'served chilled', but how cold and for how long? Cheaper whites and sweet whites need most chilling: about two hours in the fridge. Good white wines and sparklers need 60 to 75 minutes. Vintage sparklers need a bit less time.
- While white wines are much less enjoyable served without chilling, sparkling wines are *positively dangerous*. You must chill sparklers before attempting to remove the cork, or it can fly out with hazardous force.
- Don't forget the ice bucket: a receptacle containing ice and water used to be the quickest way to chill a bottle of wine (make sure all surfaces are submerged). But now there's also a wrap-around sleeve you can buy which chills in the freezer and then cools a bottle in 5 minutes. A great invention.
- Freezers can be used at a pinch; they're not ideal as the cold is rather fierce and if you leave the bottle in too long, it will freeze and possibly explode: 30 minutes is the maximum.
- Most reds should be chambre'ed, which literally means held at room temperature. When first used, room temperature meant dining room temperature (as opposed to cellar temperature); and that was before central heating. So no putting red bottles by radiators or fires! Just leave them for an hour or two in the room in which you plan to eat.

New Zealand

Key facts about New Zealand wines

- Vines were first planted in New Zealand nearly 175 years ago, but it wasn't until the mid-sixties that wine-making started to be taken seriously. Before then, gut-rot plonk was the order of the day; it's only over the last couple of decades that wines respected the world over have started to be made.
- Conditions in parts of New Zealand have proved themselves to be perfect for growing *vitis vinifera*, the wine-making vine. Because there is no pressure on space (with a population of 3,000,000 and a land mass larger than the UK), new vineyards are often sited on virgin soil never cultivated before.
- Sauvignon Blanc is probably New Zealand's most successful grape variety to date, and makes wines in the Marlborough region which can challenge any other Sauvignon Blanc in the world.
- White wines dominate New Zealand's wine industry; although Hawkes Bay in the North

Island puts out some delicious reds – Cabernet Sauvignon and Cabernet blends made in the best claret style – reds account for only about 15 per cent of the country's vinous output.

- Although wines from New Zealand only started to appear in British wine shops early in the 1980s, there are now nearly 200 different wines on sale here; the UK is not only the biggest export market for New Zealand wines, it is also the farthest away.
- New Zealand has concentrated all its export efforts on *quality*; it's not worth shipping cheap plonk half-way round the world. Consequently all New Zealand wines available in Britain are quality wines – you'll virtually never find a poor one.

Key regions

North Island

Auckland The first vineyards planted centred on North Island's most important town, although the climate here isn't ideal, being rather damp. However, for convenience, many of the key wine producers are based in Auckland, using some grapes grown locally, but also trucking in fresh-picked grapes during the cool hours of the day from all other areas in the rest of the country.

Hawkes Bay On the south-east coast, Hawkes Bay is an important area for Cabernet Sauvignon, often using the main claret grape in French restrained style (as opposed to voluptuous antipodean style). Sauvignon Blanc and Chardonnay wines are also made.

Gisborne High yields make this New Zealand's bulk wine-producing region. Although Gisborne isn't renowned for top wines, some average-to-good Chardonnays, Rieslings and the occasional Gewürztraminer are made here.

South Island

Marlborough In a beautiful spot on the north-east of South Island, Marlborough has made its name for producing concentratedly marvellous Sauvignon Blancs, with Cloudy Bay being the trailblazer. This is a key area for the future for all white wines (and a few reds).

Key wines

Sauvignon Blanc Displaying all the astringent 'green' associations with cut grass, gooseberries and flowerless herbaceous plants, but with an unusual breadth and depth, these wines have mouth-filling flavours; best sipped on their own, uncluttered by food.

Chardonnay These can be quite lean and green, more in the French than the Australian style. Some wine-makers manage to pack some peach and tropical fruit scents and flavours in, but often the wines are sold too young for these to show at their best. Best kept for two or three years after the vintage.

Cabernet Sauvignon and Cabernet/Merlot blends Can be a bit light, a little astringent and almost metallic, but after a couple of years these wines settle down to give good, bright berry scents and flavours with a strong backbone to stand up to food.

Quality classifications

A system of certified origin is being introduced (i.e. specification of region and even more precise sourcing of grapes such as a particular valley, to be allowed on the label only when the law permits). Meanwhile, New Zealand wine labels are easy to read and understand because they almost always give the grape variety, and frequently the region of origin, too.

287

The way ahead for New Zealand wines

Ideal conditions, new technology and ardent wine-makers have done miracles for New Zealand wines, pitching them up there to compete on equal terms with all the rest of the world . . . no thanks to the New Zealand government who have done little to encourage this new booming industry. Punitive taxes on wines have curbed expansion and discouraged new plantings. But the wine industry is fighting its corner fiercely, hoping to go on to bigger and still better things. Should they succeed in their objective, new funds will be freed up for further investment – which means a wider range of their gorgeous wines should come on stream, each a copybook example of the grape it's made from. If you haven't yet tried a New Zealand wine, it's a treat in store.

288

North America

Key facts about the wines of North America

- Wine is made in most states of the US and here and there in Canada, with California being by far the most important producer, responsible for 95 per cent of all US wine and an even higher percentage of wine exports. Occasionally wines from New York State on the east Coast and Washington State and Oregon in the west also find their way over to the UK.
- California makes vast quantities of wine; a single producer, E & J Gallo making more wine than the whole of Australia.
- At the quality end of things, two grapes obsess California wine-makers: Cabernet Sauvignon and Chardonnay. They also make some Pinot Noir, Merlot, Zinfandel, Grenache, and a little Syrah among reds, and Sauvignon Blanc (often called on the label Fumé Blanc), Chenin Blanc, Riesling and Colombard among whites.
- The state of California, the 'Golden State', has a very varied climate place to place, and so theoretically Californian wine-makers are capable of making wines in any style they like, including some commendable sparkling wines (often made by the French Champagne companies themselves). Wine-makers are gods in California and regrettably tend to find it less amusing to make wines for mere mortals like us; so generally California wines have pretensions to being posh and are very expensive.
- Wine has been made in California since the first settlers put down their roots there. But owing to Prohibition, the depression and the Second World War, the wine industry slipped, only restarting as a modern industry in the 1970s using the last word in wine technology and in wine-making expertise.

PACKS AND SIZES
The standard bottle of 75 cl isn't, of course, the only container for wine. It holds, for the record, six good-sized (eight small) glasses of wine.

- Half bottles, usually 37.5 cl in size, are excellent for a couple of people. Occasionally the commendable 50 cl (that is half litre) size is also found.
- The litre size is seldom used in Britain for anything other than cheap and cheerful 'party' plonk.
- Cans are handy for picnics because they don't break, but they are heavy, expensive and are not entirely inert, so they don't do the wine that much good.
- Tetrapacks of any size are preferable for picnics, though not as good as glass for serving wine at home.
- Plastic bottles seen in some supermarkets in Britain don't keep the wine marvellously, so are good only for inexpensive wines designed to be glugged down soon after bottling.
- Wine boxes have never enjoyed a good press in Britain for two reasons: 1. the wines inside have never been that marvellous and 2. the technology has never been good enough to keep the wine in good enough nick (whatever is boasted on the box). In Australia, boxes flourish with good technology and good enough wines. The answer? Buy Australian wine boxes if you fancy the idea of being able to dispense the occasional glass over a couple of weeks. The box itself is relatively expensive because of the technology designed to keep the wine fresh over a period of weeks. For instant drinking you're better off buying traditional bottles.

Quality classifications

There are legal controls on labelling which focus mainly on the area in which the grapes are grown. The lowliest wines likely to find their way to Britain will specify that they are simply from California. If at least 75 per cent of grapes are grown in a single county, such as Sonoma, that, too, may appear on the label. If they come from a small area within the county (such as Russian River in Sonoma) this, too, may appear. Not a great help, I'll admit. If a grape variety is boasted on the label, it need only constitute 75 per cent of the contents – i.e. a quarter of the grapes used can be a totally different variety.

Key wine terms on the label

- **Fumé or Fumé Blanc** Sauvignon Blanc isn't madly fashionable in California so Robert Mondavi had the brainwave of conjuring up his own name for its wines, bastardizing the name of the popular Pouilly-Fumé Sauvignon Blanc of the Loire. Fumé Blanc has been adopted widely as a name for Sauvignon Blanc wines.
- **'White'** White Zinfandel, for instance, isn't white, but pink. Because Californians considered rosé wine rather naff in concept but still enjoyed the taste, rosés made from well-known red grapes are known as 'white'.
- **Blush** An alternative name for rosé, these wines are generally fairly sweet and made from a blend of different grapes.
- **Meritage** A name coined to describe a wine made from a blend of traditional Bordeaux grapes (Cabernet Sauvignon, Merlot and Cabernet Franc).

The way ahead for North American wines

Believing their wines to be as great as any in the world, the proudest Californian wine-makers decided to market their (admittedly often marvellous) wines at fantastic prices, imagining UK customers would merely accept them for what they are. We didn't. Given the choice of a fine Burgundy and a California Pinot Noir, most of the people prepared to pay the sort of silly sums that both were asking

preferred the classic Burgundy, thank you very much. Now, driven by a threatened stagnation of sales, some companies are starting to bring their prices down, and to export more of what we want – delicious wines at reasonable prices. Look out for affordable Pinot Noirs, not just from California, but from Oregon, too. They have a piercing deliciousness of their own. Chardonnays can now be found at okay prices, too, the southern regions of California being the main source. If you like sweet wines, start experimenting! All sorts of delicious things – including sweet red wines such as Elysium – are scattered around the shops, often in the ideal half bottle size.

HOW LONG OPEN WINE KEEPS
Wine is like milk, it goes off. Stoppered with a cork in the bottle, the wine is exposed to very little oxygen and CO_2, both being necessary for microbes and bacteria, good and bad, to get to work. Take the cork out, though, and all hell is let loose.

- Wine which has been open much more than 24 hours (even if it has been recorked and kept in the fridge) begins to become oxidized and to go off.
- Unfortunately, fortified wines go off too. Fino sherry (pale and dry) should be served chilled and kept in the fridge once opened. It will then stay absolutely fresh for only about a week to ten days.
- Amontillado or 'medium' sherry and tawny port are best kept in the bottle (not decanted) and remain in good order for only three to four weeks.
- Oloroso or cream sherry shouldn't be kept, once opened, for more than two months; and that goes for ruby port, too.
- Spirits (37.5 per cent alcohol plus) are no problem; the higher alcohol level acts as a preservative so they'll keep more or less forever.
- Once wine has begun to deteriorate, there's no further use for it, not even for cooking because it will taint the food.
- There are gadgets sold to help keep wine fresh, once opened. The Vacuvin which sucks out the air so leaving a vacuum is quite effective (for only up to a week or so). Easier and better is the cannister of nitrogen gas which you spray into the neck of the bottle. It then sits on top of the wine and keeps the (lighter) oxygen away, preventing oxidation.

Portugal

Key facts about Portuguese wines

- Portugal is one of the largest (in volume terms) wine-producers in the world, but historically most of her wines have been consumed at home.
- Red wines are Portugal's strong point; she makes four times more red than white.
- Although port is Portugal's best-known wine, it accounts for only a fraction of the country's vinous output.
- Portugal has more than her share of peculiar grape varieties (peculiar to Portugal, that is) and unlike most of the rest of the wine-making world, is relying on them almost exclusively, only rarely being tempted to introduce the 'international classics' such as Cabernet Sauvignon and Chardonnay.

Portugal's best-known wines

- **Alentejo** Home to good honeyed and the pride of Portugal among traditional, velvet-smooth, mature, oaked reds, such as Tinto a Anfora. Look for Alentejo on the label.
- **Dão** Historically the reds have been rugged thunderbolts and the whites, rather coarse and unattractively old-fashioned. Now some good stuff is coming out of this area, big reds with a whisper of iron on the bouquet leading to a velvety smooth texture; vibrant and a touch tannic. Whites made with the aid of new technology are lighter and fresher with hints of honey and resin.
- **Douro** High up the Douro valley is home to port; nearer the mouth of the river is where the table wines are made, using a similar cocktail of native grapes. Reds tend to be a shade mighty with a touch of tar to them; whites can be rather nondescript, generally crisp and dry.
- **Bairrada** Red Bairradas were traditionally made to mature for a long period, but attempts have been made to bring them on stream much younger. Some have lost character and identity in the process. Older vintages, especially *Reservas* and *Garrafeiras* are best. Whites are improving all the time.
- **Vinho Verde** Means literally 'green wine'. This refers to the fact that these wines are designed to be drunk young not, in true Portuguese tradition, after years of maturation. Most of the Vinho Verdes we see in Britain are white, although many more red Vinho Verdes are actually made. Slightly sparkling, they are fresh with a high acidity. Most on the British market tend to be a bit sweet; the best examples are dry, though.

Key wine terms on the label

- *Garrafeira* The handle given to the best wines, matured for at least three years (two in wood) before bottling.
- *Reserva* Legally less lustrous than *Garrafeira*, in practice can be better. There are no minimum ageing requirements, but minimum alcohol requirements instead.
- *Vinho de Mesa* Table wine.
- *Tinto* Red.
- *Branco* White.
- *Seco* Dry.
- *Quinta* Farm or estate.

The way ahead for Portuguese wines

Combining excellent idiosyncratic grape varieties, modern equipment and talented wine-making, Portugal's potential is immense. Already the country is putting out some delicious – and very individual – wines, often at highly competitive prices. This is the place to look for something a bit different. Don't worry if you haven't heard of the wine before, give it a try. Periquita is an excellent red grape which may be mentioned either on the front label or the back label of reds. It makes gorgeously fruity, thoroughly individual wines. Muscat, too, is turning out some delicious, headily pungent, dry whites near Lisbon. An up and coming region to look for on the label is Alentejo, with its light, fruity, modern-style reds and zingy, fresh whites.

291

South Africa

Key facts about South African wines

- South African wine hasn't been on the menu for very long in Britain. Although a scattering of wines were available in the UK during the period when sanctions were imposed by most of the rest of the world, the choice was neither wide nor inspiring. Now that all things South African are becoming acceptable, the floodgates have opened to let in all comers and we can start to see what's what.
- Vines were first planted in the Cape in the mid-seventeenth century, but it wasn't until the late 1950s that table-wine making began to be taken seriously; before that South African port and sherry styles were the main preoccupation. Wine-making in South Africa has developed in isolation, without the benefit of exchange of ideas with other so-called 'New World' wine producers. Coupled with this disadvantage, South Africa hasn't (for domestic reasons) had access to good rootstock of the classic grape types. Chardonnay, for instance, is a relative newcomer to South Africa. But she now has all the will in the world to succeed in the open market and is learning fast and making confident progress.
- Chenin Blanc (also known as Steen in SA) is the mainstay among whites, making all styles of wine. In Britain you see some well-priced examples, usually more attractive than their counterparts from the Loire.
- Other white varieties offering excellent value are Sauvignon Blanc and Colombard.
- Pinotage is a peculiarly South African red variety produced from a crossing of Pinot Noir and Cinsaut. It makes some robust reds, chunky but with attractively welcoming fruit.
- Cabernet Sauvignon is behind most classy reds, traditionally working in a blend, but latterly operating highly successfully on its own, too.

Key wine terms on the label

- **Blanc Fumé** Dry white Sauvignon Blanc wine.
- **Cultivar** Grape variety.
- **Late harvest** Sweet wine made from late-harvested grapes.
- **Noble late harvest** A legal definition for a good quality sweet wine, the sweetness deriving from *botrytis* (mould – welcome mould – which concentrates the sugar in the grapes).

Legal classifications

A rectangular black and white seal is the legal guarantee that the wine is what it claims to be on the label. It officially confirms the region of origin; the vintage (only a minimum of 75 per cent of the wine must come from the declared vintage) and the grape variety (or cultivar). Again 75 per cent is the minimum requirement for a variety declared. The number ensures the history of any wine can be traced back to the grapes from which it was made.

The way ahead for South African wines

The only way for South Africa to go is onwards and upwards. Enjoying excellent conditions for grape-growing and wine-making, now that South Africa can compete openly with her wines the world over, the necessary injection of new ideas and up-to-the-minute expertise and technology should give the necessary boost to put the country up there in among the key players. The vineyards need work; some of the wine styles need streamlining (they're not always, at present, very true to type, indeed, they can be totally unrecognizable); pricing can be rather random – some wines affordable, others forbiddingly expensive. South Africa is new to the concept of competing with the world and, hungry for business, should learn fast. There should be some treats in store; cheap whites, quality reds and interesting sweeties.

South America

Key facts about South American wines

- Although Chile's wines are quite new to Britain, the Chileans have been making them, following classic French role models and using classic French vines, for more than a century. Vines were first introduced into South America 400 years ago. The modern wine industry, however, stems back to the second half of the nineteenth century when rich Chilean businessmen began to make the grand European tour. They returned with sophisticated tastes, and brought back cuttings of the classic Bordeaux vines (Cabernet Sauvignon, Merlot, Sauvignon, Semillon and a bit of Burgundian Pinot Noir) along with wine experts to craft wines for them in the French style. Shortly after this, French vineyards were devastated by the vine louse, *phylloxera*, but Chile's vineyards remained unscourged and still do to this day.
- Chile has always been acknowledged as the classy wine producer of South America.
- Argentina produces the largest quantities. Fifth largest wine-producer in the world, cheap and cheerful plonk is more her forte. She is also capable of making some good stuff at affordable prices.

Chile's key grape varieties

Cabernet Sauvignon Chile's wine industry has really been pulled up by its boot straps over the past decade or so. The local red-tinted rauli wood was used to make barrels for storing reds and traditionally-made Cabernets with rauli wood ageing in their pedigree have a peppery, bitter finish. Modern technology (and an absence of rauli wood) produces more of a zingy, almost metallic style. Cab Sauv is Chile's top grape; look beyond cheaper offerings to the classier beasts – they are showing great promise.

Merlot Generally richer than Cabernets, oak-aged versions are particularly successful.

Sauvignon Blanc Chilean Sauvignon Blanc was until very recently nondescript. Sloppy vineyard management meant other varieties would often be mixed in, confusing the character and making yet another bland, ordinary, dry white. Things are looking up in the vineyard and more of an astringent, green

character is being introduced into the wines. Worth looking out for.

Chardonnay New areas are being developed for growing Chardonnay, only recently introduced into Chile. Watch this space! Some good things are just round the corner.

Argentina's key grape varieties

Cabernet Sauvignon the classic red grape makes simple, well-priced wines, fruity but uncomplicated.

Malbec New wine-making methods are working miracles with the local fruit; look out for this southern French type.

Torrontes Argentinian whites can be a bit coarse and undistinguished, but this local grape variety, either acting on its own or in blends (look out for it on back labels) introduces an enticing spiciness and a pungence of its own.

Key wine terms on the label

- *Special* Two years old.
- *Reserva* Six years old.
- *Pago* Single estate.
There are no legal classifications to speak of, so look for grape varieties you recognize to help determine style.

The way ahead for South American wines

Chile

Having roared into prominence on British wine shelves with the internationally famous grape varieties being offered at good affordable prices, Chile may have made some unfortunate decisions recently. Her wine-producers have got together with the intention of re-launching their wines on our market as classy, quality wines at not such affordable prices. There's a lot of competition out there and it's debatable whether they will still be quite so appealing after the price hike. Certainly some class-act wines are being made, but that's only part of the business.

Argentina

The Falklands war knocked Argentina for six. Argentine wines were doing very nicely on the British market at the bottom end of the price scale until wham, as the battleships set sail from English shores, Argentine produce suddenly wasn't welcome any more. Wines are creeping back on to the shelves now and creeping up the quality and price ladder, too. As yet, though, price tags aren't as ambitious as those from neighbouring Chile. And most of the wines are fine.

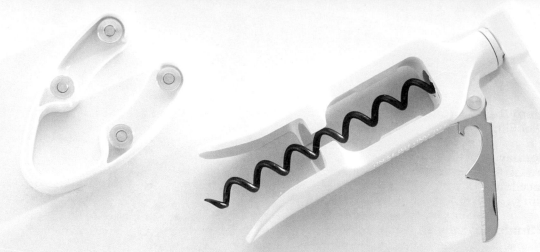

Spain

Key facts about Spanish wines

- Spain has a larger vineyard area than anywhere else in the world, but makes only half the volume of wine put out by either France or Italy.
- The world's most widely planted grape is the virtually unheard of Airen, the white grape dominating the colossal vineyards of Spain's vast (virtually rainless, by the way, contrary to the saying) central plain called La Mancha.
- Although Rioja is synonymous with quality wine from Spain, it is in fact only one of 40 quality wine-producing areas (or *Denominaciones de Origen*) in Spain, each with its own official controls.
- The vine-attacking louse, *Phylloxera*, the scourge of European vineyards in the late nineteenth century, effectively wiped out Bordeaux before it later went on to cross the Pyrenees to attack Spain. So Bordeaux wine-makers dashed south to Rioja and Navarra introducing a strong French influence to wine-making there before phylloxera arrived.
- Cava is the name given to Spain's top sparkling wines made by the same labour-intensive method as Champagne.
- Don Darius and all the other 'Dons' that appear on our wine shop shelves, modest but characterful reds and whites displaying inviting oaky characteristics, have been such a runaway success that they have turned the focus of the wine shop shelves back on to Spain again after a long lull.
- Sherry comes from Spain. If no other country (i.e. Cyprus, South Africa) appears on the label it is Spanish and it is the best. There are several styles. Fino is dead dry and pale (one of the driest wines in the

world), delicious served straight from the fridge. Amontillado is nut-coloured and also has a nutty taste. Most in this country is 'medium' although it can be found dry. Oloroso is rich-coloured and rich-tasting, usually very sweet (i.e. cream) although it, too, can be found in a dry style.
- Sherry may be Spain's best-known vinous export, but it in fact represents only 4 per cent of her production. Countless Spaniards have never tried it.

Key wines to try

Spanish red wines have historically been more to British taste than their whites, which at the cheaper end of the scale can be rather coarse and often over-sulphured. New technology has cleaned up the whites quite a bit, but often by sacrificing any personality for the wine. A middle road is now being pursued.

Good whites to try Try 'Don' this and 'Don' that, which tend to be ordinary table wines from any wine area, but jollied along by some oak character. La Mancha whites are often good and clean, crisp, dry whites. Valencia makes some excellently priced, seemingly orange-scented and flavoured, sweet Moscatel de Valencias. White Rioja comes in two styles: new squeaky clean, almost anonymous whites such as Marqués de Cáceras, and old-style (recently re-introduced) types with some oak ageing. If the front label doesn't make the style clear, look at the back label.

Good reds to try Excellent value is offered by typically jammy-sweet, soft reds with a bit of oak character coming from Valdepeñas, La Mancha and Utiel-Requena. Navarra makes some well-priced wines in the Rioja vein. Meanwhile Rioja itself has become a bit pricey at the mature *Reserva* end of things, but cheaper examples, having gone through a dull patch, now show promise as good easy-drinking reds.

Quality classifications

Vino de Mesa is the lowliest grade, simply meaning table wine.

Vinos de la Tierra is equivalent to French *Vin de Pays*, i.e. country wine with a bit of local character.

DO (*Denominacion de Origen*) is ascribed to a wine from a particular area which conforms to all the standards, grape varieties, etc. for that area.

DOC (*Denominacion de Origen Controllata*) is the top rating, at present allowed for Rioja only.

Key wine terms on the label

- *Tinto* Red.
- *Blanco* White.
- *Rosado* Pink.
- *Dulce* Sweet.
- *Seco* Dry.
- *Joven* Young wine.
- *Sin Crianza* Without ageing, i.e. young and simple. This term is being replaced by *joven*.
- *Crianza* The first step on the maturation ladder; the wine has some oak ageing.
- *Reserva* This means the wine has been aged in wood for some time; it then has to mature in the bottle, too.
- *Gran Reserva* The term ascribed to top wines aged for a minimum period in both oak barrels and in bottle.

The way ahead for Spanish wines

The first Spanish wines to trickle over to Britain were cheap and often not very cheerful plonk. So-called Spanish Burgundy, Spanish Sauternes and their successors in the shape of big brands such as Corrida and Don Cortez did nothing for the country's vinous reputation. When we discovered Rioja, though, we were turned on to something *very* different. Here was a class-act wine. For a long time there was only Rioja at the top of the quality scale and cheap plonk at the bottom. Rioja prices then soared, but with the injection of new technology and wine-making expertise, other wine-making areas started to make good wines, too, at good prices. Sometimes 'international' grape varieties back up the local types. Look out for wines from Penedés (particularly made by Torres), Costers del Segre (Raimat's the name to look out for), Ribera del Duero, Rueda and Navarra.

United Kingdom

Key facts about English wines

- All wines made from fresh-picked grapes grown in the open air in England and Wales are called 'English'. 'British' wine is the name given to wine made here from grape concentrate imported from abroad and reconstituted with tap water before being made into wine.
- There are 400 or so vineyards in southern Britain, about eighty large enough to make wine commercially.
- Vines are thought to have been introduced to Britain by the Romans, continuing to be grown, for better or worse, until the Second World War. The industry restarted, with new confidence, in the 1950s.
- Germany was taken as the role model for the new plantings. At first German varieties and German wine styles dominated, but gradually English wine acquired its own identity.
- Because of our cool climate, England makes more white wine than red, although many

vineyards are having increasing success with their reds; Pinot Noir particularly.

- The most widely planted grape variety is Müller-Thurgau, followed by Seyval Blanc.
- There is an embryonic sparkling wine industry. It should have a great future, since southern England enjoys the same geology and the same chalk hills as Champagne in France. Sparkling wines respond well to cool weather conditions, too. The only snag could be the British mentality which might not be painstaking enough to put sufficient effort into producing top-flight sparklers. The best types should declare 'traditional method' on the label.

What English wines are like

English white wines fall roughly into two styles: the medium, German-inspired styles and the greenly astringent, dry types. However, whether medium or dry, there is an identifiable Englishness to them all. Nettley, green and scented like new bracken shoots is a good description. Increasingly sophisticated wine-making techniques are introducing some new oak barrels for fermenting or ageing some wines. But still the very Englishness of them (and it's nothing to be ashamed of, rather the reverse) shows through.

Legal classification

Until very recently, all English wines have been obliged, by EC law, to call themselves simply 'table wine', the lowliest quality rating of any wine. However, wine-makers have been keen to introduce some quality classification, not least because we will be prevented from planting any more vineyards if we remain wholly in the table wine class, in accordance with EC regulations. So a pilot scheme has been introduced, promoting wines which pass relevant tests to the status of Northern Counties Quality Wine or Southern Counties Quality Wine.

Key wines to try

Thames Valley Vineyards, with their Australian wine-maker, triumphed in the annual English wine competition in 1992 – look out for their wines. Because to date English wine operations have been too small to supply big chains of wine shops or supermarkets, English wine has tended to be available only on a local scale. This is changing now – look in your local wine shop, restaurant *and* supermarket. If you haven't tried an English wine yet, mend your ways and try one now.

The way ahead for English wines

Price has been a stumbling block for our home-grown wines. Imagining they should come cheap, customers overlooked the fact that they are almost all the equivalent of château-bottled and hand-crafted. There's no bulk industry in the UK. However, with some bigger vineyard holdings coming on stream and some successful co-operatives drawing on the fruit from several different growers, cheaper wines are now available, breaking the £3 barrier for the first time. English wines are now ready to be taken seriously, and the whites especially can compete on equal terms with the wines of the world. Sparklers could follow suit.

297

IDEAL GLASSES
The shape and design of wine glasses is important. Just one shape will do, or the same shape in different sizes, if you like.

- The ideal wine glass is a tulip-shaped bowl – that is narrowing slightly towards the lip – on a stem. Traditionally you'd have a larger one for red wine than for white.
- For sparkling wine, the saucer shape (alleged to have been modelled on Marie Antoinette's breast) is hell. It loses all the bubbles instantly into the air and has no room at all for the bouquet to collect. It is also perilously easily spilt. Instead a tall flute is best, again ideally tapering a little towards the brim.
- For sherry and port you need a tulip 'bud', as it were; the same principle as the tulip-shaped wine glass with a bowl narrowing towards the lip on a stem, but smaller, and possibly more elongated and narrower. Schooners you sometimes see in pubs filled to the brim are murderous to sherry. There's no room for the bouquet to collect and, they are easily spilt.
- No wine or fortified wine glass should be poured more than a half to two-thirds full. If you are doing a tasting of the wine, pour the glass only one-third full to leave plenty of room for the wine to be swirled and for the bouquet to collect.

White wine   **Red wine**

Sherry   **Champagne**

CORKSCREWS
New designs of corkscrews are developed every year; they're a booming gift market. Some work, others dismally don't. No matter how simple or complicated the mechanics, successful corkscrews share some simple design features in common.

- The spiral, that is the screw itself, must have an open helix; you should be able to post a toothpick down the middle of it.
- It should definitely not be solid like the screw it is named after. If it is solid, particles of cork are displaced as it makes its clumsy way through the cork and they fall into the wine.
- An attached blade or foil cutter is handy to discourage you from blunting the tip by removing the capsule with it.
- An efficient levering device, although not essential, usually helps to guide the cork out straight and minimizes the likelihood of breaking it. The Screwpull range of corkscrews (one is shown here) are some of the best.
- Should a cork break, a secondary device with two parallel prongs of unequal length is useful as a back-up. Even with a broken cork it seldom fails.

All good corkscrews should have an open helix. A good test of this is to slide a toothpick down the middle of it

A Screwpull corkscrew with attached foil cutter

Lever for broken corks

Here are twenty-one recommended menus designed for you to entertain your family and friends. All menus use recipes that are in the book but don't forget that the *Recipe Index* at the back will give you lots more suggestions.

easy entertaining

We have designed each menu so that the flavours and the colours balance. They are divided into the four seasons and in each case we have given some advice as to what can be prepared in advance. Wine tips are included, selected to partner the main course.

SPRING

Two dinner parties

Melon, Prawn and Yoghurt Salad (see page 43)
Turkey Polpette (see page 89)
with Beans Amandine (see page 126)
and Buttered Noodles
Soufflé Omelette (see page 58)

Advance preparation:
– make the salad and chill
– make the polpette and re-heat

> **English wine would match the turkey well, or Hungarian Riesling.**

Cheese and Onion Quiche (see page 207)
Crafty French Roast Chicken (see page 68)
Gooseberry Custard Fool (see page 231)

Advance preparation:
– make the quiche and re-heat
– make the gooseberry fool and chill

> **Chicken takes either red or white wine comfortably; try either a *cru* Beaujolais such as Morgon, or a pungent white such as German Morio Muskat.**

A Sunday lunch

Moules Marinières (see page 48)
Garlic and Herb Roast Lamb (see page 178)
with Petits Pois à la Française (see page 125)
and Sauté Potatoes (see page 131)
Rhubarb Fool with Lemon Thins (see pages 240, 222)

Advance preparation:
– prepare peas and re-heat
– make the fool and chill
– make the lemon thins

> **Merlot is a soft, at best sweetly fruity, red grape. Try one from southern France; the grape will unusually be boasted on the label.**

A Greek meal

Greek Salad (see page 107)
Moussaka (see page 120)
Apple Baklava (see page 213)

Advance preparation:
– prepare the salad then dress it later
– assemble the moussaka ready for the oven
– make the baklava; it is best eaten cold

> **The piney note in Greek Retsina is the perfect foil for the oiliness of Moussaka, or you could go for a hearty Mediterranean red such as Fitou.**

SUMMER

A summer lunch

Carrot and Coriander Soup (see page 12)
Smoked Salmon Quiche (see page 208)
with cucumber salad
and a green salad (see page 107)
Raspberry Cream Crowdie (see page 239)

Advance preparation:
– make the soup the day before and re-heat
– make the raspberry cream and chill

A zingy, herbaceous Sauvignon Blanc would stand up for itself and not be overwhelmed by the smoked salmon. Chile is a good, well-priced source. Or try South African Colombard.

A cold summer lunch

Potted Shrimps and Wholemeal Bread (see pages 43, 198)
Waldorf Salad (see page 76)
French Fruit Flan with Crème Pâtissière (see pages 211, 213)

Advance preparation:
– make the potted shrimp the day before
– make the pastry the day before

An exotic companion for the Waldorf Salad is Madeira Sercial (which is dry). Or try Irsay Oliver, a spicy white from Czechoslovakia.

A summer dinner party

Salmon and Dill Moulds (see page 38)
Poussin with Cracked Wheat and Apricots (see page 156)
Exotic Fruit Salad in a Melon Basket (see page 234)

Advance preparation:
– make the salmon moulds
– make the fruit salad

Try a luscious oaked Chardonnay from North America or Australia.

A Mediterranean meal

Gazpacho (see page 122)
Italian Veal Meat Loaf (see page 182)
Strawberries in Orange Juice (see page 240)

Advance preparation:
– make the gazpacho
– prepare the strawberries

Don't pour the wine until after the first course; it will murder it. Then go for a soft Italian red such as a Dolcetto or a Teroldego Rotaliano.

A fish dinner

Caesar Salad (see page 108)
Haddock Dieppoise (see page 32)
Simple Pavlova (see page 225)

Advance preparation
– wash and dry the lettuce and store in a polythene bag in fridge
– make the pavlova meringue, keep in an air-tight tin

Wait until the main course before pouring the wine, then go for a white Graves, an oak-aged Sauvignon Blanc (often called Fumé Blanc in the New World) or an Australian Semillon.

AUTUMN

Two lunch parties

Crab Cakes (see page 46)
with Mushroom Gratin (see page 132)
and a green salad (see page 107)
and Wholemeal Bread (see page 198)
Middle Eastern Oranges (see page 235)

Advance preparation:
– prepare the shaped crab mixture, ready to
fry at the last minute
– make the fruit salad

**White wine with zip to it: try
Bourgogne Aligoté or a Chardonnay
from northern Italy (Alto Adige) or
southern France.**

Pumpkin and Tomato Soup (see page 11)
Hot Boiled Gammon (see page 184)
with Leeks au Gratin (see page 119)
and Pease Pudding (see page 184)
Scandinavian Apple Cake (see page 228)

**An interesting contrast would be
provided by dry, white Muscat; look
out for examples from Hungary and
Portugal.**

A Mediterranean meal

Tuscan Bean Soup (see page 11)
Osso Bucco (see page 189)
Baked Apples (see page 228)

Advance preparation:
– make the soup and re-heat

**The Italian classic would be the
mighty red Barolo, made from the
Nebbiolo grape, or the slighter
Barbaresco.**

An autumn dinner

Smoked Mackerel Pâté (see page 38)
French-Style Daube (see page 167)
with Mashed Potatoes (see page 130)
and a green salad (see page 107)
Blackberry Tart (see page 231)

Advance preparation:
– make the pâté the day before
– make the daube and re-heat
– make the pastry for the tart

**Southern French red would be the
true partner; try Bandol or the fruity
Côtes de Frontonnais.**

WINTER

An alternative Christmas dinner or New Year's feast

Neapolitan Terrine (see page 39)
Roast Goose (see page 90)
with Red Cabbage with apples (see page 115)
and Potato and Celeriac Mousse (see page 118)
Walnut and Lemon Tart (see page 212)

Advance preparation:
– make the fish terrine
– make the red cabbage and re-heat
– make the tart, to be eaten cold or warmed
through at the last minute

**If you want to splash out, go for the
wonderful Syrah-based northern
Rhône reds, Hermitage or St Joseph.
Crozes-Hermitage and Châteauneuf-
du-Pape could be cheaper bets.**

301
....

A fruit dinner

Chicken Livers Sautéd with Grapes (see page 78)
Pheasant with Walnuts and Pomegranates (see page 100)
Pears Belle Hélène (see page 236)

Advance preparation:
– poach the pears in syrup
– make the ice-cream

 Pinotage, a South African grape cross, offers robust flavours and plenty of fruit. It's a good choice with this menu.

A winter lunch

French Pickled Mackerel (see page 37)
Bacon Pudding and Mrs Beeton's Tomato Sauce (see page 185)
Apricot Fool (see page 230)

Advance preparation:
– mackerel must be made at least 3 days in advance
– make the tomato sauce and re-heat
– make the apricot fool and chill

 In Mrs Beeton's day ale would have accompanied this bacon dish. We have a much wider choice of ales in our shops today – try a traditional ale or porter, usually a little sweet; it will go well with the mackerel too.

A game dinner

Winter Salad (see page 108)
Marinated Roast Haunch of Venison (see page 93)
with Creamed Savoy Cabbage (see page 114)
Apple and Almond Tart (see page 227)

Advance preparation:
– prepare the winter salad
– make the apple tart to be eaten cold or re-heated

 Big-flavoured wines such as good Fitou or Rioja reserva.

A Central European meal

Borscht (see page 12)
Beef Stroganoff (see page 163)
with Rice (see page 150)
Pancakes with Cherry Jam (see pages 60, 242)

Advance preparation:
– make the borscht and re-heat
– make the pancakes and layer between sheets of greaseproof paper to stop them sticking together

 French red Burgundy would be great, or look out for a Pinot Noir from Alsace or Romania.

Three vegetarian menus

Artichokes (see page 123)
Lasagne with Ricotta and Aubergines (see page 144)
Sautéed Apples with Almonds and Apricot Preserve (see page 230)

Advance preparation:
– make the lasagne and re-heat

 A juicy red with plenty to say for itself such as Australian Shiraz.

Provençal Grilled Tomatoes (see page 121)
Bean Cassoulet (see page 128)
Pear Tart (see page 237)

Advance preparation:
– make the pastry (but the tart is best warm from the oven)

 Californian Zinfandel is a good partner for this vegetarian menu.

Crisp Fried Aubergines (see page 120)
Couscous (see page 155)
Lemon and Lime Sorbet (see page 232)

Advance preparation:
– make the couscous
– make the sorbet

 A lusty wine to cope with the deep flavours – French Syrah or Minervois.

In keeping with our straight-forward approach, this chapter contains what we believe to be the key equipment every kitchen should have. If you are equipping a kitchen from scratch, here is what you need to know.

the crucial kitchen

1. Pans

No kitchen should be without:
- 2 frying pans – 1 large and 1 small;
- 4 saucepans – 1 large, 1 medium, 1 small and 1 milk (with lip and broad base)
- 2 casseroles – 1 large and 1 small;
- 1 steamer;
- 1 wok;
- 2 roasting pans;
- 2 racks – 1 meat and 1 cooling rack for cakes and bread.

Stainless steel-covered aluminium saucepans are the best. Cast iron or plain aluminium are fine but go for a non-stick surface. Look for 'long-life' non-stick that can take metal utensils. Should we be talking copper? No – far too expensive. Remember that some cookers, including halogen and ceramic hobs, require flat-bottomed saucepans, and glass saucepans will prevent these hobs working properly.

Casseroles. Our first choice is vitreous or enamelled. Ovenproof, glazed earthenware will do.

With saucepans, and indeed all other equipment (particularly knives), the best you can afford is what you should buy. Anything really cheap is a false economy.

2. Tools – Electrical

A food processor is essential. It should have a strong motor and a good bowl capacity [1 litre (1¾ pints) minimum].

Food mixers are useful for large quantities. In the absence of a food mixer, a hand-held electric whisk is a good idea.

And finally . . . an electric kettle.

Hand mixer

Blender

Food processor

3. Tools – Manual

Some people are gadget-mad. Their annual visit to the Ideal Home Exhibition results in the multiple purchase of gadgets that thereafter lie neglected in the back of the kitchen drawer. But here are the manual tools we regard as essential:

- a set of wooden spoons, a plastic spatula, a fish slice, a slotted spoon, a pair of meat-handling forks, a ladle, a 'swivel' potato peeler, a 'bedspring' whisk (called a 'coil' whisk);
- a large metal colander with generous handles, a sieve with a minimum 18 cm (7 inch) diameter;
- an apple corer, a jam funnel and a lemon juicer;
- a can opener that makes a safe cut below the rim of the lid leaving no jagged edges;
- 2 mixing bowls (large and small), a measuring jug and a salad spinner;
- a set of scales (they do not need to be electronic);
- a pepper grinder;
- a set of skewers.

Swivel peeler

304

Coil whisk

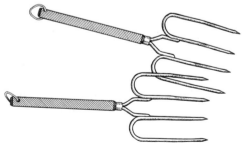

Meat handling forks

Salad spinner

4. Knives

The following are mandatory:
- a carving knife [25–30 cm (10–12 inches)];
- a chef's knife [20–25 cm (8–10 inches)];
- a general purpose knife [10–15 cm (4–6 inches)];
- a paring knife [7.5 cm (3 inches)];
- a bread knife;
- a serrated knife for fruit etc.;
- a palette knife;
- a sharpening steel.

Carving knife

Chef's knife

General purpose knife

Paring knife

Bread knife

Fruit knife

Palette knife

Sharpening steel

The following are optional:
● a Chinese-style chopper;
● a fish filleting knife;
● a cheese knife;
● a grapefruit knife.

Chinese-style chopper

Fish filleting knife

Cheese knife

Grapefruit knife

The correct position for sharpening a knife

If you can't face sharpening your own knives you can buy knives that have a self-sharpening sheath and some stainless knives guarantee a sharp blade for a number of years. Butchers and fishmongers (if you get on the right side of them) will sharpen your knives for you.

5. Stoves, ovens and hobs

Appearance and decoration is down to you. That aside look for the following features:

Stoves and hobs

● Controllable heat that can be turned on or off instantly (e.g. gas, halogen, induction);
● a low heat, simmer position;
● completely stable pan bases;
● easily understood controls;
● controls out of reach of children (if you have them).

Ovens

● Shelves that are stable when pulled out;
● a door that will stay open (fold-down are best);
● a self-cleaning facility;
● a grill that heats to a high temperature and that is at a convenient height;
● a grill pan with safe handles which do not get too hot to hold.
Be aware that fan ovens require a different way of cooking and are, in our belief, less versatile.

Agas and similar cookers

● Be aware that these, too, require a different style of cooking (but many serious cooks swear by them).
● Your kitchen must be big enough and with good ventilation.

305

Advice on design and materials

Handles should be:
● comfortable to hold;
● non-slip when wet;
● dishwasher and hot water-proof.
Handles are made from wood, plastic or a variety of resins. All are fine so long as they satisfy the above criteria.
Blades: The all-round best material for the blade is sharpened stainless steel. Specialists prefer carbon but it rusts easily and requires much more maintenance.

Sharpening knives

There are a number of mechanical and electrical devices available, but the simplest and most useful method is to use a steel. Here is a safe method. Hold the steel down vertically with its point touching a solid surface. At about 35 degrees to the surface pretend you are cutting a slice of cheese off the steel with your knife – make 3 or 4 'cuts' on one side and 3 or 4 on the other. Our illustration shows the angle the knife should be to the steel.

6. Surfaces

Go for easy-clean surfaces in your kitchen e.g. marble, Corian, slate, formica. **Avoid** tiles and wood as they are difficult to clean and unhygenic.

The modern way to avoid cross-contamination (see page 66) is to have five colour-coded chopping boards. Plastic is the best material but don't scour it as it will trap food and smells. Coloured plastic boards are not ideal to see what you are doing but you can buy boards with different coloured handles. The best colour code is:

● green – for fruit and vegetables;
● red – for raw meat and poultry;
● blue – for fish;
● white – for cooked foods;
● yellow – for dairy products.

Ensure that near your oven and hob you have a surface on which you can put hot pans safely.

7. Design

If you are designing a new kitchen, adopt the principle of 'dirty through to clean'. The areas of activity in the kitchen should ideally progress like this:
1. Rubbish near the door.
2. Surface where raw, dirty foods are prepared.
3. Sink for washing up and cleaning.
4. Surface for cooked foods to be served up.
This progression is designed to keep raw and cooked foods apart.

Top shelf: dairy products

Middle shelf: cooked meat

Bottom shelf: raw meat

Drawer: fruit and vegetables

FACT FILE **The problem with fridges is that we rely on them for most of our food storage but we do not use them well and some older ones are unreliable. See the diagram of the fridge for maximum temperatures for each shelf. Use a fridge thermometer to check it if you are not sure. Then store foods in the fridge as illustrated to avoid cross-contamination.**

This index has been included to help you plan your meals. As well as listing all the recipes for starters, main meals and desserts, you will also find a list of vegetarian recipes and recipes for cakes, breads, biscuits, sauces, dressings, pastry and preserves.

recipe index by course

index

Page numbers in *italic* refer to illustrations

311
·············